INSPIRE / PLAN / DISCOVER / EXPERIENCE

DENMARK

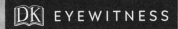

DENMARK

CONTENTS

DISCOVER 6

Welcome to Denmark 8

Reasons to Love Denmark 10

Explore Denmark 14

Getting to Know Denmark 16

Denmark Itineraries 22

Denmark Your Way 30

A Year in Denmark 50

A Brief History 52

EXPERIENCE COPENHAGEN 58

Central Copenhagen North 70

Central Copenhagen South 90

Christianshavn and Holmen 118

Beyond the Centre 126

EXPERIENCE DENMARK 142

Northwestern Zealand 142

Southern Zealand
and the Islands 176

Funen 194

Southern and
Central Jutland 204

Northern Jutland 226

Bornholm 242

Greenland and
the Faroe Islands 256

NEED TO KNOW 268

Before You Go 270

Getting Around 272

Practical Information 276

General Index 278

Phrase Book 286

Acknowledgments 287

Left: Warehouses in Ebeltoft, Central Jutland
Previous page: Lighthouse off the coast of Southern Jutland
Front cover: Boats and tenements on Nyhavn, Copenhagen

DISCOVER

Sun setting over Copenhagen

Welcome to Denmark 8

Reasons to Love Denmark 10

Explore Denmark 14

Getting to Know Denmark 16

Denmark Itineraries 22

Denmark Your Way 30

A Year in Denmark 50

A Brief History 52

WELCOME TO
DENMARK

Buzzing bars and restaurants bounding colourful city canals. Great stretches of sand dunes illuminated by sublime skies. Working windmills nestled in picturesque meadowland. Whatever your dream trip to Denmark includes, this DK Eyewitness Travel Guide is the perfect companion.

1 An artful New Nordic dish at Restaurant Substans in Aarhus.

2 Viking ship at Roskilde Vikingeskibsmuseet.

3 Traditional timber and grass roof houses on the Faroe Islands.

Follow in the footsteps of the Viking Danes as you explore this utterly enchanting country – from the castles of Zealand to the beaches of Skagen. Denmark has moved on from its fearsome Viking empire, and is today regarded as the benchmark for progressive politics, sustainability, design and lifestyle, best embodied in the art of *hygge*. Embrace this Danish concept when wild swimming in Silkeborg Lake District, enjoying a bike ride around Bornholm, or marvelling at the Northern Lights in Greenland, Denmark's spectacular, autonomous hinterland.

Craving the bustle of a city? You're spoiled for choice. Effortlessly cool Copenhagen is chock full of world-class restaurants, cutting-edge architecture and Instagram-worthy canals. In historic Helsingør you'll discover both cobbled streets and contemporary art, plus the formidable Kronborg Slot, the setting of tragic masterpiece *Hamlet*. To the north, artistic Aarhus rivals Copenhagen with its dynamite dining and innovative art installations, while port city Aalborg marks the start of fjord country.

With so many different experiences and regions on offer, Denmark can seem over-whelming. We've broken the country down into easily navigable chapters, with detailed itineraries and comprehensive maps to help plan the perfect adventure. Add insider tips, and a Need To Know guide that lists all the essentials to be aware of before and during your trip, and you've got an indispensable guidebook. Enjoy the book, and enjoy Denmark.

REASONS TO LOVE
DENMARK

It oozes history. Its scenery is breathtaking. It's effortlessly stylish. Ask any Dane and you'll hear a different reason why they love their country. Here, we pick some of our favourites.

1 WILD BEACHES OF SKAGEN

The ethereal beauty of drifting dunes and wild seascapes at Jutland's northernmost tip has long been captured by painters. Take some time out to enjoy this rugged landscape.

SCREEN-STEALING SCENES 2

Makers of Nordic Noir dramas keep returning to Denmark and it's easy to see why. Follow in the footsteps of great detectives and explore the country's beguiling scenery for yourself.

3 SMØRREBROD

Sourdough rye bread piled high with succulent shrimp or tender roast beef, and garnished with colourful flourishes; *smørrebrød* is an unmissable lunchtime tradition throughout Denmark.

CYCLING IN COPENHAGEN *4*

Copenhagen is the world's most bike-friendly city, with more than 60 per cent of locals cycling along the city's pretty canals and extensive bike paths. Rent a bike and join them.

LOUISIANA MUSEUM OF MODERN ART *5*

Marvel at works by the likes of Asger Jørn and Giacometti set against the stunning backdrop of the Øresund Sound. This is one of the greatest modern art experiences in the world *(p146)*.

AARHUS *6*

Move over Copenhagen; Denmark's cultural capital is a showstopper *(p208)*. Dine out at one of Aarhus's stellar restaurants and check out innovative artworks like Ron Mueck's *Boy*.

ENCHANTING AMUSEMENT PARKS 7

Child-like joy thrives at Denmark's many wonderlands. Marvel at Legoland's mini-brick masterpieces, stroll under Tivoli's sparkling lights and revel in Bakken's rollercoasters.

THE MAGIC OF 8
H C ANDERSEN

H C Andersen's magical storytelling has long captured imaginations, and his greatest works were inspired by his home country, from *The Little Mermaid* to *The Ugly Duckling*.

9 VIKING HERITAGE

The word "Viking" comes from a Scandi term meaning to travel. The Danes might have traded their longships for bikes but there are many reminders of the ancient seafarers.

10 DANISH DESIGN

Simple forms, clean lines, pops of colour and unimpeachable functionalism; Denmark's ultra-cool interior and fashion design is world renowned, and it's yours for the taking.

BORNHOLM'S CULINARY SCENE 11

Foodies flock to this island paradise cast in the Baltic Sea to eat well, whether at Michelin-starred, New Nordic powerhouses or traditional, rural smokehouses.

HYGGE 12

The Danish art of cosiness – *hygge* – can involve a candlelit drink with friends in winter, or a harbourside picnic in summer. Danes value slowing down and savouring the moment.

EXPLORE

DENMARK

This guide divides Denmark into eight colour-coded sightseeing areas: Copenhagen, Northwestern Zealand, Southern Zealand and the Islands, Funen, Southern and Central Jutland, Northern Jutland, Bornholm, and Greenland and the Faroe Islands, as shown on the map below. Find out more about each area on the following pages.

Hirtshals

Hjørring

Brønderslev

Hanstholm

Aalborg

Thisted

Limfjorden

Mors

Fur

NORTHERN JUTLAND
p226

Nykøbing Mors

Salling

Nissum Bredning

Skive

Hobro

Struer

Viborg

Randers

Holstebro

Silkeborg

North Sea

Ringkøbing

Herning

Ringkøbing Fjord

SOUTHERN AND CENTRAL JUTLAND
p204

Skanderborg

Horsens

Vejle

Varde

Kolding

Middelfart

Esbjerg

Fanø Bugt

Ribe

Haderslev

Rømø

Aabenraa

Tønder

Sønderborg

Flensburg

GERMANY

0 kilometres   40

0 miles   40

N

Skagen

Frederikshavn

Læsø

Aalborg Bugt

Anholt

Halmstad

Grenå

K a t t e g a t

Ängelholm

Aarhus

S W E D E N

Samsø

Helsingør ○ Helsingborg

Frederiksværk

Hillerød ○ Hørsholm

Frederikssund ○

Holbæk ○

COPENHAGEN
p58

Kalundborg ○

**NORTHWESTERN
ZEALAND**
p142

Roskilde ○

Malmö

Køge Bugt

Sorø ○ ○ Køge

Slagelse ○ Ringsted ○

FUNEN
p194

Odense ○

Nyborg ○

Næstved ○

Faaborg ○

**SOUTHERN ZEALAND
AND THE ISLANDS**
p176

*B a l t i c
S e a*

Svendborg ○

Stege ○

Rudkøbing ○

*K i e l
B a y*

○ Nakskov

Nykøbing F. ○

Gedser ○

0 km 800
0 miles 800

N

Greenland

Svalbard

*Greenland
Sea*

*Barents
Sea*

**GREENLAND AND
THE FAROE
ISLANDS**
p256

ICELAND

Arctic Circle

Faroe Islands

FINLAND

NORWAY

SWEDEN

ESTONIA   RUSSIA

IRELAND

UK

**Area of
main map**

BORNHOLM
p242

FURTHER TERRITORIES

GETTING TO KNOW
DENMARK

A clutch of islands set around a narrow peninsula, Denmark is considerably smaller than its Nordic neighbours and yet bursts with charisma. From the rural farmland of Southern Zealand up to the icy outpost of Greenland in the north, each region has its own distinct personality.

COPENHAGEN

PAGE 58

On the east coast of Zealand is Denmark's capital of Copenhagen, the King of Scandi cool. Flocks of locals can be seen navigating their famously laid-back city by bicycle, stopping to chat, drink coffee and revel in the Danish art of *hygge*. Peppering the city are green spaces and superlative restaurants that embody Copenhagen's culinary prestige, not forgetting a wealth of art galleries, design-led stores and a nostalgic amusement park. There's a whiff of regal grandeur, too, with royal guards marching from Rosenborg Slot to Amalienborg, the home of the Danish monarchy. All of this is connected by a network of canals and waterways, with colourful Nyhavn the most iconic. Lined with veteran barges, its cobbled quayside thrums with locals and visitors rubbing shoulders as they eat, drink and put the world to rights.

Best for
Cutting-edge fusion cuisine, cycling, museums and galleries, bars and café culture

Home to
Amalienborg Slot, Tivoli, Rådhus, ARKEN Museum

Experience
The magic of Tivoli at night, when the pleasure gardens are festooned with fairy lights

NORTHWESTERN ZEALAND

It's easy to see why this part of Denmark's largest island lured early Viking settlers and, later, medieval aristocrats. Here deep blue inlets that create perfect natural harbours carve their way into a fertile heartland and calm, shallow waters – pleasantly warm in summer – lure swimmers to its northern beaches. Royal castles, formidable fortresses and noble mansions are dotted around its sandy shores and idyllic meadows, where cattle graze in lush fields. This bucolic region is a magnet for cyclists, walkers and nature lovers.

Best for
Modern art, history, royal castles

Home to
Louisiana Museum, Helsingør, Roskilde, Fredriksborg Slot

Experience
A bike ride along on the beautiful Fjordstien cycle path

$\rightarrow$

PAGE 176

SOUTHERN ZEALAND AND THE ISLANDS

Sandy beaches and lively amusement parks lure families to Southern Zealand with attractions like Bon Bon-Land and Lalandia offering all-weather activities for everyone. Those looking for more natural beauty won't be let down. Imposing cliffs rise between golden sandy strands on the islands of Falster and Møn, watched over by shrieking seagulls. On the Susa river, swans swim beside canoeists between forested banks, and history buffs delight in the churches and castles of Vordingborg and Koge.

Best for
Family attractions, sunbathing on beaches, coastal scenery

Home to
Stevns Klint, Møns Klint, Maribo, Liselund Slot

Experience
Gin and wine tastings at artisan distilleries and vineyards

PAGE 194

FUNEN

It's easy to see why Funen is called the "Garden of Denmark". Lush pastures and fruit-filled orchards are the keynotes of a hinterland dotted with opulent manors and formidable castles. Odense, the island's largest city, is a cultural hotspot famed as the birthplace of national treasure and literary legend H C Andersen, and Egeskov Slot is one of Denmark's most magnificent castles. Off Funen's long, sandy coast, the tiny island of Aero has postcard-pretty villages, and tranquil Langeland is perfect for gentle bike rides among windmills and old-fashioned farms.

Best for
Exploring pretty villages, beautiful beaches, castles and medieval history

Home to
Odense, H C Andersens Hus, Egeskov Slot, Valdemars Slot

Experience
Testing you navigation skills by finding your way around Nyborg Slot's intricate maze

PAGE 204

SOUTHERN AND CENTRAL JUTLAND

Cyclists and walkers are guaranteed pleasant and scenic excursions in Southern and Central Jutland. Culture vultures head to lively Aarhus, chock-full of bars and cafés where locals gather to drink, chat and listen to music. Historic Ribe offers a time-hop back to the Viking Age and the western isles of Aero and Jomo have their own cultural heritage. For families, it's all about the mini-brick-metropolis of LEGOLAND®, where colourful characters, rides and shows are a crowd-pleasing attraction.

Best for
Medieval towns, scenic countryside, castles and Viking heritage

Home to
Aarhus, Ribe, LEGOLAND®

Experience
Panoramic views from the technicolial walkway crowning ARoS Aarhus Kunstmuseum

→

NORTHERN JUTLAND

Long, sunlit summer days brighten Denmark's "land of light" at the northern tip of Jutland. Colossal, luminous skies, where seabirds and waterfowl wheel above North Sea combers and rolling moorland, have attracted painters since the 19th century. Budding historians can plunge into the world of the Vikings at Lindholm Hoje and Fyrkat, while lively university town Aalborg has both a historic centre and a more youthful vibe. Head here to sample akvavit, its potent signature spirit.

Best for
Beachcombing, spectacular vistas, postcard-pretty fishing harbours, experiencing café life in Aalborg

Home to
Aalborg, Limfjorden, Skagen

Experience
Hair-raising thrills on the roller coasters of Farup Sommerland

BORNHOLM

Figs, vines and mulberries flourish in the mellow microclimate of Denmark's sunniest island. Bornholm, sitting on its own in the sheltered waters of the Baltic Sea, is a much-loved holiday destination with Danes but little-visited by other nationalities. The island's coasts are an amalgam of rugged cliffs and sandy beaches. Its verdant hinterland is dotted with distinctive medieval churches and pretty villages, home to skilled artisans and artists.

Best for
Summer sun, natural heritage, round churches

Home to
Osterlars Rundkirke, Joboland, Madkulturhuset Gaarden, Bornholms Kunstmuseum

Experience
Gentle cycle tours through meadows, fields and forests

PAGE 256

GREENLAND AND THE FAROE ISLANDS

Adventurers seeking unique experiences on land and at sea will find them among the rocky shores and icy waters of Denmark's two remotest territories. The Faroes, a cluster of 18 isles off the coast of Scotland, are home to sheep-farmers and fisherfolk. Puffins, fulmars and kittiwakes flock along the archipelago's rugged cliffs, and whales and seals in its waters. Even more remote is Greenland, where green coasts fringe an icy outpost from which glaciers flow down to Arctic fjordlands.

Best for
Adventure, epic scenery, wildlife, snow

Home to
Nuuk, Kangerlussuaq, Qaanaaq, Torshavn, Vestmanna Bird Cliffs

Experience
Dog sledding over Arctic fjords and – if you're lucky – a glimpse of the Northern Lights

→

1 The spire of Vor Frelsers Kirke, Christianshavn.

2 Tapestry of Queen Margrethe at Christiansborg Slot.

3 Coffee Collective.

4 Warpigs in Vesterbro.

Denmark brims with travel possibilities, from two-day tours around its capital to intrepid expeditions exploring the country's enchanting rural landscapes. These itineraries will help you to chart your own course.

2 DAYS

in Copenhagen

Day 1

Morning Avoid the morning crowds and head for a relaxed breakfast among locals at Parterre *(p123)* in Chistianshavn. Afterwards, check out the 95-m (312-ft) golden spiral tower of Vor Frelsers Kirke, and meander past two of Copenhagen's most colourful, picture-perfect houses: No 4 Overgaden Oven Vandet and No 3 Sofiegade *(p124)*. Cross Knippelsbro bridge on foot to the island of Slotsholmen.

Afternoon Explore the regal Christians-borg Slot complex *(p98)*; tour the royal reception rooms and marvel at 1,000 years of history, as woven into immense tapestries in the Throne Room. When your stomach starts to rumble, leave the palace and make your way down Gammel Strand, and ask for a table at local institution Schønnemans *(www.restaurant schonnemann.dk)*. Relish *smørrebrød* with schnapps pairings, before climbing the spiral ramp of the Rundetaarn astronomy tower *(p105)*. After descending, browse Copenhagen's flagship stores on Strøget for Danish design.

Evening Head to a dinner reservation at Palægade *(p83)* and conclude the evening by strolling back down Gammel Strand for sophisticated cocktails at the world-ranked and mysteriously unmarked bar Ruby *(p109)*.

Day 2

Morning A visit to Coffee Collective *(p132)*, in Torvhallerne food hall, is an ideal way to kickstart the day. Browse the food stalls and stock up on picnic supplies before walking to the idyllic Botanisk Have *(p86)* for a peaceful encounter with 13,000 species of plant life. The lacy Victorian Palmehus (Palm glass house) is especially striking. Finish breakfast among the greenery before continuing toward Nørrebro *(p133)*.

Afternoon For quirky, independent shops and Instagram-perfect alleys, explore Elmegade, Jægersborgade and Blågårds-gade in diverse and dynamic Nørrebro. Each street is packed with cool boutiques, tempting cafés, and destination restaurants. If you're unsure about where to stop, head for an impeccable lunch at Mirabelle *(www.mirabelle-bakery.dk)*, one of Copenhagen's best bakeries.

Evening Pay your respects to author H C Andersen and philosopher Søren Kierkegaard at Assistens Cemetery in Nørrebro before saddling up and cycling south to Vesterbro. Take your time sipping craft beer at pubs such as Warpigs and Mikkeller *(p132)* before winding up the evening at Ideal Bar in the design-savvy music venue VEGA *(Enghavevej 40)*, where a good night is guaranteed.

←

1 Inside the Louisiana Museum of Modern Art.

2 Frederiksborg Castle.

3 A pretty cottage in Gilleleje.

4 Restoration work at Roskilde Vikingeskibsmuseet.

4 DAYS
in Zealand

Day 1

Morning Rise early and drive to one of the best contemporary art museums in the world – the Louisiana Museum of Modern Art *(p146)*. The abstract sculpture garden, framed by the Øresund Sound, is stunning.

Afternoon Continue on to scenic Humblebæk and lunch at the waterfront Restaurant Sletten *(p164)* followed by a stroll on the beach. Drive 17 km (11 miles) north to Domain Aalsgaard *(p168)*, a small seaside vineyard and Denmark's first certified winery – perfect for tastings.

Evening If time and alcohol levels allow, enjoy the sound of the surf at Kronborg Slot *(p150)*, perched on the tip of Helsingør before settling in at the eccentric Kyhns Guesthouse *(www.kyhnsgaestehus.dk)*.

Day 2

Morning Drive to Hornbæk home to the Danish Riviera's most popular beach – the name means "surf beach" – and makes for a perfect morning walk. Move on to Gilleleje *(p164)*, the Riviera's most charming, sleepy village, and explore its small lanes with clusters of thatched houses leading to the historic harbour.

Afternoon For an unpretentious, freshly caught fish lunch head to Restaurant Brasseriet *(www.brasseriet-gilleleje.dk)*, then follow the seaside trails between Gilleleje and Tisvildeleje for good bird-watching opportunities.

Evening Drive along the gorgeous coastal road of Strandvejen to Tisvildeleje. Here you'll find the historic 1896 beachside resort of Helenekilde Badehotel *(p167)*. Stop here for the night and enjoy the sun setting over the terrace.

Day 3

Morning Head to Troldeskoven, or The Trolls' Forest, the starting point for exploring around Tisvildeleje, part of the vast Kongernes Nordsjælland National Park. It's an eerie area of ancient trees, bent and twisted into bizarre shapes.

Afternoon Drive 30 km (18 miles) southeast to Frederiksborg Slot *(p160)*, Christian IV's grand Renaissance castle in Hillerød, with lavishly decorated rooms and splendid portraiture. Lunch on Danish classics at Spisestedet Leonora, in the former castle stables, and relish the view before explore the romantic gardens.

Evening Pick up a bottle from Vexebo Vin *(Veksebovej 9)*, Denmark's hottest natural winemaker, before heading south down to Roskilde *(p154)* to check into 300-year-old Zleep Hotel *(p156)*.

Day 4

Morning Join locals for a leisurely coffee at Kaffekilden *(www.kaffekilden.net)* before strolling past the UNESCO-ranked Domkirke toward the harbour.

Afternoon Time travel to the world of the Vikings at the renowned Vikingeskibs-museet *(p158)*, where five sunken longships have been brought back to life by archaeologists. Enjoy interactive history lessons in Viking culture, and sail on one of the vessels up the Roskilde fjord.

Evening Dine at New Nordic gem Mumm *(www.mummros kilde.com)*, then enjoy a craft beer at edgy Klosterkælderen *(www. klosterkaelderen.beer)*.

7 DAYS
in Jutland and Funen

Day 1

Start by wandering the cobbled streets of fairytale author H C Andersen's hometown, Odense (p198). Denmark's third largest city has a lovely centre full of painted manor houses and Andersen-themed attractions, including his childhood home and the H C Andersen Museum. Enjoy lunch at bistro No. 61 (www.restaurant. no1.dk) before meandering along the city's fairy tale trail, lined with fantastical sculptures. For dinner, mmoks (www. mmoks.dk) serves New Nordic small plates with impeccable wine pairings.

Day 2

Get your caffeine fix and a croissant at Nelle's Coffee (www.nellesbar.dk), Odense's favourite for latte art and organic carbs, before getting on the road. Cross the Lille Bælt strait to Jutland, head west, and take the ferry from Esbjerg to Fanø (p222), the tiny idyllic Wadden Sea islet. After a 12-minute ride you're on white sand beaches populated by seal colonies. Sip a beer at Fanø Bryghus (www.fanoebryghus.dk), a renowned craft brewery, then scoop up

some local ham, cheese and bread from Rudbecks family deli (www.udbecks.dk) and enjoy a picnic by the water.

Day 3

Take a morning ferry back to the peninsula and cross Jutland, stopping at Jelling (p219). Here you'll find two UNESCO-listed rune stones from the 10th century, which mark key turning points in Denmark's monarchy. Once you've had your fill of history, continue one hour northeast to Aarhus (p208), Denmark's fast-growing cultural capital and dine at Substans (p208), a New Nordic powerhouse.

Day 4

Kick off with a walk high above the city in the rainbow-hued tunnel on top of ARoS Kunstmuseum (p210). Designed by Olafur Eliasson, it's one of the most spectacular immersive art installations and most photographed spots in Denmark. View Danish modernists and other greats in the permanent collection before lunching

1 H C Andersen's childhood home.

2 Seals on Fanø beach.

3 Substans restaurant in Aarhus.

4 Olafur Eliasson's *Your rainbow panorama* atop the ARoS Kunstmuseum, Aarhus.

5 Sand dunes along Råbjerg Mile.

on local seasonal food at ARoS Wine and Food Hall. Wander the attractive centre, including narrow, half-timbered Møllestien, then head to Aarhus Food Hall for a *smorgasbord* of local and international cuisine and Mikkeller beer.

Day 5

Drive due north one hour to Fyrkat *(p238)*, a former Viking fort castle with reconstructed buildings and interactive demonstrations, including falconry, weaponry and meal preparation. Continue north to Skagen *(p234)* at the tip of the Jutland peninsula. Check into 19th-century hotel Brøndums *(www.broendums-hotel.dk)*, where the Skagen painters gathered out in their heydey, and enjoy a leisurely meal at its restaurant, featuring original Madame Brøndum recipes. End the day with a stroll on Sønderstrand Beach.

Day 6

Soak up the morning view of the Kattegat Sea from Sønderstrand before stepping into Skagens Museum *(p234)*, where the

Skagen School painters' canvases perfectly capture the landscape. Make your way to Grenen *(p234)*, the curving arch of sand at the ultimate tip of the peninsula, where the North Sea (Skaggerak) and the Baltic Sea (Kattegat) clash, to marvel at the power of the waves. Meander back into the lovely streets of Gammel Skagen and end the day at a buzzy seafood restaurant on the harbour.

Day 7

Brave the wilder west coast, with its bigger beaches and bigger waves, where Danes drive right onto the wide white-sand beaches of Kandestederne and Skiveren. Lounge and paddle awhile, then head to the mighty Råbjerg Mile *(p236)* where Denmark's tallest sand dunes offer exercise and wide views. Ruths Brasserie *(www.ruths-hotel.dk)* will replenish your energy with French cuisine.

→

1 Traditional dwellings in Tinganes, Tórshavn.

2 Artfully presented scallops at Koks.

3 Puffins on Kalsoy.

4 Múlafossur waterfall.

3 DAYS
in the Faroe Islands

Day 1

Morning Explore the Faroese capital Tórshavn *(p266)* on Streymoy island, strolling the winding, narrow pathways in the Á Reyni district, where the Viking turf-roofed homes are tightly nestled. Stop by Panamé coffee shop and Vaglið bookshop and maybe pick up hand-knits at Guðrun & Guðrun on Niels Finsens gøta.

Afternoon Stock up on picnic supplies and drive half an hour northwest to the legendary Vestmanna bird cliffs *(p266)*. Boat tours run from May to September (advance booking advised) and are a great way to see the deep grottoes, soaring cliffs, the nesting site of thousands of sea birds.

Evening Head back to Tórshavn for a memorable meal at Koks *(p266)*, the islands' most innovative restaurant (reservations essential).

Day 2

Morning Set off early to Klaksvík, a drive of 1 hour and 20 minutes, to shop for hiking snacks before catching the ferry to magical Kalsoy island *(p266)*, dubbed "the flute" due to its thin shape. Ridged with 13 peaks and 11 valleys, and home to just 150 people, it's truly unique. Sip a coffee and take in the views on the scenic 20-minute boat ride.

Afternoon The 5-km (3-mile) round-trip hike to the lighthouse at Kallur, Kalsoy's northern tip, affords astonishing views. Start from the village of Trøllanes, where there's parking and a trail map. Along the way, in addition to sheep, look out for Kalsoy's rich bird life, including puffins, storm petrels and black guillemots. At the top are epic views of craggy cliffs, wild seascapes and verdant valleys.

Evening Catch the late afternoon ferry back to Klaksvik, to dine on classic Faroese dishes at the cosy yet elegant Áarstova *(www.aarstova.fo)*.

Day 3

Morning Breakfast at the Brell café *(9 Vaglið)* in Tórshavn, with options like berry tarts and *smørrebrød*, then drive to the island of Vágar *(p266)*. The third largest of the Faroe archipelago, it has charming villages and awe-inspiring natural attractions. Start at Sandavágur, a 13th-century town on the south coast and two-time winner of best-kept village in the Faroes.

Afternoon Continue on to tiny, pictur-esque Gásadalur, tucked between lush, green fields and jagged montains. This village, which was inaccessible to cars until 2004, has just 24 residents but is famous for the beautiful Múlafossur water-fall a short walk away. The mighty cascade plummets off the side of the island straight into the Atlantic ocean. From here you can also spy tiny Mykines island.

Evening Back in the car, head back to base camp in Tórshavn for an evening meal at Ræst *(www.raest.fo)*, the island's New Nordic hotspot. The name is the Faroese word for the fermentation which dominates traditional regional cuisine, and this trendy-rustic restaurant applies the concept to lamb and seafood, house-made bread, seaweed beer and desserts.

The Art of New Nordic

New Nordic cuisine uses age-old methods of cooking with new techniques, plus fresh, seasonal ingredients from Scandinavia's fruitful countryside. Inputs are sustainably sourced and, in some instances, foraged. You're spoiled for choice when it comes to New Nordic in Copenhagen (p68) but there is so much beyond the captial. Highlights include Slots-køkkenet (p175) in North-western Zealand and Substans in Aarhus (p211), both popular with food critics.

→

Beautiful New Nordic dish at Aarhus' Substans, and interior of noma (inset)

DENMARK FOR
FOODIES

Denmark may be small, but it's a world culinary destination. The country has a whopping 31 Michelin stars, and is famous for igniting the New Nordic movement. There is much more gourmet goodness besides and, whether it's fine dining or comfort food, Danes take pride in their cuisine.

Classic Cuisine

Traditional Danish cuisine is comforting, revolving around pork, herring, rye bread and root vegetables. At lunchtime, smørrebrød is the perpetually popular choice. Flæskesteg is Denmark's national dish, consisting of a roast pork joint with crackling and parsley sauce, and Frikadeller (pork and veal meatballs) is another time-honoured hot dish. If you're looking for heartier fare, head to the likes of Kolvig (p213) in Aarhus and Rønnede Kro (p185) in Southwestern Zealand.

←

Seasoning traditional smørrebrød laden with freshwater prawns

↑ Foraging for fresh ingredients in Denmark's wild and green landscape

Foraging For Food

Wild food is wildly popular across Denmark, foraged by pros and amateurs alike. Spots like Nordisk Spisehus *(p211)* in Aarhus and Kadeau *(p123)* in Copenhagen forage for ingredients. Learn more at www.nordicfoodlab.org.

(p211) ... *(p123)*

INVENTION OF SMØRREBROD

Food historians debate whether *smørrebrød* (open sandwiches) are of medieval or 19th-century origin, but the gist is the same. When lunch was the most important meal of the day, workers heaped toppings such as fried fish, marinated herring, bacon and mushrooms, on stale bread. When soaked by the topping, the bread was so tasty, they ate that too. Of the 300-plus types, a classic Bornholmer is a sourdough rye slice with smoked herring, raw onion and egg yolk. A New Nordic spin could have toppings of beef tartar, pickled beetroot, potato crisps, capers, cress and a mustard emulsion. The perfect pairing: Danish beer and schnapps.

Shoppers stopping at food stalls in Copenhagen's Torvehallerne ↑

On the Street

Pølsebod (hot dog stands) have long been a cultural institution in Denmark, serving sausages topped with ketchup, mustard and sautéed onions. You'll also find gourmet hot dog stands at food halls, which have proven wildly popular in Denmark's cities, with the likes of Aarhus Central Food Market *(p211)* and Copenhagen's Torvehallerne *(www.torvehallernekbh.dk)*. When you're ready for a sweet snack, be sure to try *æbleskiver* (fluffy pancake balls), the perfect pick-me-up.

Modern Masters

When it comes to modern art, Denmark's artworks are often housed in buildings as striking as the collection inside. ARoS Kunstmuseum *(p210)* in Aarhus is topped with *Your rainbow panorama*, a 360-degree rooftop walkway by artist Olafur Eliasson. Inside, the collection includes Denmark's avant garde CoBrA movement and the Neue Wilden group. The seafront Louisiana Museum *(p146)* woos art lovers with its extraordinary international collection of contemporary and modern art from the likes of Asger Jorn, Picasso, Giacometti and so many more.

→

The attractive exterior of the ground-breaking Louisiana Museum

DENMARK FOR
ART LOVERS

Denmark's art galleries celebrate the emotive scenes captured by artists for centuries, including works belonging to the Golden Age and Skagen School. Exciting contemporary art can also be found in urban public spaces, from street art in Copenhagen to installations in Aarhus and Helsingør.

Inspired by Nature

Denmark's stunning nature and wildlife were largely immortalized on canvas from 1880, when Realism and Naturalism reigned supreme. The most famous exponent was the Skagen School, with artists such as Peder S Krøyer and Anna and Michael Ancher capturing the sunlight and seascapes of Northern Jutland on canvas. Visitors can soak up the inspiring landscape for themselves in Skagen *(p234)* and admire the school's artworks at Skagen Museum. Bornholm saw a similar movement, with works by painters Edvard Weie and Karl Isakson displayed at Bornholms Kunstmuseum *(p252)*.

←

Summer Evening near Skagen by Peder S Krøyer

The Golden Age

Copenhagen's Statens Museum for Kunst (p76) has Denmark's most comprehensive collection of masterpieces from the Golden Age (1800-1850), a period so-named for the surge in national creativity. The museum houses paintings by Golden Age giants like Nicolai Abildgaard, C W Eckersberg, L A Ring and Vilhelm Hammershøi. Learn more about the movement at Ny Carlsberg Glyptotek (p96) in Copenhagen, Fuglsang Kunstmuseum (p190) in Southern Zealand and Ribe Kunstmuseum (p212).

In the Garden Doorway by L A Ring, displayed at the Statens Museum for Kunst ↓

↑ Modern art displayed in the airy interior of Louisiana Museum

---

💬 INSIDER TIP
Street Art

Construction sites, bridges and so much more are treated as canvases in the capital, especially in Nørrebro and Vesterbro. Urban Explorer CPH offers great street art tours *(www.urbexplorer.dk)*.

Sculpture Spaces

Copenhagen has a museum dedicated to Berthel Thorvaldsen, the most renowned Danish sculptor and a leading Neo-Classical sculptor in Europe. Thorvaldsens Museum (p112) contains stone works, sketches and objects of antiquity that inspired the master. For modern and abstract pieces, the outdoor waterfront sculpture park at Louisiana (p146) has works by Jean Arp and Max Ernst. Also just outside the capital is ARKEN Museum (p130), which offers creative experiences interacting with provocative pieces in nature.

←

Neo-Classical sculptures lining the walls of Thorvaldsens Museum

Oar-some Ships

Roskilde's Vikingeskibs-museet *(p158)* houses the ancient skeletons of five vessels sunk near Roskilde in the mid-11th century. In the boatyard, Viking tools and experimental archaeology are being used to reconstruct the ships. Replica boats even take visitors out sailing on Roskilde fjord from April to October. Those preferring dry ground will enjoy the Viking craft workshops here.

←

Inside the boatyard workshop at Roskilde's Vikingeskibsmuseet

DENMARK AND THE
VIKING TRAIL

The name "Viking" comes from the Old Norse for "to travel," suggesting that the Vikings saw themselves as explorers. Today, adventurers visit Denmark in search of reminders of this ancient civilization. From sailing on a recon-structed ship to feasting in a long hall, here are ideas for getting started.

TOP 3 VIKING EVENTS

Jelling Viking Market
Viking horse shows and craft fair, plus Viking skills to try, and trips on a Viking ship in early July *(www.vikinge marked-jelling.dk)*.

Moesgaard Viking Moot
Late July in Aarhus sees a Viking market with reenactments *(www. vikingetraeffet.dk)*.

Jels Viking Pageant
Fierce swordfighting and spicy romance presented in an open-air theatre in July. *(www.jelsvikinge spil.dk)*.

Burial Rites

Dating from between 400 and 1000 AD, Lindholm Høje *(p238)* near Aalborg is a burial site with 700 stone-marked graves. A Viking village once stood just to the north and thanks to a sand drift that covered the area in 1000 AD, the remains are well preserved. Findings are imaginatively displayed at the Lindholm Høje Museum.

→

Stones circling graves at Lindholm Høje, Northern Jutland

Fyrkat Farmstead

A recreated Viking farmstead near Fyrkat fortress *(p239)*, in Northern Jutland, shows how farms supported defensive positions. The farm is authentically built and costumed staff demonstrate Viking crafts such as silverwork and weaving. Children can don costumes and let off steam on a Viking-themed playground.

🔍 HIDDEN GEM
Reading Runes

In Jelling *(p219)*, 10th-century runes reveal much about ancient Danish monarchy, mainly the character of Harald Bluetooth (who gave the name to wireless tech).

↑ An attractive thatched building at the Fyrkat Viking Center

Re-enactments in Ribe

The jewel in Jutland's Viking crown is Ribe *(p212)*, the country's oldest town, founded in around 700 as a Viking marketplace. Ribes Vikinger *(p213)* is an informative museum, but the era is best depicted at Ribe Vikingecenter *(p213)*, which has a longhouse with workshops and re-enactments. Hands-on activities include coin making, falconry, woodcarving, archery, swordplay, and cooking.

←

Traditional helmet used during Viking re-enactments at Ribe Vikingecenter

Vikings in the Capital

The Nationalmuseet in Copenhagen *(p100)* houses all manner of Viking treasures, from jewellery and coins to weaponry, giving a sense of the lives of these ancient people. Be sure to pay a visit to the bronze Viking figures atop a column in Rådhuspladsen *(p103)*.

→

A dazzling array of Viking jewellery at the Nationalmuseet

Awesome Architecture

Bold shapes, sustainable materials and an abundance of natural light characterize modern Danish architecture. In Copenhagen the glass Black Diamond at Det Kongelige Bibliotek *(p113)* and the mighty Øresund Bridge *(p137)* are both arresting sights. The Iceberg apartment buildings in Aarhus *(p210)* are striking and wonderfully airy inside, while The Wave in Vejle *(p222)* is softer in its design but no less striking.

→

The clean silhouettes of The Wave in Vejle, Southern Jutland, and the impressive Øresund Bridge *(inset)*

DENMARK FOR
DESIGN LOVERS

Perhaps Denmark's most influential cultural export is its style, which never seems to go out of style. Clean, simple lines, minimalism and functionalism pervade clothing, interior and furniture design. Here are some elements to look out for in this effortlessly cool country.

Cool Ceramics

Denmark has produced elegant ceramics for centuries. Royal Copenhagen *(www.royalcopenhagen.com)*, established in 1775, epitomises classic Danish porcelain with its simple, dainty patterns, while design-forward Kähler Ceramics *(www.kahlerdesign.com)* has preferred pops of colour since 1889. Inge Vincents *(www.vincents.dk)* represents the new generation of Danish ceramics, with paper thin and carefully twisted porcelains.

←

Royal Copenhagen's ceramic wears, complemented with pops of colour

Modish Museums
Designmuseum Danmark *(p80)* in Copenhagen has an gorgeous collection of applied arts plus a museum store for design-savvy souvenirs. Trapholt in Kolding *(p224)* also houses cool design exhibits.

↑ Chairs displayed in Designmuseum Danmark

↑ One of Copenhagen's stricking, elevated cycle bridges

Stylish Yet Sustainable
In the last few decades Copenhagen has been reimagined as a green city with fewer cars and many bikes. Attractive, effective bridges and innovative urban parks demonstrate the city's commitment to becoming more sustainable while retaining a dynamic design approach. The striking cyclist bridges of Inderhavnsbroen *(p125)* and Cirkelbroen *(p125)* capture this.

Craft Brewers

The capital's craft beer allstars are Mikkeller *(www.mikkeller.dk)*, To Øl *(www.toolbeer.dk)* and Amager *(www.amager bryghus.dk)*. Carlsberg *(www.carlsberg.com)* also has a house craft label, Jacobsen, which can be enjoyed at its Copenhagen brewery *(p132)*. Outside of Copenhagen, craft beer aficionados are excited about island brewing, such as Fanø Bryghus on Fanø *(p222)*, Ugly Duckling Brewing on Funen *(p194)*, Svaneke on Bornholm *(p248)*. Speciality beers can also be found at small brewpubs.

$\rightarrow$

To Øl's buzzing BRUS brewpub and bottle shop in Copenhagen

DENMARK
ON TAP

Beer has been part of Danish culture for 5,000 years. Carlsberg and Tuborg once dominated, but craft brewing has grown faster than wild yeast in sour beer. With more than 150 microbreweries, Denmark has become an artisan beer destination.

Where to Head

City-trippers are spoiled for choice, with 90 per cent of breweries in the greater Copenhagen area and more popping up across Danish cities. Basement Beer *(www.basementbeerbar.dk)* is the go-to bar in Aalborg, while Odense has the playful Anarkist Beer & Food Lab *(www.the odorschiotzbrewing.co)*. In Aarhus, head to Mig og Ølsnedkeren *(www.olsnedkeren.dk)*.

$\leftarrow$

Exposed barrels at a micro-brewery in Copenhagen

King Carlsberg

In the early 19th century, Jacob Christian Jacobsen studied the art of brewing in Bavaria before returning to his native Denmark with a supply of yeast in a hat box. Little did Carlsberg know that his would become a household name, nor that his Copenhagen brewery would become a popular tourist attraction. Head to the achingly cool neighbourhood of Vesterbro *(p132)* to visit the brewery. A handful of craft brewers are on its doorstep if you fancy a tipple afterwards.

← A bike carrying cans of Carlsberg in Copenhagen

TOP 3 PUBS WITH A VIEW

Skagen Bryghus
The northernmost brewery of Denmark has seafood pub grub and views of the ocean *(skagenbryghus.dk)*.

Halsnæs Bryghus
On the Danish Riviera, this brewpub has floor-to-ceiling windows looking on to Hundested Harbour *(www. halsbryg.dk)*.

Svaneke Bryghus
The restaurant at this organic, sustainable waterfront brewery has a seasonal menu as enticing as its brews *(www.svaneke bryghus.dk)*.

Maverick Mikkeller

Mikkel Borg Bjergso, founder of Mikkeller *(www.mikkeller. dk)* and the pioneer of the Danish craft beer movement, is responsible for brewing some of the most distinctive beers in the world. The former teacher doesn't own his own brewery, instead guest-brewing at other Danish breweries and creating beers for 40 shops and bars worldwide. You'll find a number of dedicated Mikkeller bars across Copenhagen, plus two in Aarhus *(p208)* and one in Odense *(p198)*.

Did You Know?

Denmark's popular Christmas Beer release party takes place on 1st November.

↑ Zany designs decorating Mikkeller craft beer cans

On Your Bike

Gentle, flat terrain and bike paths make Denmark ideal for family cycling. You can take bikes aboard ferries to islands like Falster and Møn where traffic is light. Copenhagen has more bikes than people, so experience the city like a Copenhagener on a locally invented Christiania bike, with a cargo area for the tots.

←

Cycling with a child trailer along a coastal path on Falster

DENMARK FOR
FAMILIES

Denmark is made for family holidays. From the imaginative amusement parks of Tivoli, LEGOLAND® and Bakken, and the country's many interactive Viking experiences, to the stretches of sandy beaches and numerous cycling opportunities – there's something for kids of all ages.

Animal Encounters

Walk on the wild side at Wadden Sea National Park by starting at Vadehavscentret *(p213)* in Ribe. The visitor centre has hands-on exhibits. Esbjerg *(p223)*, in Southern Jutland, is home to seal colonies, while Rømø *(p222)* offers a porpoise and seal safari. Knuthenborg Safari Park *(p192)* and Copenhagen Zoo *(p128)* are both home to all manner of animals.

Riding High

Denmark has an enviable collection of amusement parks. Big and little kids alike flock to Billund's LEGOLAND® (p214) to build and play. With interactive rides, cities built entirely from mini-bricks and opportunities to build your own masterpiece, there is something for everyone. In Copenhagen, Tivoli (p94) continues to enchant families with its twinkling pavilions, fairy-tale-themed rides and carnival games. Those looking to make a splash will love Lalandia waterpark (p186), while historic Bakken (p162) has welcomed families since the 16th century!

$\rightarrow$

Flying through the air on the chair swing ride in Tivoli, Copenhagen

Time Travel

Follow in the footsteps of the infamous Vikings. In Roskilde you can watch boat-builders reconstruct Viking long boats at the Vikingeskibs-museet (p158) and even sail the high seas on a reimagined vessel. Ribe (p212) and Fyrkat (p238) offer warrior training, falconry shows, archery, coin and jewellery making, and more.

$\leftarrow$

Learning about craftsmanship at Vikingeskibsmuseet, Roskilde

Life's A Beach

Denmark has over 7,000 km (4,350 miles) of coastline and some great beaches. Top family-friendly sands include Amager Strandpark (p138) close to Copenhagen, the shallow and calm waters of Marielyst (p189), and beautiful Hornbæk (p164). Around Skagen (p234), Sønderstrand and the Kattegat coast beaches are known for gentle waters.

↑ Watching a young elephant at Copenhagen Zoo

$\rightarrow$

Running over a sandy dune in Denmark

In the Beginning

Andersen was born in Odense in 1805, and today the city honours their most famous resident. See the desk at which he penned his magical tales at HC Andersens Hus and visit his simply furnished childhood home at HC Andersens Barndomshjem (p198). A ticket will get you into both if you visit on the same day.

←

HC Andersen's writing desk at HC Andersens Hus, in Odense

DENMARK AND
HC ANDERSEN

The magical fairytales of Hans Christian Andersen have become the stuff of legend. The writer was born in Odense, lived in Copenhagen and loved Helsingør, leaving behind countless reminders of his life's work. Explore the scenes that inspired him as you follow his literary trail.

TOP 4 HC ANDERSEN ACTIVITIES

Fairy Tale Trail, Odense
Discover 15 fairytale sculptures dotted around Odense (www. visitodense.com).

Summer Show, Odense
Catch a performance of a classic Andersen tale at Den Fynske Landsby (www.visitodense.com).

HC Andersen Bicycle Tour, Copenhagen
Cycle from landmark to landmark (www. copenhagenbicycles.dk).

Ugly Duckling Beer Tasting
Tastings inspired by Andersen (www.ugly duckling brewing.dk).

Did You Know?

It is understood that Anderson was dyslexic and this gave him a unique writing style.

A summer open-air performance of a fairytale story ↑

Literary Landscape

Andersen took inspiration from the landscape, giving a magical angle to Denmark's wildlife and people. The idea for *The Ugly Duckling* came to him in handsome Ringsted *(p182)* while on Funen *(p194)* he wrote the poem *I am a Scandinavian*. Danes have added to this landscape, such as with a number of Andersen-inspired statues in Odense.

→

Bjørn Nørgaard's *The Trinity*, depicting the three sides of H C Andersen

Life in Copenhagen

Having failed as an actor, Andersen turned to his pen. He lived along vibrant Nyhavn *(p104)* and borrowed books from the Rundetaarn library*(p105)* for inspiration. Copenhageners are fiercely proud of their links to the writer. You can visit his grave in Assistens Kirkegård in Nørrebro *(p133)*, statues of him in Kongens Have *(p87)* and Rådhuspladsen *(p103)* and, of course, greet the haunting Little Mermaid *(p82)*.

Cycling in Copenhagen

Copenhagen's 13 km (8-mile) Harbour Circle route follows both sides of the harbour, from Nyhavn in the north to Sluseløbet in the south. It's connected by six design-savvy, car-free bridges. Visit Copenhagen *(www.visit copenhagen.com)* has details of self-led cycling tours, and you can check out our itinerary on p64.

←

Cycling along Copenhagen's Inderhavnsbrøen

DENMARK
BY BIKE

When in Denmark, do as the Danes do and cycle. Predominantly flat terrain and brilliant infrastructure mean cycling is at the heart of Danish living, both in city centres and rural outposts. It's also an affordable and fun way to see the country. Here are some tips to get you started.

Romantic Rides

If you're looking for a romantic cycle, Bornholm *(p242)* is best. The island is the sunniest part of Denmark, and bike trails snake through forests, quaint towns and along gorgeous coastal paths. Stop at Kadeau *(p251)* for dinner before a night at the gorgeous Stammershalle Badehotel *(p249)*. Turn to p254 for ideas on a cycle route.

Pedal in Pastures

Funen island *(p194)* is known as the garden or orchard of Denmark, and its verdant landscape certainly makes for a gorgous bike ride. More than 1,000 km (620 miles) of cycling routes lead through beautiful pastures and woodland, past castles and mansions, and alongside the Baltic coast. Its main city of Odense *(p198)* has 540 km (335 miles) of bike paths and free city bike rental. Visit the tourist office *(www.visitfyn.com)* for more infomation and itinerary suggestions.

$\longrightarrow$

Looking out to sea on a lovely sand beach on Funen

The Ancient Road

The Ancient Road *(www.haervej. com)* follows the hilltops of the Jutland Ridge for 450 km (280 miles), leading all the way down to the German border. This is a scenic journey dotted with historic monuments and is popular with both expert cyclists and hikers.

$\longleftarrow$

Mountain bikers planning their journey on the Ancient Road

Wheel-y Wild

Adventurers should head for Jutland's wild west coast, home to Denmark's most panoramic cycle route *(www. northsea cycleroute.dk)*. A particularly scenic stretch is the 42 km (26 mile) road from Nymindegab to Bork Havn, finishing at the town of Nørre Nebel. Though the landscape is truly tranquil, a good bike and stamina are recommended for this particular route.

$\uparrow$

A quiet road snaking through cornfields in Bornholm

$\longrightarrow$

Gorgeous views from a sand dune in Lønstrup

Beachside Abodes

When it comes to romantic places to stay beside the sea, you're spoiled for choice. Along the Danish Riviera, in Northwestern Zealand, turquoise waters and white sands could be yours at a number of bathing hotels frequented by royalty and celebs, such as idyllic Helenekilde Badehotel *(p167)*. Gilleleje *(p164)* is a pretty fishing village that beckons with its houses leading down to the water, and nearby Hornbæk *(p164)* is a lovely resort.

←

Sun setting over a wooden pier in Hornbæk, Northwestern Zealand

DENMARK FOR
BEAUTIFUL BEACHES

No matter where you are in Denmark, you're never far from the sea. Better still, Denmark has some of the loveliest beaches in Europe, from secluded island beaches and the white sands of the Danish Riviera, to the glittering sunlight of Skagen in the north. There's a bathing spot for every occasion.

Idyllic Islands

Denmark's islands offer every type of beach, with Bornholm *(p242)* particularly rich in sandy stretches and Funen *(p194)* boasting 1,100 km (684 miles) of coastline. Rømø *(p222)*, off the coast of Southern Jutland, has a 12-km (7-mile) sand beach, while Fejø and Femø *(p158)* in Southern Zealand have many private beaches.

Sandy Balka Beach, on the lovely island of Bornholm ↑

TOP 3 EATERIES WITH A WATERSIDE VIEW

Restaurant Kadeau, Bornholm
This Michelin-star restaurant is set right on the beachfront in Aakirkeby (www.kadeau.dk).

Stud!o, Copenhagen
The stylish dining room at this New Nordic gem looks out over the city harbour (www.thestandardcph.dk).

Hotel Fredriksminde, Præstø
The restaurant here is praised by critics and has a gorgeous terrace by the sea (www.frederiksminde.com).

Romantic Retreat

The sunlight of Denmark's northernmost beaches in and around Skagen (p234) are legendary. Grenen beach at the jagged tip of the peninsula is a dramatic scene (though banned to swimmers), while the calm waters of Skagen Sønderstrand are best for a romantic evening walk.

↑ Seals resting on Grenen beach in Skagen, Northern Jutland

Wild Wild West

Thrill-seekers of all ages should head for Jutland's wild and windswept west coast, where adventure awaits off the beaches – from surfing and sailing to paddle-boarding. A surf community is growing around Klitmøller, not far from the calmer waterways of Limfjorden (p230). In the south, Rømø (p222) is great for kitesurfing.

←

Surfing the boisterous waves off Klitmøller, in Northern Jutland

Urban Beaches

Copenhagen's coolest harbour swim area is Havnebadet Islands Brygge (p137), which has three pools, diving boards and a BBQ area, while Krøyers Plads (p124) in Christianshavn has a pier beside great eating and drinking spots. Families will enjoy Amager Strandpark (p138), a long coastal beach on the city's southern island.

→

Sunbathing alongside one of Copenhagen's canals in summertime

Did You Know?

Nikolaj Coster-Waldau, who plays Jaime Lannister in *Game of Thrones*, is Danish.

Alicia Vikander and Mads Mekkelsen in A Royal Affair ↑

DENMARK FOR
INSPIRATION

Denmark might be small but it excels at big stories. Prolific actors, directors and screenwriters have hailed from this part of Scandinavia, and the country's brooding landscape has inspired blockbuster TV series. Here's how best to experience the screen-stealing scenery.

Nordic Noir

Characterized by thriller narratives, unhurried plots and brooding cinematography, Denmark has made a killing exporting Nordic Noir TV series, and inspired various spin-offs. Copenhagen formed the backdrop of *The Killing* and *Borgen*, while the Øresund Bridge *(p137)* played an integral role in *The Bridge*. Follow in the footsteps of your favourite detective on a tour *(www.nordictours.com)*.

→

Actress Sofie Gråbøl on the set of *The Killing* in famous Faroe knitwear

💬 INSIDER TIP
Like Sarah Lund

Fancy the hand-knitted jumper made famous by *The Killing*? Head to Gudrun & Gudrun in Tórshavn on the Faroe Islands *(www.gudrun gudrun.com)*.

Move Over Hollywood

Forget London and L A and head to Denmark for screen-worthy scenes. The story of one of the first sex-change operations, *The Danish Girl* (2015), was filmed around Nyhavn *(p104)* while period romp *A Royal Affair* (2012) took inspiration from Christiansborg Slot *(p98)*. Director Lars Von Trier shot the murderous, star-studded series *The House That Jack Built* (2018) in a forest north of Copenhagen, having previously filmed Björk here in *Dancer in the Dark* (2000). Outside of the capital, *Babette's Feast* (1987) was shot in Vendsyssel, Northern Jutland.

Baroness Karen von ↑
Blixen-Finecke, also
known as Isak Dinesen

Out of Denmark

Baroness Karen Christenze von Blixen-Finecke (1885-1962) is one of Denmark's most loved 20th-century international authors. She wrote two of her most revered works, *Out of Africa* and *Babette's Feast* under the pen name Isak Dinesen. These were made into films, the former winning seven Oscars. At Blixen's Rungstedlund home *(p163)*, you can see furniture from her Kenya farm, including Denys Finch Hatton's favourite chair and the chest given to Blixen by her butler, Farah.

↑ Charming exterior of
Rungstedlund, Karen
von Blixen's home

A YEAR IN
DENMARK

JANUARY

Winter Swimming Festival *(late Jan)* "Icebreakers" frolic in the freezing sea.

Winter Food Fest *(late Jan)* Restaurants in Odense present gourmet treats.

△ **Copenhagen Fashion Week** *(late Jan)* The Nordic region's biggest fashion event.

FEBRUARY

△ **CycleCross World Championships** *(early Feb)* Top riders tackle cycling's most rugged, muddy event over rough pavements in Bogense.

Mad Design Live *(early Feb)* The very latest designs in Scandinavian homes and furniture are on display in Bolig.

World Cup TÖLT *(mid- to late Feb)* International dressage competition featuring Icelandic horses.

MAY

SPOT Music Festival *(early May)* The streets of Aarhus host 200 bands, from folk to rock.

Copenhagen Marathon *(19 May)* One of Scandinavia's biggest, most popular marathons.

△ **Aarhus Classic Car Race** *(late May)* Old Bugattis race vintage Formula One cars.

DISTORTION *(late May)* Over 100,000 hip hop and dance music fans throng Copenhagen streets.

JUNE

Skagen Music Festival *(early Jun)* One of Denmark's oldest folklore and folk music festivals.

Copenhell *(mid-Jun)* Copenhagen's four-day celebration of heavy-metal music and motorcycles.

△ **St Hans** *(23 Jun)* An ancient, country-wide celebration in which effigies of witches are burned.

Roskilde Rock *(late Jun)* Denmark's big rock fest.

SEPTEMBER

△ **Aarhus Food Festival** *(early Sep)* Tastings of regional specialities in Aarhus restaurants.

Tour de Gudenå *(7 Sep)* An annual kayak race across the scenic lake at Silkeborg.

Nykøbing Honky Tonk *(7 Sep)* Jazz festival.

OCTOBER

△ **Tivoli Halloween** *(second half of Oct)* Witches, lanterns and pumpkins galore, plus treasure hunts and seasonal menus.

MARCH

△ **Fastelavn** *(3 Mar)* Traditional Danish festival where children dress in costumes and smash suspended containers of sweets.

Horse and Rider *(early Mar)* The Danish Warmblood Stallion Show is hosted alongside an equestrian equipment trade fair in Herning.

World Championships of Women's Curling *(mid-Mar)* Held on the ice at Silkeborg, this is one of Scandinavia's most popular sport events.

APRIL

△ **International Viking Market** *(late Apr)* In Ribe, actors in Viking costume recreate a traditional medieval market, practice ancient crafts and fight mock battles.

JULY

Nibe Festival *(early Jul)* Camping and concerts.

Esbjerg Tall Ships Race *(mid-Jul)* High-masted vintage sailing ships visit Denmark for four days.

△ **Moesgaard Viking Moot** *(late Jul)* Scandinavia's biggest Viking re-enactment.

Copenhagen Opera Festival *(late Jul)* Arias echo in the capital as the divas come to town.

AUGUST

Esbjerg International Chamber Music Festival *(two weeks in Aug)* Music lovers from around the world attend performances, and masterclasses are offered to aspiring musicians.

Hans Christian Andersen Festival *(mid- to late Aug)* The city of Odense is populated with Ugly Ducklings, Little Mermaids and Snow Queens, all in costume and in character.

△ **Aarhus Festival** *(late Aug)* Denmark's second city delights in theatre, music, art and cuisine, with events all across the city.

NOVEMBER

St Morten's Day *(10 Nov)* Everyone in Denmark dines on goose or duck to celebrate an ancient tale about a priest hiding among a flock of geese to escape being named bishop.

△ **Hans Christian Andersen Christmas Market** *(late Nov)* An open-air market in Odense, featuring all kinds of crafts based on characters from Andersen's beloved books.

DECEMBER

△ **Three Days of Christmas** *(24–26 Dec)* Denmark counts Christmas as three days, each with special rituals and treats, and all official holidays.

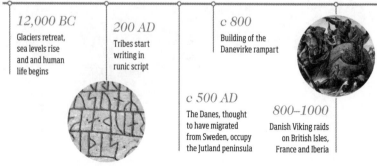

A BRIEF
HISTORY

Despite a history of pillaging, invasion and plague, Denmark has evolved through centuries of religious and social conflict into one of the world's most enviable and egalitarian democracies. And despite rain every other day, Danes are among the happiest people on earth.

Earliest Denmark

Denmark was shaped by climate. The first signs of human life date from the end of the Ice Age when glaciers retreated and rising sea levels divided the land into its present array of islands and fjords. In around 8300 BC temperatures began to rise. Tundra gave way to forests and local tribes hunted reindeer rather than fish and seals. The oldest preserved human body in Denmark is the Koelbjerg Man, who is thought to date back to around 8,000 BC. The bog body of a 25-year-old, named the Elling Woman, who died 2,400 years ago, shows evidence of ritual sacrifice.

1 A 16th century map of Denmark.

2 The Tollund Man bog body at the Museum Silkeborg.

3 A 19th century sketch of the Danevirke.

4 Carved rune stone at the Viking Museum in Bork, Ringkoebing Fjord.

Timeline of events

12,000 BC
Glaciers retreat, sea levels rise and and human life begins

200 AD
Tribes start writing in runic script

c 500 AD
The Danes, thought to have migrated from Sweden, occupy the Jutland peninsula

c 800
Building of the Danevirke rampart

800–1000
Danish Viking raids on British Isles, France and Iberia

The Great Wall of Denmark

By 500 AD, Scandinavian tribes had coalesced and one people was formed on the Jutland peninsula. Their greatest achievement was the Danevirke, a wall that stretched for 30 km (19 miles) and stood 6 m (20 ft) high. The brainchild of Godfred, King of Jutland (r 804–810), this rampart was the epitome of late Nordic Iron Age technology and was largely successful in repelling invaders. It is now on German soil, in the state of Schleswig-Holstein.

The Viking Age

As the population grew, expeditions were launched in search of new shores and resources. From about 700 to 1000 AD, Viking Danes and their Scandinavian counterparts murdered, enslaved and assimilated the peoples of their discovered lands, returning home with spoils of war and putting Scandinavia on the map as a powerful empire. Viking Danes sailed the globe, reaching Newfoundland, Kiev and Constantinople, and further establishing settlements in Iceland and Greenland. English King Alfred fought off Danish conquest in the south but the Vikings gained control in the north, and many left Denmark for the northern British Isles.

↑ *The Ancestor*, a 19th-century engraving of a Viking Dane

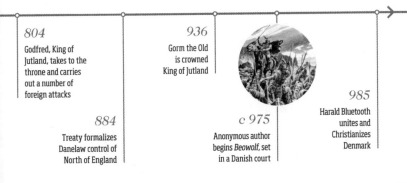

804
Godfred, King of Jutland, takes to the throne and carries out a number of foreign attacks

884
Treaty formalizes Danelaw control of North of England

936
Gorm the Old is crowned King of Jutland

c 975
Anonymous author begins *Beowolf*, set in a Danish court

985
Harald Bluetooth unites and Christianizes Denmark

Christian Era

In 936, Gorm the Old was crowned king of Jutland, but it was Gorm's son, Harald Bluetooth (r 958–986), who united Denmark and embraced Christianity in around 980. Bluetooth immortalized his achievement in Denmark's most cherished artifact, the Jelling Stone (p219). Bluetooth's grandson, Canute the Great (r 1016–1035), ruled as the monarch of Denmark, Norway and England until his death, marking the end of the Viking Age.

The Kalmar Union and Lutheran Reformation

Denmark's next defining moment came in 1363, when Princess Margaret I married Norway's King Håkon. From the age of 27 Margaret was the undisputed ruler of Denmark, albeit in the name of her infant son, Olaf. When he died suddenly in 1387, Margaret was once more declared regent, before she nominated Erik of Pomerania as king of all Scandinavian nations in 1397. This was the foundation of the Kalmar Union, which would last until 1523. Around this time, the Lutheran Protestant Reformation swept through Denmark: monasteries were dissolved and Lutheranism was made the state religion, and remains so today.

QUEEN MARGARET I (1353–1412)

Denmark's first queen united and ruled Scandinavia without challenge, from 1389 to 1412. She was a popular monarch, celebrated for her wisdom, energy and morality. War with Sweden persisted after her death.

Timeline of events

1016
King Canute reigns over Denmark, Norway, Sweden, England and Finland

1035
Death of Canute marks end of the Viking Age

c 1160
City of Copenhagen founded as herring port

1227
Swedish victory at Bornhøved signals end of Danish dominance

1349–1350
Bubonic plague kills two-thirds of the population

1397
Norway, Sweden and Finland united under Danish rule in Kalmar Union

Absolute Monarchy

In the years that followed, Danish kings embarked on a series of disastrous religious wars. Encouraged by England, Christian IV (1577–1648) waded into the Thirty Years War in 1625, only to lose land, money and morale. In 1658, his son Frederick III (1609–1670) lost all of Denmark's territories in Sweden. He then declared himself absolute ruler, breaking with the Danish tradition of an elected king, and in 1665 stipulated that all future kings would be hereditary. Kings continued to rule as absolute monarchs until 1848.

Enlightenment

A peace treaty with Sweden signed in 1720 marked the beginning of the longest war-free period in Denmark's history. This period saw the economy grow and a new sense of Danish nationalism emerge, inspired by the French Enlightenment. Frederick VI (1768–1839) ushered in a series of reforms: land was broken up and distributed among the working classes, landowners were given roles in government and compulsory education was introduced for children under the age of 14.

① The Jelling Stone.

② Margaret I crowning Erik of Pomerania.

③ King Frederick III of Denmark and Norway.

④ The 1720 Battle of Grengam concludes war with Sweden.

Did You Know?

Since 1513, Denmark has alternated kings called Frederick and Christian.

1523
End of the historic Kalmar Union

1536
After civil war, Lutheranism becomes the official religion

1660
Absolutist hereditary monarchy installed

1658
Treaty of Roskilde costs Denmark last territories in Sweden

1720
War with Sweden ends; Denmark's population totals 700,000

1729
Greenland becomes province of Denmark

The Golden Age

In spite of a British attack of Copenhagen at the start of the 19th century, which left citizens starving, Denmark experienced an unprecedented flourishing of culture. The capital was rebuilt and the country delighted in the fairy tales of Hans Christian Andersen, the philosophical musings of Søren Kierkegaard, the music of Niels W. Gade and the Romantic paintings of Christoffer Wilhelm Eckersberg. In the second half of the century Denmark lost its territories of Schleswig and Holstein to Prussia and Austria and, in 1864, declared permanent neutrality.

World Wars

Denmark maintained its neutrality during World War I, although combatants sank one-third of its commercial fleet nonetheless. Once more declaring itself neutral at the outbreak of World War II, the Germans invaded in "peaceful occupation". The Danish government cooperated but, by 1943, ordinary Danes were openly resistant, blowing up railways and ferrying Danish Jews to neutral Sweden by fishing boats. When Germany surrendered in 1945, Resistance movement leaders formed a new government.

1. *Bella and Hanna Nathanson, C W Eckersberg (1820).*
2. *A group of Danish resistance fighters, 1945.*
3. *Danish krone coins.*
4. *Queen Margrethe II of Denmark.*

1924

The year Nina Bang became the first female minister of Denmark, and one of the first in the world.

Timeline of events

1814
Denmark goes bankrupt and cedes Norway to Sweden

1816
The Faroe Islands become a county of Denmark

1940
Denmark "peacefully" occupied by Germany troops

1951
Christine Jorgensen receives the world's first widely publicised gender reassignment surgery, in Copenhagen

Post-War Denmark

After the war, Denmark was recognized as a member of the Allied Forces and joined the UN and NATO, abandoning neutrality. A new constitution in 1953 embraced women as heirs to the throne, and Queen Margrethe II ascended the throne in 1972 following the death of her father, Frederick IX. In 1973, Denmark became the first Scandinavian country to join the EU; however, in 2000, 53 per cent of the country voted to reject the eurozone.

Denmark Today

Denmark is consistently ranked as one of the most desirable countries to live in, topping the World Happiness Report. It's widely regarded as a tolerant society, with high standards of living; social services are exemplary and citizens are strong advocates of the environment, women's rights and sexual liberation. It hasn't all been plain sailing, however. Denmark has hit headlines due to rising crime, declining education and health-care standards, and strict immigration and asylum policies. In 2015, Lars Løkke Rasmussen formed a minority government as prime minister, later forming a coalition with other conservative parties.

QUEEN MARGRETHE II (1940-)

Thanks to new laws Queen Margrethe inherited the throne ahead of her uncle, becoming the second queen in the country's history. Her role as monarch is largely ceremonial. She's a talented artist and works under the name Ingahild Grathmer. She illustrated the Danish edition of *The Lord of the Rings*.

1973
Denmark joins the European Union

2006
International furore over Danish cartoons depicting the prophet Mohammed

2018
Islamic face veil is made illegal in public, sparking controversy

2012
Same-sex marriage legalized; Denmark launches the world's biggest wind turbine

2019
General election due to be held in June

EXPERIENCE
COPENHAGEN

Enjoying Sydhavnen canal's scenery

Central Copenhagen North............70

Central Copenhagen South...........90

Christianshavn and Holmen..........118

Beyond the Centre............................126

EXPLORE
COPENHAGEN

This guide divides Copenhagen into three colour-coded sightseeing areas, as shown on the map below, and an area beyond the city centre. Find out more about each area on the following pages.

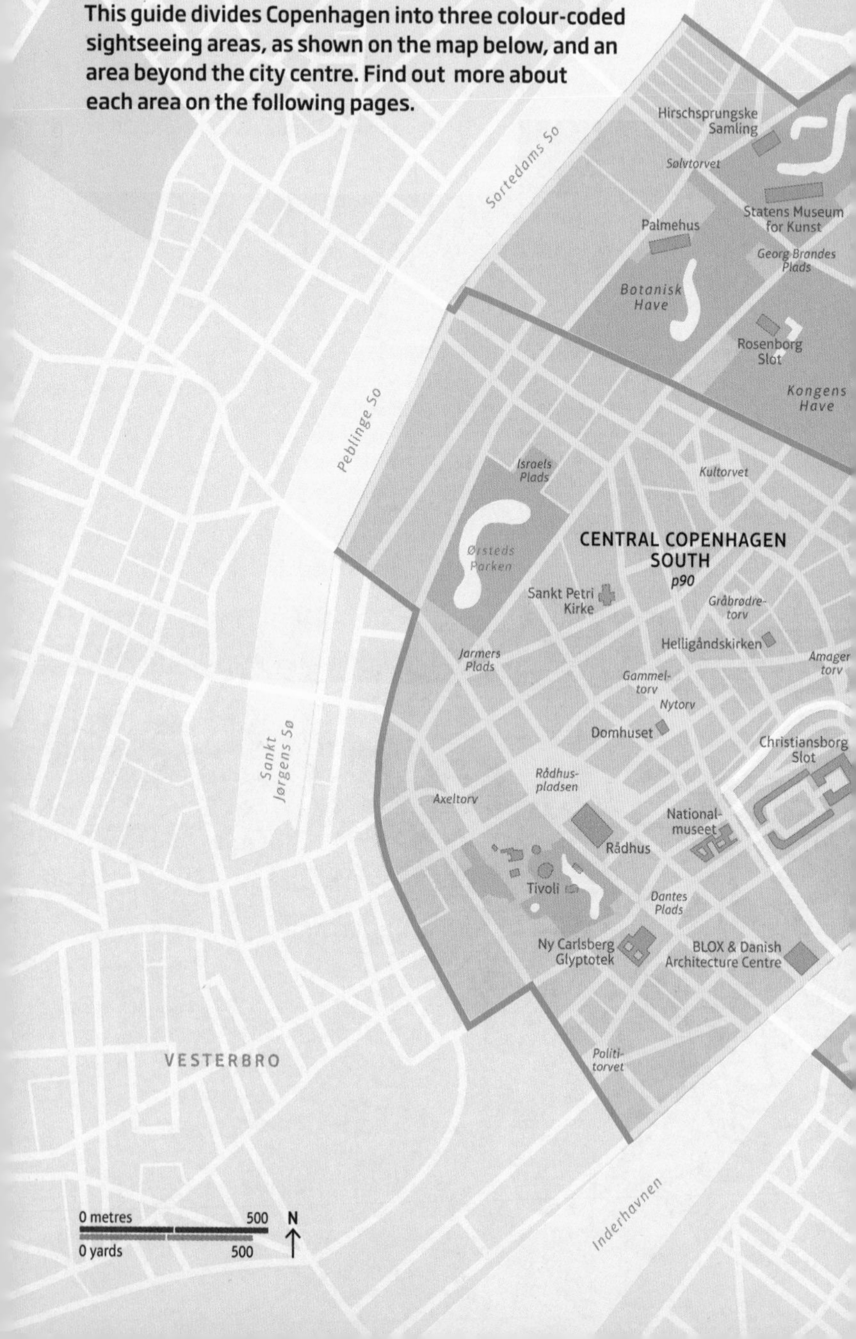

Sortedams Sø

Hirschsprungske Samling

Sølvtorvet

Statens Museum for Kunst

Palmehus

Georg Brandes Plads

Botanisk Have

Rosenborg Slot

Kongens Have

Peblinge Sø

Israels Plads

Kultorvet

Ørsteds Parken

CENTRAL COPENHAGEN SOUTH
p90

Sankt Petri Kirke

Gråbrødre-torv

Helligåndskirken

Amager torv

Jarmers Plads

Gammel-torv

Nytorv

Domhuset

Christiansborg Slot

Sankt Jørgens Sø

Rådhus-pladsen

Axeltorv

National-museet

Rådhus

Tivoli

Dantes Plads

Ny Carlsberg Glyptotek

BLOX & Danish Architecture Centre

VESTERBRO

Politi-torvet

Inderhavnen

| 0 metres | 500 |
| 0 yards | 500 |

N

The Little Mermaid

Østre Anlæg

Eidsvoll Plads

Kastellet

CENTRAL COPENHAGEN
NORTH
p70

FREDERIKSSTADEN

Inderhavnen

Nyholm

Designmuseum
Danmark

Marmorkirken

Davids
Samling

Amalienborg
Slot

Operaen

Frederiksholm

Kongens
Nytorv

Skuespilhuset

Nyhavn

Det Kongelige
Teater

Inderhavnen

Krøyers
Plads

Arsenalvej

Slots-
plads

CHRISTIANSHAVN
AND HOLMEN
p118

Stadsgraven

Det Kongelige
Bibliotek

Christiania

Christians
Kirke

Vor Frelsers
Kirke

CHRISTIANSHAVN

AMAGERBRO

DENMARK

COPENHAGEN

GETTING TO KNOW
COPENHAGEN

Copenhagen is regarded one of the world's most liveable cities and it's easy to see why. Situated on the Øresund, Copenhagen's location is unsurpassed - it's possible to tour the canals by boat and walk to most major sights, while the city's infrastructure supports a contingent of enthusiastic local cyclists.

PAGE 70

CENTRAL COPENHAGEN NORTH

First-time visitors make a beeline for historic Central Copenhagen North. At its heart is Amalienborg Slot, the Danish royalty's official home, which is surrounded by decadent mansions, with Rosenborg Slot a short walk away.

Best for
Castles, royal connections, art galleries

Home to
Amalienborg Slot, Statens Museum Kunst

Experience
The Changing of the Guard at Amalienborg Slot

PAGE 90

CENTRAL COPENHAGEN SOUTH

Best known for the colourful quayside of photogenic Nyhavn, this area buzzes with locals and tourists alike. Shoppers descend on Strøget, jam-packed with boutiques and high-street names, while culture vultures flock to the museums.

Best for
Museums and galleries, shopping, café culture

Home to
Tivoli, Ny Carlsberg Glypotek, Nationalmuseet

Experience
Thrills and spills on the rollercoasters of Tivoli

PAGE 118

CHRISTIANSHAVN AND HOLMEN

These islands comprise the most diverting district of Copenhagen, and by far the most ethnically diverse. Here Vor Frelsers Kirke pierces the sky, its spire offering braver visitors a staggering view across the city. The islands have tended to attract experimental endeavours, most famously the "free state of Christiania", an alternative community since 1971. Bicycles are as prevalent as anywhere in the city, but the islands' network of canals means waterbuses are also a great way to get around.

Best for
Photogenic bridges, New Nordic dining, counter culture

Home to
Christiania, Vor Frelsers Kirke, Krøyers Plads

Experience
The incredible city views from the spire of Vor Frelsers Kirke

PAGE 126

BEYOND THE CENTRE

To get a real sense of life as a local, you need to head beyond the centre. Great starting points are the vibrant neighbourhoods of Vesterbro and Nørrebro, which are a short cycle from central Copenhagen. Once you get a taste for their laid-back village vibe and intoxicating mix of restaurants and cultural sights, you won't want to leave. Even further afield, you can escape to a wealth of green spaces and golden beaches where there are many opportunities for walks, swims and picnics.

Best for
Cool neighbourhoods, beautiful scenery, coffee

Home to
Fredriksberg Have, ARKEN Museum

Experience
An unforgettable New Nordic meal at Noma

→

1 Cycling through Copenhagen's historic streets.

2 Elevated bridge in Fisketorvet.

3 A barman mixing cocktails at LIDKOEB, Vesterbro.

4 A live gig at VEGA, Kødbyen.

1 DAY BY BIKE

in Copenhagen

Morning

A trip to Copenhagen wouldn't be complete without a day spent exploring on a bike saddle. Traversing the city centre isn't intimidating if you follow the basic guidelines; stay to the right in your bike lane and pay close attention to traffic lights. Pick up your ride from one of the many central rental agencies such as Copenhagen Bicylces *(www.copenhagen bicycles.dk)* in Nyhavn *(p104)*. Alternatively, Bycyklen *(www.bycyklen.dk)* provide electric bikes with GPS, which you can pick up at docking stations all over the city, once you've registered as a user online. Start by cruising along the colourful, bustling Nyhavn harbourfront, Copenhagen's most famous area, and once the stomping ground of H C Andersen. Take Inderhavnsbroen *(p125)*, the newest cyclist and pedestrian bridge, across the canal and soak up the gorgeous views. On arrival in pretty Christianshavn, lock up your bike for a breakfast feast at 108 *(p123)*, a canalside Michelin-starred restaurant and café with mouth-watering pastries and coffees. If you feel like kicking back on the canal, Krøyers Plads *(p124)*, just by 108, is a great hotspot to linger. Get back on your bike and pedal for six minutes to Baroque Vor Frelsers Kirke *(p122)*. It's worth scaling the church spire's gold spiral staircase for the best view in Copenhagen.

Afternoon

Cross over Cirkelbroen *(p125)*, a striking cyclist bridge designed by Danish artist Olafur Eliasson to resemble ships at sea. Dismount here for photos before pedalling 15 minutes south to the city's favourite waterfront playground of Havnebadet Islands Brygge *(p137)*. This ex-industrial area has been converted into a waterside park and makes for a great sunbathing spot in summer. Cross Bryggebroen and Cykelslangen, both stunning cycle bridges, the second of which leads you into the heart of Vesterbro *(p132)* and the hip Kødbyen, the city's meatpacking district. Stop to lunch on the world's best Scandi-Mexican fusion tacos at Hija de Sanchez *(p139)* by former ex-Noma chef. After lunch, browse the local scene, especially independent and up-and-coming design stores before cycling slightly north to the twinkling lights of Tivoli *(p94)* for nostalgic revelry at dusk. Alternatively, if Tivoli is closed for the season, park up your bike and stay in Kødbyen, the heart of Copenhagen's nightlife, bursting with craft beer bars, cocktail clubs and all-night dance parties.

Join the Club

Kødbyen in Vesterbro (p132) has the highest concentration of night clubs, with top picks like Jolene (Flæsketorvet 81–85), Bakken (www. bakkenkbh.dk) and KB3 (www. kb3.dk). In central Copenhagen, Culture Box (www.culture-box.com) is considered the best electronic music venue while The Jane (Gråbrødretorv 8) is perfect for a chilled night out.

←

Locals socializing at Bakken, in Kødbyen

COPENHAGEN
AFTER DARK

Copenhageners are famous for their laid-back attitude, but this doesn't stop them from partying into the early hours. Whether you enjoy live jazz in a smoky bar, dancing the night away at a club night or indulging in cocktails with friends, the city has an intoxicating mix of nights out.

Copenhagen Live!

Denmark's capital excels at live music. VEGA (www.vega.dk) is the most famous venue, hosting big and up-and-coming names year round. For classical music, head to Tivoli (p94) and Operaen (p123). Rust (www.rust.dk) is the spot for indie and electronica, while jazz jam sessions draw crowds to Sofiekælderen (www. sofiekaelderen.dk) and Jazz Montmartre (www.jazzhusmontmartre.dk).

→

Music fans enjoying a set at local legend VEGA

Raise the Bar

Swanky watering holes abound, tucked discreetly on canal side streets. Must-visit cocktail bars include Lidkoeb (www.lidkoeb.dk) and Ruby (p109), ranked in the top 50 World's Best Bars. Craft beer fans are spoiled for choice; check out p38 for ideas. Danish wine is also having a moment and Den Vandrette Natural Wine Bar (p109) is a great starting point.

$\longrightarrow$

Interior of stylish Ruby, serving quality drinks and cocktails (inset)

Did You Know?

Locals make eye contact when making a toast – be sure to do the same.

LGBT+ NIGHTS OUT

Copenhagen is one of the world's most gay-friendly cities, and LGBT+ travellers will be made to feel welcome by locals. Copenhagen Pride (www.copenhagen pride.dk) takes place in August and LGBT+ film festival Mix Copenhagen (www. mixcopenhagen.dk) in October. For gay-friendly nightlife, head to Rådhuspladsen (p103) where bars like Oscar Bar & Cafe (Regnbuepladsen 9) are great for an evening drink. More about LGBT+ nightlife can be found at www.lgbt.dk and www.out-and-about.dk.

Smørrebrød Staples

Classic dining rooms such as Ida Davidsen (www.idadavidsen.dk), Restaurant Sankt Annæ (p83) and Schønnemanns (www.restaurant schonnemann.dk) serve a staggering 300 varieties of these open-face sandwiches. In-demand upstarts such as Aamaans (www.aamanns. dk) and Restaurant Palægade (p83) reinvent classics with foraged ingredients and heritage meat, even making their own schnapps pairings. For more about this traditional Danish lunch in areas outside of Copenhagen, turn to p30.

→

Colourful and fresh
Smørrebrød ingredients
at Aamaans

COPENHAGEN FOR
FOODIES

Copenhagen is one of the world's great foodie destinations, and its restaurants offer everything from 20 mind-blowing courses at a Michelin-starred New Nordic restaurant to a traditional, open-faced sandwich with schnapps. The questions is, where will you begin?

Food Halls and Pop Ups

There are three food halls to tempt foodies. Elegant Torvehallerne (www.torvehallerne kbh.dk) has everything from a Mikkeller bottle shop to gourmet food stalls selling picnic supplies. The Tivoli Food Hall (p95) has fun spins on high-end cuisine. Reffen, on Refshaleøen island (p136), is a cool waterfront market with rotating stalls.

←

Enjoying the waterfront
scenery of Reffen food hall

A Copenhagen Caffeine Fix

As one of the top five coffee-consuming nations worldwide, Denmark is passionate about coffee and cafés that embrace the art of *hygge*. Coffee Collective *(p132)* has several branches, all with great, laid-back vibes and superb coffee made from house-roast, single-origin beans. Beloved by chefs, Copenhagen Coffee Lab *(www.copenhagen coffeelab.com)* has cracked the alchemy of the perfect coffee. Prolog Coffee *(p132)* in Kødbyen and Forloren Espresso *(p87)* in central Copenhagen, are both cosy spots, perfect for a reviving cup after a day of sight-seeing.

EAT

Don't miss eating at these New Nordic gems.

Relæ
⬛ Jægersborggade 41
🕐 Sun, Mon, L Tue–Thu
🌐 restaurant-relae.dk

Ⓚ Ⓚ Ⓚ

No. 2
⬛ Nicolai Eigtveds Gade 32 🕐 Sun
🌐 nummer2.dk

Ⓚ Ⓚ Ⓚ

Höst
⬛ Nørre Farimagsgade
🕐 Lunch 🌐 cofoco.dk

Ⓚ Ⓚ Ⓚ

← Coffee Collective's service bar in Torvehallerne food hall

NOMA AND NEW NORDIC

Rene Redzepi, chef and co-owner of two-Michelin star restaurant noma *(p123)*, is credited with refining the New Nordic culinary movement, which is based on seasonal and regional ingredients, innovative cooking techniques and artful presentation. Noma has topped the World's 50 Best Restaurants list four times, and reopened a new, highly sought after restaurant in 2018. Although it's difficult to secure a reservation, noma has spawned more accessible New Nordic eateries throughout the city. Stand outs include 108 *(p123)*, Amass *(p139)*, Barr *(p123)* and Relæ.

Best Bakeries

A clutch of visionaries have taken carbohydrate-rich indulgences to new heights. Meyers Bageri *(www.meyersmad.dk)* launched the city's organic baking movement and has spots in Nyhavn and Nørrebro. In Fredriksberg, Hart Bageri *(p139)* is the hot newcomer and supplies to noma. Nørrebro's Mirabelle *(www.mirabelle-bakery.dk)* is the king of sourdough, while sister eatery Bæst *(p139)* excels at wood-fired pizzas.

↑ A tray of tempting sweet pastries at Meyers Bageri, in Nørrebro

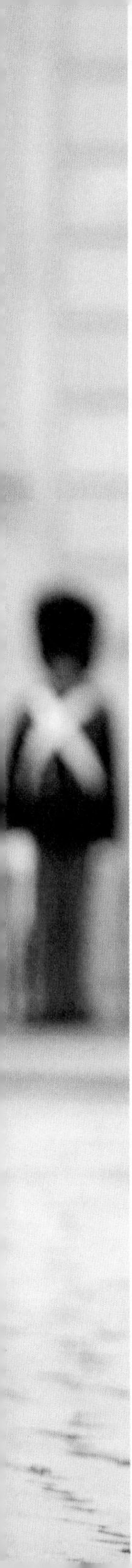

The Danish Royal Guard, Amalienborg Slot

CENTRAL COPENHAGEN NORTH

Central Copenhagen North is characterized by its stately residences and generous open green spaces. A glance at a map of Copenhagen reveals a sense of planning and order in the northern sector's streets, something that is missing in the meandering medieval streets further south. Denmark's "builder king" Christian IV is responsible for the pentagon-shaped Kastellet constructed in 1626 with five bastions and outlying earthworks. Still officially a military headquarters, the massive fortress is primarily used as a public park. It is the city's foremost symbol of the Copenhagen ethos of stability, practicality and public service. The next Frederick, Frederick V, contributed his own cultural masterpiece, the district of Frederiksstaden, considered one of the Rococo masterpieces of Europe. This complex also includes Amalienborg Slot, the Danish royal palace that actually comprises four individual palaces. Today's predominantly Neo-Classical style buildings date from the Danish Golden Age of the 19th century. Pedestrian zones and cycle paths testify to the city's pledge to become carbon neutral by 2025.

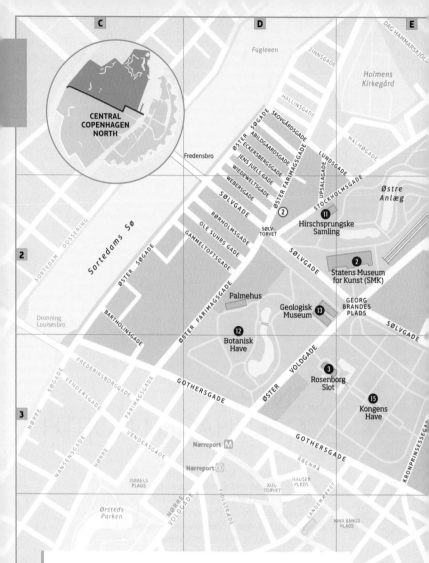

CENTRAL COPENHAGEN NORTH

Must Sees

1. Amalienborg Slot
2. Statens Museum for Kunst (SMK)
3. Rosenborg Slot
4. Designmuseum Danmark

Experience More

5. The Little Mermaid
6. Kastellet
7. Sankt Albans Kirke
8. Marmorkirken
9. Medical Museion
10. Gefionspringvandet
11. Hirschsprungske Samling
12. Botanisk Have
13. Geologisk Museum
14. Davids Samling
15. Kongens Have

Eat

1. Rebel
2. Aamanns Establissment
3. Restaurant Palægade

Drink

4. Forloren Espresso

Stay

5. Babette

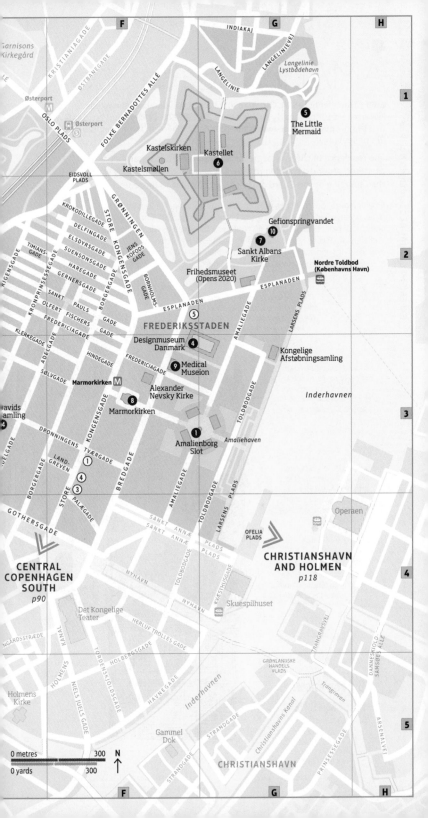

① 🦽 🚶

AMALIENBORG SLOT

📍F3 **🏛 Amalienborg Slot, Christian VII's Palace, Amalienborg Slotsplads**
🚇 Nørreport **Ⓜ Kongens Nytorv** **🚌 1A, 19, 26, 29, 650S** **🕐 Museum: May, Sep & Oct: 10am–4pm daily; Jun–Aug: 10am–5pm daily; Nov–Apr: 10am–3pm Tue–Sun**
🌐 amalienborg.dk

The residence of Queen Margrethe II comprises four separate palaces clustered around a cobbled piazza. Get a sense of royal life by watching the Changing of the Guard and visiting the palace's museum.

Amalienborg's four buildings were intended as mansions for four wealthy families but, when Christiansborg Slot burned down in 1794, Christian VII bought one of four palaces and made it his residence. Designed by Nicolai Eigtved, Christian VII's Palace is renowned for its Great Hall, which has splendid Rococo woodcarvings and stucco decoration. Since 1885, the palace has been used mostly for royal guests and ceremonial purposes. Check online for tour times.

The palace gallery has a beautiful ceiling and is the work of C L Fossati. The French architect Nicolas-Henri Jardin designed the furniture.

The tiled stove in the Velvet Chamber comes from Lübeck. The wall hangings were presents from Ludwig XV to an important high court official.

Don't miss the elegant Great Hall, an example of the artistry of Nicolai Eigtved, and is Denmark's most beautiful Rococo chamber.

All the palace statues were renovated in the 1970s by sculptor Eric Erlandsen with the help of the SMK (p74).

The entrance hall has been renovated to appear as it would have done when the palace was first built.

Did You Know?

The Changing of the Guard happens here every day at noon.

↑ Statue of Frederick V
standing outside
Amalienborg's palaces

*Royal guards, sporting bearskin
hats, stand watch, day and night,
in front of the palace.*

↑ Christian VII's Palace,
part of the Amalienborg
Slot complex

↑ Neo-Classical details in the golden yellow
Gala Hall, Amalienborg

FOUR PALACES

The name Amalienborg
actually refers to an
earlier palace, built in
1669 by Frederick III for
his young bride Sophie
Amalie. The present
complex is unique for
being made up of four
palaces. These are
Christian VII's Palace,
Christian VIII's Palace,
Frederick VIII's Palace
and Christian IX's
Palace. The equestrian
statue of Frederick V in
the piazza reputedly
cost as much as the
entire complex.

2 🛹 🎨 🖼 🛍

STATENS MUSEUM FOR KUNST (SMK)

📍E2 🏛Sølvgade 48-50 🚉Østerport, Nørreport Ⓜ️Nørreport, Kongens Nytorv 🚌6A, 26, 42, 150S, 184, 185 🕐11am-5pm Tue-Sun (to 8pm Wed) 🌐smk.dk

The National Gallery is a veritable *smorgasbord* of Danish and European art. Among the plethora of painters represented within SMK's walls are artists from Denmark's Golden Age and members of the Skagen School, plus Old Masters and modern giants.

The palatial National Gallery is Denmark's largest art gallery. Danish artists from the Golden Age include Christoffer Wilhelm Eckersberg and Constantin Hansen, and from the Skagen School you'll see works by Peder Severin Krøyer, and Anna and Michael Ancher. Bruegel, Rubens and Rembrandt are among SMK's Old Masters while Picasso and contemporary installation art represent the 20th and 21st centuries. Weekend workshops encourage children to make their own art, and the gallery offers a number of guided tours; check online for details.

GALLERY GUIDE

On the ground floor, contemporary art exhibitions are held in the X-Room, while Sculpture Street is the venue for contemporary Danish and international sculpture. The museum's permanent collection is on the first floor and in the New Wing, which is linked to the main museum by an atrium. The museum also has a number of spaces reserved for temporary exhibitions on particular artists or eras. The museum café, Kafeteria, opened in 2018 and is a lovely, modern space for a coffee and light bite.

↑ The impressive façade of SMK, fronted by gardens and a fountain

Gallery Highlights

View from Dosseringen (1838)

▽ Christen Købke was unique for painting quaint and suburban scenes on a grand scale.

Interior in Strandgade (1901)

▽ Vilhelm Hammershøi was famous for his subdued artworks that often depicted interiors.

A Sculptor in his Studio (1827)

△ This painting by Wilhelm Ferdinand Bendz shows sculptor Christen Christensen at work.

Havest (1885)

△ Danish artist Laurits Andersen Ring painted rural labourers in an increasingly industrial world.

Studying an artwork
by Walter Dahn at
Copenhagen's SMK

③ ⊘ ▢ ▢

ROSENBORG SLOT

D3 **Øster Voldgade 4A** **Ⓢ Ⓜ Nørreport** **5A, 6A, 26, 150S, 173E, 184, 185** **Mid-Apr-May, Sep-Oct: 10am-4pm daily; Jun-Aug: 9am-5pm daily; Nov-mid-Apr: 10am-3pm Tue-Sun** **rosenborgcastle.dk**

This exquisite royal palace could have been plucked from one of H C Andersen's fairy tales, with its turrets and gables and sprawling gardens. Built for Christian IV, inside is a treasure-trove of royal objects and armoury but the showstopper at Rosenborg is its underground treasury, home to the crown jewels and other royal regalia.

The Dutch-Renaissance brick palace was built from 1606–24 on the orders of Christian IV to serve as a summer residence. Rosenborg was used by successive monarchs until the early 18th century, when Frederick IV built a more spacious palace at Frederiksberg. In the early 19th century Rosenborg was opened to the public as a museum and it remains one of the most popular attractions in Copenhagen. Visitors can stroll around 24 royal rooms.

The Marble Hall's Baroque decor was commissioned by Frederick III. The Italian decorator Francesco Bruno clad the walls with imitation marble.

The Great Hall is adorned with 17th-century tapestries and a collection of 18th-century decorations. This includes three silver lions that guarded the throne.

The spire-topped tower is one of the city's most loved landcmarks.

Equestrian paintings, portraits, and a series of 17th-century floral watercolours by Maria Merian can be found in the tower stairway.

A 17th-century silver lion that guards thrones in the Great Hall ↓

Christian IV's Winter Room has a fine collection of Dutch paintings and a speaking tube connected to the wine cellar below.

Studying royal artifacts housed inside the grand Dutch-Renaissance palace of Rosenborg (inset)

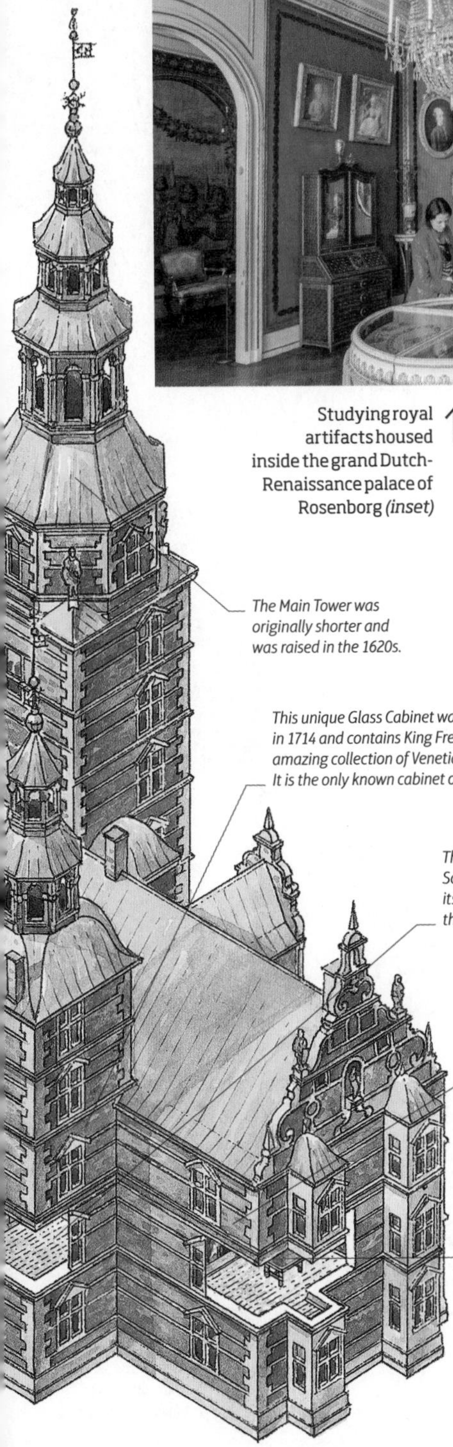

The Main Tower was originally shorter and was raised in the 1620s.

This unique Glass Cabinet was designed in 1714 and contains King Frederick IV's amazing collection of Venetian glass. It is the only known cabinet of its kind.

This Chinese Drawing Room was used by Sophie Hedevig, sister of Frederick IV. One of its most distinctive items is a guitar bearing the princess's monogram.

The third floor was completed in 1624 and was designed to provide space for the magnificent, long Banqueting Hall.

The table standing at the centre of Frederick IV's Royal Chamber was given to the king by the Grand Duke of Tuscany in 1709. The rock crystal chandelier is probably from Vienna.

← Grand exterior of the royal palace Rosenborg Slot in Copenhagen

④ 🏛 🎨 📷 🛍

DESIGN-MUSEUM DANMARK

📍 F3 🏛 Bredgade 68 Ⓢ Østerport Ⓜ Kongens Nytorv
🚌 1A, 15 🕐 11am–6pm Tue, Thu–Sun; 10am–9pm Wed
🌐 designmuseum.dk.

In a city revered for its cool approach to design, Designmuseum Danmark celebrates the history of applied arts and industrial design. At the heart of the museum's permanent and temporary exhibitions is the humble chair, a key example of design evolution.

Designed by architects Nicolai Eigtved and Lauritz de Thurah, this grand 18th-century building was the city hospital until its closure in 1919 (philosopher Søren Kierkegaard died here in 1855). Today it's Denmark's largest and most comprehensive study of Danish and international design. The museum's extensive collection includes fashion, textiles and poster art and celebrates Danish innovators such as Arne Jacobsen, Kaare Klint and Poul Henningsen. There's even an exhibition of beer labels.

The star attraction is the museum's permanent exhibition entitled "The Danish Chair: An International Affair". This tunnel of pieces tells the story of the chair – one of the strongest representatives of the development of design, and a key reason why furniture design has made Denmark famous worldwide. The museum archive holds collections of drawings that show the stages of design by pioneers of design. The shop is an excellent port of call for the design savvy, and a great source of ceramics, textiles, books and gifts.

↑ Grand façade of Designmuseum Danmark, fronted by trees

Notable Designs

1924
Kaare Klint, the father of Danish Modern, founds the Royal Academy of Fine Arts Copenhagen.

1926
Poul Henningsen, a functionalist architect, designs the PH-lamp, which prevents visual glare with three concentric shades.

↑ Exploring the Danish Chair exhibition, which includes a 1960s section *(inset)*

1949

▽ Hans Wegner, the "Master of Chairs", designs the Wishbone chair with a "Y" back. Inspired by a Chinese child's chair, it's still a bestseller today.

1963

▽ Grete Jalk designs laminated plywood furniture, including the GJ nesting tables and GJ chair. Sleek and inexpensive to produce, her designs expand the reach of Danish Modern in the US and UK.

1927

△ Kaare Klint's Red Chair forms a series of chairs. It displays his perfect use of geometry as chairs slot perfectly around a dining table.

1958

△ Arne Jacobsen creates the iconic Egg chair for the Royal Hotel Copenhagen, perhaps the most sought-after chair.

↑ Langelinie promenade flanked by greenery, not far from the Little Mermaid

EXPERIENCE MORE

5
The Little Mermaid

📍G1 🏛Langelinie
Ⓢ Østerport 🚌26
🅦 mermaidsculpture.dk

The tiny figure of the Little Mermaid *(Den Lille Havfrue)*, sitting on a rock and gazing wistfully at passing ships, is probably Denmark's best-known monument. The sculpture, commissioned by Carl Jacobsen, head of the Carlsberg brewery, was inspired by the ballet version of *The Little Mermaid*, which in turn was based on Hans Christian Andersen's tragic tale about a young mermaid who falls in love with a prince.

The sculptor, Edvard Eriksen (1876–1959), wanted to model the statue on Ellen Price, a prima ballerina who had played the part of the mermaid in the Royal Theatre production of the ballet. However, the dancer refused to pose nude. As a result, the sculptor's wife, Eline Eriksen, modelled instead.

The final bronze cast was placed at the end of the harbour promenade next to the Kastellet in 1913. Since then, the sculpture has fallen victim to various protesters and pranksters. In 1964 her head was cut off; some time later she lost an arm, and in 1998 she lost her head once again. In 2003, she was removed from her perch using explosives, and she has been a frequent victim of paint attacks, but again the Danish authorities have stepped in to restore the mermaid.

Note that the Little Mermaid is some distance from other sights and is always busy with snap-happy tourists. Having said this, a stroll along the bucolic Langelinie promenade is a pleasant way to reach her.

THE STORY OF THE LITTLE MERMAID

The heroine of Andersen's tale is a young mermaid who lives beneath the waves with her five sisters. The mermaid rescues a prince from a sinking ship and falls in love with him. Desperate to be with the prince, she is seduced by a wicked sea witch into giving up her beautiful voice in return for legs so that she can go ashore. However, the witch warns, should the prince marry another she will die. The prince adores his new, mute lover, but in the end he is forced to marry a princess from another kingdom. Before the wedding takes place, the mermaid's sisters offer her a magic knife. All she need do is stab the prince and she will be free to return to the water. The mermaid cannot bring herself to murder him and, as dawn breaks, she dies.

6
Kastellet

📍G1 Ⓢ Østerport 🚌1A, 15, 20E, 26 ♿Grounds only
🅦 kastellet.info

A fortress was first built on this site in 1626, but a Swedish attack in 1659 revealed its numerous weak points and the defences were rebuilt on the orders of Frederick III. The final structure, completed in 1664 and dubbed the Kastellet (Citadel), consisted of a fort in the shape of a five-pointed star. It was surrounded by high embankments and a large, deep moat.

In the 19th century it was partially demolished and rebuilt once more, serving as a prison. The prisoners' cells were built against the church so that the convicts, unseen by the public, could participate in Mass by peering through small viewing holes cut into the walls. During World War II it was taken over by German forces, who built a bunker and used it as their headquarters.

It is now used by the Danish military, although the grounds and ramparts are freely open to visitors, who can enter via two walkways to the north and south. The surprisingly serene atmosphere inside the walls makes the Kastellet the perfect place for a quiet stroll, taking in the windmill and colourful barracks. The peace and quiet may be interrupted

> The surprisingly serene atmosphere inside the walls makes the Kastellet the perfect place for a quiet stroll, taking in the windmill and colourful barracks.

by military drills, and you may see the mounted Guard Hussars in full parade uniform. For tours of the grounds call 33 11 22 33.

7

Sankt Albans Kirke

◉ G2 ⌂ Churchillparken 🚌 1A, 15 🕐 Summer: 10am–4pm Mon–Fri, 1pm–4pm Sun 🌐 st-albans.dk

This church was built in 1887 to serve the city's Anglican community after religious freedom was granted. It is named after Saint Alban, a 4th-century Roman soldier who converted to Christianity and suffered a martyr's death. Notably, it is the only Anglican church in Denmark. Situated close to the Gefion fountain, along Langelinie promenade in Churchillparken, the elegant Gothic church was a gift from Britain's Edward, Prince of Wales, who was vying for the hand of Princess Alexandra, the daughter of Christian IX. They married in 1863 and the prince ascended to the throne as Edward VII in 1901. Services are held in English and the congregation often includes tourists.

EAT

Rebel
Fabulous cuisine without the loftiness of other New Nordic restaurants. Don't be afraid to quiz the sommelier on wine options.

◉ F3 ⌂ Store Kongensgade 52 🌐 restaurantrebel.dk

Ⓚ Ⓚ Ⓚ

Aamanns Establissment
Here you can expect artfully crafted *smørre-brød* at lunchtime and reinvented classics for dinner.

◉ D2 ⌂ Øster Farimagsgade 12 🕐 Mon, Tue D 🌐 aamanns.dk

Ⓚ Ⓚ Ⓚ

Restaurant Palægade
With chef alumni from the top New Nordic and *smørrebrød* restaurants and a four-course tasting menu, it's no wonder Palægade is a hotspot.

◉ F3 ⌂ Palægade 8 🕐 Sun D 🌐 palaegade.dk

Ⓚ Ⓚ Ⓚ

← Sankt Albans Kirke overlooking the deep moat of the Kastellet

Spectacular domed interior of Copenhagen's grand Marmorkirken ↑

8

Marmorkirken

🅰 F3 🏛 Frederiksgade 4
🚌 1A, 15, 19, 26 🕐 Church:
10am–5pm Mon–Thu &
Sat, noon–5pm Fri & Sun;
dome: 3pm Sat & Sun
(Jun–Aug: 1pm daily)
🅦 marmorkirken.dk

The vast dome of the Baroque Frederikskirken, also known as Marmorkirken or the Marble Church, leads many visitors to suspect that its architect, Nicolai Eigtved, based his design on St Peter's Basilica in Rome. The church was named after Frederik V, who wanted to celebrate his family's 300 years of Danish rule by building a new district

---

GREAT VIEW
Climb Marmorkirken

For some of the most impressive views over Central Copenhagen, especially Amalienborg Slot and the Operaen across the harbour, few places can beat the top of the copper-green dome (the largest in Scandinavia) of the stunning Marble Church.

---

in the city of Copenhagen – Frederiksstaden – with the church as its focal point. When work began, in 1749, the plan was to construct the church out of marble imported from Norway (hence its alternative name). However, it quickly became apparent that the cost of such a venture would exceed the financial resources of the treasury, and work was abandoned in 1770.

A century later the building was completed using more easily sourced Danish marble. The most obvious feature of the church is its dome – one of the largest in Europe. Visitors can climb the 260 steps to the top of the bell tower. Inside the church are frescoes by Danish artists and a wonderfully ornate altar. Outside, the building is encircled by statues of Danish scholars and saints.

9

Medical Museion

🅰 F3 🏛 Bredgade 62
Ⓢ Østerport 🚌 1A, 15, 19
🕐 10am–4pm Tue–Fri,
noon–4pm Sat & Sun
🅦 museion.ku.dk

A combined museum and research unit of the University of Copenhagen, the Medical Museion was founded by a private initiative in 1907. It marked the 50th anniversary of the founding of the Danish Medical Association with a public exhibition of historical medical artifacts. The museum remained public until 1918, when it was taken over by the university.

The museum's main site is on Bredgade in the former Royal Academy of Surgeons building, which dates from 1787. Visitors can expect to see ongoing exhibitions of human remains and medical devices as well as installations by individual curators. The centrepiece of the museum, however, is the anotomical theatre, where students in days gone by would gather to observe the dissection of corpses and learn about human anatomy. The Medical Museion has one of the largest and richest historical collections of medical artifacts in Europe, with up to 250,000 pieces. There is also a large image collection, a document archive and a historical book collection. A satellite exhibition is located at the university's Faculty of Health and Medical Sciences, in the Panum building on Blegdamsvej, 2 km (1 mile) from the Medical Museion.

10

Gefionspringvandet

📍 G2 🚌 1A, 15

Built in 1908 by Danish sculptor Anders Bundgaard, the impressive Gefion fountain is one of Copenhagen's largest monuments. Its main feature is a statue of the Scandinavian goddess Gefion. According to legend, the king of Sweden promised to give her as much land as she could plough in one night. Gefion, who took him at his word, turned her four sons into oxen and harnessed them to a plough. By the morning she had covered a fairly sizeable chunk of Sweden, which she picked up and threw into the sea, forming the island of Zealand. The hole left behind became Lake Vänern (whose shape somewhat resembles that of Zealand).

---

11 ♨️ ⓜ

Hirschsprungske Samling

📍 D2 🏛 Stockholmsgade 20
Ⓢ Østerport 🚌 6A, 14, 26, 42, 94N, 150S, 184, 185
🕐 11am–4pm Wed–Sun
🌐 hirschsprung.dk

The Hirschsprungske Samling is one of Copenhagen's finest museums and owes its existence to the patronage

↑ Learning about Danish art history in Hirschsprungske Samling

of Heinrich Hirschsprung (1836–1908), a Danish tobacco baron and supporter of Danish artists. The collection has been on display since 1911 and is housed in a Neo-Classical building by Østre Anlæg park.

The collection includes works by prominent Danish artists from the first half of the 19th century, otherwise known as the Golden Age. This includes pieces by Christoffer Wilhelm Eckersberg, Christen Købke, Wilhelm Ferdinand Bendz and Nicolai Wilhelm Marstrand, plus further pieces from the late 19th and 20th centuries.

A free tour at 2pm on Sundays highlights the works of a different artist each week and lasts around 45 minutes.

← Gefionspringvandet, depicting the goddess Gefion and her four oxen at work

12

Botanisk Have

D2 **Gothersgade 128** **M** **Nørreport** **6A, 14, 42, 150S, 184, 185, 350S** **May–Sep: 8:30am–6pm daily; Oct–Apr: 8:30am–4pm daily** **botanik.snm.ku.dk**

Some 13,000 species of plants are gathered in the Botanical Gardens, including many native Danish plants as well as some highly exotic specimens collected from around the world. The garden was established in 1872, on the grounds of old town fortifications. Bulwarks have been turned into rockeries, and the moat that once surrounded the fortified walls is now a lake filled with water and marsh plants.

The gardens have much to offer. There are perennial and annual plants, ancient trees and 27 greenhouses, one of which contains more than 1,000 varieties of cactus. Elsewhere, you can see coffee and pineapples growing, and a butterfly house is open in summer. Don't miss the roof-top walk in the steamy palm house. The café outside the palm house offers magnificent views of the garden.

13

Geologisk Museum

D2 **Øster Voldgade 5-7** **M** **Nørreport** **6A, 26, 42, 184, 185** **10am–5pm Tue-Sun** **geologi.snm.ku.dk**

Standing close to the eastern end of the Botanisk Have, the Geological Museum opened in 1893 and occupies an Italian Renaissance-style building. Its stone decorations include rosettes, columns and arches.

Among the earliest exhibits are the meteorites on display in the courtyard, the biggest of which was found in Greenland in 1963 and is the sixth largest

1600

The year that the Botanisk Have was founded by royal charter.

in the world. You'll find other exhibits devoted to butterflies, dinosaurs and the solar system, and two individually decorated rotundae. Colourful stones and rock crystals are on sale in the museum shop.

14

Davids Samling

E3 **Kronprinsessegade 30** **M** **Nørreport** **1A, 15, 19, 26, 42, 43, 350S** **1-5pm Tue–Sun (to 9pm Wed)** **davidmus.dk**

Christian Ludvig David (1878–1960), the founder of this museum, was a lawyer who in 1945 set up the C L David Foundation and Collection with the idea of sharing his fine collection of artwork, furniture and crafts. David's great-grandfather had owned the building from 1811 until 1830, and David acquired it in 1917 – a century after his family had lived there – making it his home until his death in 1960. The foundation bought the neighbouring building, at Kronprinsessegade 32, in 1986. The museum is best known for its extensive collection of

↑ Palatial palm house reflected in a pond at Botanisk Have

Islamic art, including items from Spain, Persia, India and elsewhere. Among the many treasures, some of which date as far back as the 7th century, are silks, ceramics, jewellery and ancient daggers inlaid with jewels. The museum also houses a small collection of Danish paintings and sculpture, as well as 18th-century English, French and German furniture. There is also a collection of Danish silver dating from the 17th and 18th centuries. Visitors are welcome to borrow an info-tablet and an audio guide for free from the reception to learn more about the texts in the Islamic collection.

15
Kongens Have

📍 E3 🕐 7am–dusk daily

The King's Garden was established by Christian IV in 1606 as the private gardens of Rosenborg Slot (p78) and is Copenhagen's oldest park, retaining most of its original layout. In the 17th century the gardens supplied the royal court with fresh fruit and vegetables, plus roses to adorn the royal apartments.

Today, the shady public gardens, criss-crossed by paths and with numerous benches, are one of the best places in the capital for walking and relaxing. As well as the grassy open spaces, quiet corners, rose gardens and fountains, you can also find one of Copenhagen's most famous monuments: a statue of Hans Christian Andersen enchanting a group of children with some of his magical fairy tales.

DRINK

Forloren Espresso
A stone's throw from Marmorkirken, caffeine aficionados flock to this hidden gem for single-origin espressos and impeccable latte art.

📍 F3 🏠 Store Kongensgade 32 🕐 Sun 🌐 forlorenespresso.dk

Ⓚ Ⓚ Ⓚ

→ Bronze statue of Hans Christian Andersen in Kongens Have

A SHORT WALK
AROUND AMALIENBORG SLOT

Distance 1.5 km (1 mile) **Time** 20 minutes
Nearest metro Kongens Nytorv

In the late 18th century, Frederick V made Amalienborg Slot the focal point of a new, smart district, named Frederiksstaden in his honour. Today, the sense of royal history is tangible and visitors flock here for the pomp and ceremony. Stately buildings and wide thoroughfares lead to Amalienborg Slot, the official residence of Queen Margrethe II. Onlookers stop to watch the Changing of the Guard at noon, with the new palace guards marching to the palace from the barracks on Gothersgade at 11:30am.

The **Medical Museion** *(p84) is housed in the former Danish Academy of Surgery and has on display some gruesome human remains as well as an old operating theatre.*

Alexander Nevsky Kirke *is a Russian Orthodox church and was completed in 1883. It was a gift from Tsar Alexander III to mark his marriage to a Danish princess.*

Also known as Frederikskirken, **Marmorkirken** *(p84) is just west of Amalienborg. Its huge dome rests on 12 pillars and is one of the biggest of its kind in Europe, measuring 31 m (102 ft) across.*

FREDERICIAGADE

BREDGADE

FREDERIKSGADE

Consisting of four almost identical buildings, **Amalienborg Slot** *(p74) has been the main residence of the Danish royal family since 1794.*

←

The impressive dome of Copenhagen's Marmorkirken

Studying chairs through the ages ↑
at the Designmuseum Danmark

**CENTRAL COPENHAGEN
NORTH**

*Around
Amalienborg Slot*

Locator Map
See more detail on p72

● START

The **Designmuseum Danmark** building first
served as the city hospital in the 18th century,
and today it provides an exhibition space to
showcase Danish design (p80).

Sankt Ansgars Kirke is on the site of a
Roman Catholic chapel and was once used
by Copenhagen's foreign population. The
present building was completed in 1842.

0 metres   50   N
0 yards   50   ↑

AMALIEGADE

FREDERICIAGADE

TOLDBODGADE

TOLDBODGADE

**Kongelig
Afstøbningssamling**, or
*Royal Cast Collection, has
over 2,000 sculpture casts,
including a copy of the Venus
de Milo and copies of statues
from the Acropolis.*

Amaliehaven is a modern park,
donated to the city by the A P
Møller shipping company in 1983.
The gardens are next to Nyhavn
and are a popular place for a walk.

○ FINISH

Thorvaldsens Museum reflected in a water feature

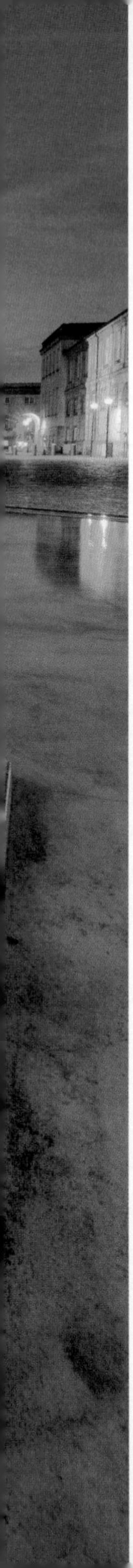

CENTRAL COPENHAGEN SOUTH

This is arguably Copenhagen's oldest district, showing signs of Viking settlement during the 10th century. Christian IV enlarged the district in the 17th century but decades of trouble were to follow. These streets endured various sieges by the Swedes, followed by extensive fires and plague in the 18th century. The old, weathered walls fell thanks to massive bombardment from Britain's Lord Nelson at the beginning of the 19th century. Major expansion and redevelopment in 1850 and again in 1901 opened up the area's avenues. Nyhavn, with its brightly painted five- and six-storey 17th-century mansions fronting the waterside, typifies the stolid charm of this district. In 1962, Strøget became Europe's first modern pedestrian-only boulevard, and is still the longest such street in the world. Home today to the Danish Parliament, Copenhagen University and Tivoli, Central Copenhagen South is Denmark's cultural, political and social heart.

CENTRAL COPENHAGEN SOUTH

Must Sees

1 Tivoli
2 Ny Carlsberg Glyptotek
3 Christiansborg Slot
4 Nationalmuseet
5 Rådhus

Experience More

6 Rådhuspladsen
7 Nyhavn
8 Charlottenborg Slot and Kunsthal Charlottenborg
9 Rundetaarn
10 Det Kongelige Teater
11 Kongens Nytorv
12 Skuespilhuset
13 Nikolaj Kunsthal
14 Gråbrødretorv
15 Kunstforeningen GL STRAND
16 Helligåndskirken
17 Sankt Petri Kirke
18 Højbro Plads
19 Universitet
20 Vor Frue Kirke
21 Folketinget
22 Nytorv
23 Ripley's Believe It or Not!
24 Thorvaldsens Museum
25 Børsen
26 Krigsmuseet
27 BLOX & Danish Architecture Centre
28 Det Kongelige Bibliotek

Eat

1 Studio
2 Schønnemanns
3 Admiral Gade 26

Drink

4 Ruby
5 Den Vandrette Natural Wine Bar
6 Ved Stranden
7 Café Det Vide Hus

Stay

8 Hotel Nobis
9 Hotel Nimb
10 Hotel D'Angleterre

1 ⚔ 🍴 📷 🛍

TIVOLI

📍C6 🏠Vesterbrogade 3 Ⓢ Central 🚌1A, 2A, 5C, 6A, 9A, 34, 37, 66, 250S 🕐Mid-Apr-mid-Sep, last 2 weeks in Oct, mid-Nov-end Dec: 11am-10pm daily (to midnight Fri & Sat) 🌐 tivoligardens.com

It's not surprising that Walt Disney was inspired to build his own amusement park after visiting Copenhagen's Tivoli. At the heart of the city for more than 175 years, these imaginative gardens have something for everyone, including hair-raising roller coasters, nostalgic fair games and star-studded concerts.

When Tivoli first opened in 1843 it had only two attractions: a carousel pulled by horses and a roller coaster. Today it's an altogether grander affair. Part amusement park, part cultural venue, part wonderland, Tivoli is one of the most famous places in Denmark and much loved by the Danes, who regard it as one of their national treasures. Situated in the heart of the city, this dream-like garden is planted with almost 1,000 trees and blooms with 400,000 flowers during the summer. At night,

when it's lit by a myriad of coloured fairy lights, Tivoli is a truly magical sight. Thrill-seekers are spoiled for choice when it comes to rides (at an additional cost) but there is much more besides, from free performances and kids' play areas to a wealth of dining options.

> **At night, when it's lit by a myriad of coloured fairy lights, Tivoli is a truly magical sight.**

Boating beside the impressive pagoda in Tivoli's Orient area ↑

Seasonal Guide

INSIDER TIP
Cheap Eats

If you're splashing cash on rides, eat in Tivoli Food Hall in the Bernstorffsgade corner of the gardens. Here you can try fast food with a Danish accent at Bobba-bella, Asian-fusion snacks at Kung Fu Street Food, or organic Icelandic at Glo.

↑ Musician Nile Rodgers performing with Chic at Tivoli

Spring

▽ Tivoli's season opens with a bang in April. Weekly pyrotechnics, indoor and open-air concerts, marching bands and blooming flowers turn the park into a veritable fairyland from now until autumn.

Summer

Tivoli is at its lively, colourful (and busiest) best in midsummer, when hundreds of thousands of blooms line its paths. The longer hours of daylight make al fresco dining and outdoor entertainment - such as outdoor concerts - a real summer delight.

Autumn

▽ It's all about pumpkins and ghosts when Tivoli opens for a two-week Halloween season. Mainly for kids, the fortnight features stalls selling costumes, a trick-or-treat night and the Monster's Parade.

Winter

More than one million lights brighten Tivoli's six-week Christmas season, and seasonal treats tempt in the park's dozens of cafés and restaurants. There's a special fireworks display on New Year's Eve. The winter fun doesn't stop there; Tivoli's ice rink is a favourite with locals when the park opens in the new year.

← Snowy scenes and twinkling Christmas decorations

2 🜂 Ⓜ 🖵 🛍

NY CARLSBERG GLYPTOTEK

📍D6 🏠Dantes Plads 7 🚌1A, 2A, 5C, 6A, 32, 73, 94N, 173, 250S, 602, 613, 866 🕐11am–6pm Tue–Sun (to 10pm Thu) 🚫1 Jan, 5 Jun, 24 & 25 Dec
🌐glyptoteket.dk

This stellar museum comprises Mediterranean antiquities and 19th-century artworks, but the jewel in its crown is the central conservatory, chock-full of exotic flora, towering palms and bewitching sculptures.

Ny Carlsberg Glyptotek is a world-class collection of more than 10,000 treasures, including Ancient Egyptian art, Greek and Roman sculptures and a huge collection of Etruscan artifacts. Alongside its ancient antiquities is a wealth of Danish paintings and sculptures from the Golden Age, and exquisite works by French Impressionist masters such as Degas and Renoir. It has grown from the fine collection of sculptures (glyptotek) donated by Carl Jacobsen, founder of the New Carlsberg Brewery (p132). Today the museum consists of three architecturally different buildings, the first built in 1897 and the last added in 1996. The Winter Garden and its café were designed, as the name implies, as a pleasant, green space for the hard winter months. At its centre is Kai Nielsen's emotive Water Mother sculpture.

> INSIDER TIP
> **Classical Concerts**
>
> Enjoy musical performances alongside statues of ancient heroes in the Central Hall. Performed by leading classical ensembles, concerts are held August to September and cost about 75 Kr.

GALLERY GUIDE

The horseshoe-shaped Dahlerup Building (1897) contains mainly Danish and French sculpture. Ancient artifacts from the Mediterranean and Egypt are found via the Winter Garden in the Kampmann Building (1906). The Larsen Building (1996), rising within one of the court-yards of the Kampmann Building, houses French painting. The Glypto-tek's famous café is in the Winter Garden on the ground floor.

←

Visitors sitting around Kai Nielsen's *Water Mother* in the Glyptotek's Winter Garden

↑ Exterior of the historic Ny Carlsberg Glyptotek at dusk

→

Little Dancer of Fourteen Years by Edgar Degas (c 1880)

3 🖐 ✍

CHRISTIANSBORG SLOT

📍 E5 🏛 Christiansborg Slotsplads 🚌 1A, 2A, 11A, 14, 26, 40, 66
🕐 10am–5pm Tue–Sun (May–Sep: daily) 🚫 4, 12 & 18 Jun, 9 Jul
🌐 christiansborg.dk

While Amalienborg is the home of the Danish monarchy, Christiansborg is Denmark's political and judicial nerve centre. This impressive complex comprises the Folketinget (Parliament), Prime Minister's office and Supreme Court, plus some 11th-century ruins.

The royal family lived on this site before the fire of 1794 and some rooms are still used by the Queen for state dinners, banquets and receptions. The magnificent Royal Reception Rooms, which are richly decorated with art, chandeliers, gold and marble, are open to the public. Tours of the Reception Rooms take place at 11am (Danish) and 3pm (English). Don't miss the underground ruins of medieval castles (additional ticket required).

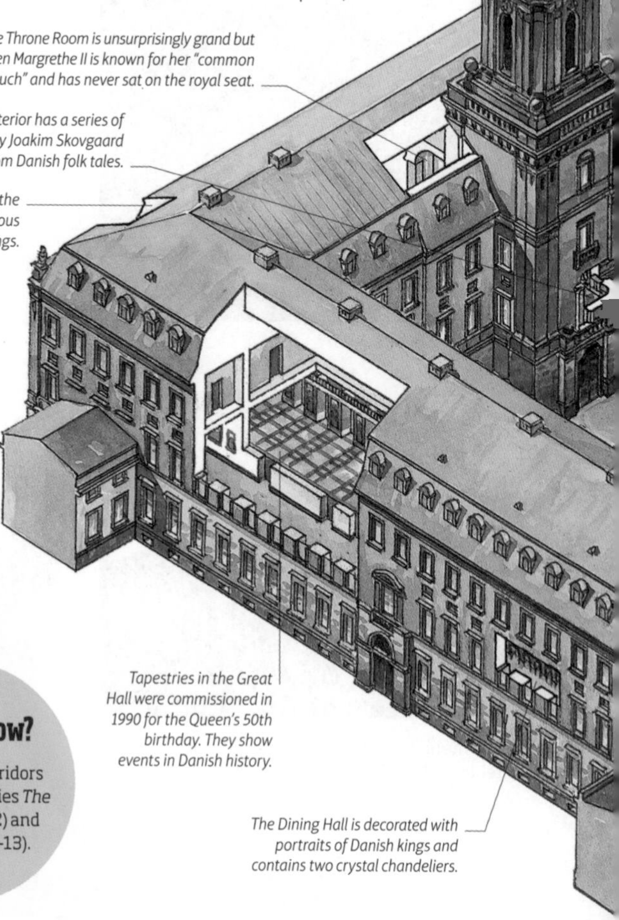

The Throne Room is unsurprisingly grand but Queen Margrethe II is known for her "common touch" and has never sat on the royal seat.

The tower's interior has a series of tapestries created by Joakim Skovgaard depicting scenes from Danish folk tales.

Completed in 1924, the Velvet Room has luxurious velvet wall linings.

→
The impressively grand complex of Christiansborg Slot, Copenhagen

Tapestries in the Great Hall were commissioned in 1990 for the Queen's 50th birthday. They show events in Danish history.

Did You Know?

The palace's corridors starred in TV series *The Killing* (2007–12) and *Borgen* (2010–13).

The Dining Hall is decorated with portraits of Danish kings and contains two crystal chandeliers.

Colourful tapestries lining the Great Hall, and the palace's façade punctuated by its tower *(inset)*

*A small portion of the vast royal collection is housed in the Library. The remaining volumes are at **Amalienborg Slot** (p74).*

Bertel Thorvaldsen's frieze depicting Alexander the Great entering Babylon is displayed in the Alexander Room.

GREAT VIEW
Tallest Tower

Christiansborg has the tallest tower in the city, standing at 106 m (348 ft), and the views from the top are sensational. It's free to enter but get there early – it gets busy.

4 ⊗ ☺ 🛍

NATIONALMUSEET

📍 D5 🏠 Ny Vestergade 10 🚌 1A, 2A, 6A, 12, 15, 26, 29, 33, 650S 🕙 10am–5pm Tue-Sun 🌐 natmus.dk

Stone Age tools, Viking treasures, Inuit clothing and medieval art galore – the encyclopedic National Museum provides a detailed understanding of Denmark's rich history and culture.

Aside from items relating to Danish history, this prestigious museum houses artifacts from all over the world. From Egyptian jewellery and mummies to recreated 19th-century living quarters and a wonderful display of historic toys, it's worth allocating several hours for a visit to the museum. There's a good children's section too, where kids can try on armour or "camp out" in a Bedouin tent. All exhibits are labelled in English.

Gallery Guide

The Nationalmuseet is housed in a Rococo-style mansion, which was once the palace of the Crown Prince. The museum collection is spread over four floors, with pre-history, Viking

> **There's a good children's section too, where kids can try on armour or "camp out" in a Bedouin tent.**

The bright and airy interior of Copenhagen's Nationalmuseet ↑

↑ Palatial exterior of the Nationalmuseet, overlooking a canal

Antiquities

▽ Greek pottery, Etruscan jewellery and Egyptian mummies are on display in the Egyptian and Classical section. There is much more besides, including items from Africa, India and Japan.

treasures and the Children's Museum on the ground floor. The Middle Ages shares the first floor with Ethnography, which continues on the second floor. Here you'll also find exhibits of toys and the history of the Danes. You can meet Egyptian mummies on the third floor. Restaurant Smör is fairly formal, with table service only, and serves excellent Danish cuisine.

Inuit Culture

▽ Included in the ethnographic section are rooms devoted to the Inuit. These contain many clothing, including a suit made of bird feathers, as well as tradit- ional kayaks and harpoons.

14,000

The number of years of covered in the Nationalmuseet.

Bronze Age

▽ Denmark's pre-history is told in this fascinating section. These Bronze Age helmets date from around the 9th century BC and were found in Viksø, Zealand.

5 Ⓜ

RÅDHUS

Ⓒ C5 Ⓐ Rådhuspladsen 1 Ⓢ Central Station 🚌 6A, 11, 26, 29, 33
🕐 9am-4pm Mon-Fri, 9:30am-1pm Sat; World Clock: 8:30am-
4:30pm Mon-Fri, 10am-1pm Sat Ⓦ kk.dk

Looming large in the central Rådhuspladsen is City Hall.
Don't be put off by the building's austere exterior or
municipal role; it's free to step inside the Rådhus and,
for a small cost, you can climb the tower.

The red-brick Rådhus, which opened in 1905, was designed
by Danish architect Martin Nyrop (1849–1921), and inspired by
both Italian buildings and elements of Danish medieval architecture. Its main hall, which is used for exhibitions and official
events, is decorated with statues of Nyrop as well as three
other prominent Danes – Bertel Thorvaldsen, H C Andersen and
Niels Bohr. Join a guided tour for a small fee. Tours in English
take place at 1pm Monday to Friday and 10am on Saturday.

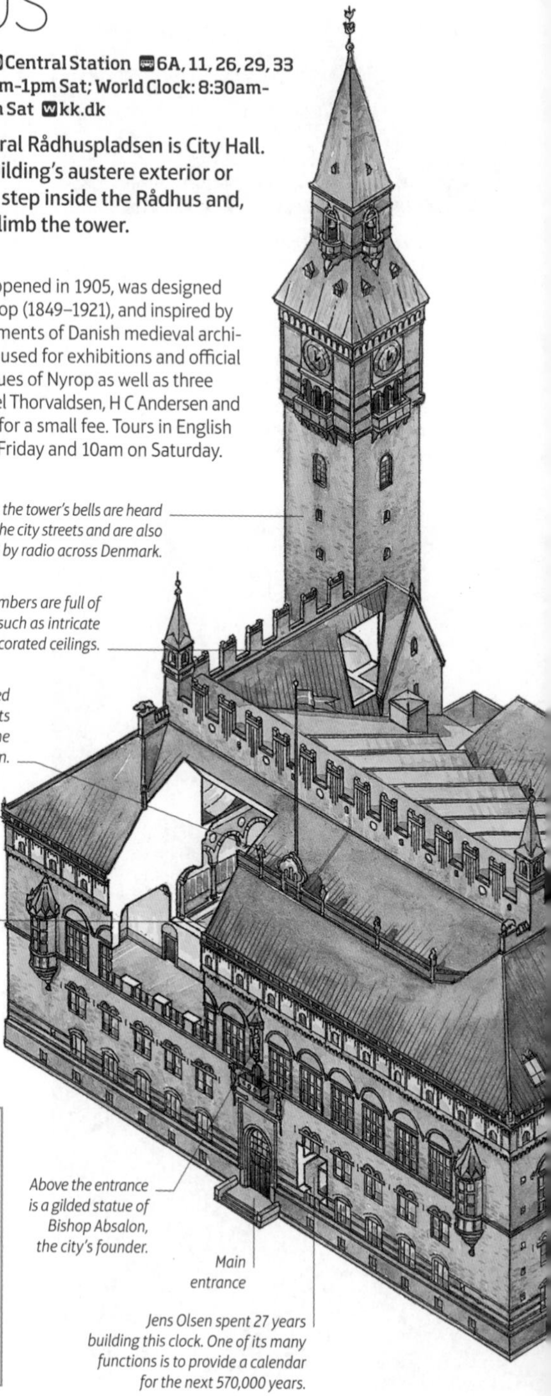

The peals from the tower's bells are heard
throughout the city streets and are also
transmitted by radio across Denmark.

The Rådhus rooms and chambers are full of
architectural flourishes such as intricate
brickwork, mosaics and decorated ceilings.

Copenhagen's emblem hasn't changed
much since the 13th century. It consists
of three castle towers, waves of the
Øresund and the sun and moon.

This vast, rectangular Main
Hall on the first floor is flanked
by cloisters and topped with a
glazed roof. It has Italianate
wall decorations and a number
of sculptures.

⛰ GREAT VIEW
Climb the Tower

This is one of the city's
tallest buildings. Climb
302 stairs to the top of
the 105-m (344-ft) tower
and you'll be rewarded
with stellar views
across the capital. Here
you'll also find the clock.

Above the entrance
is a gilded statue of
Bishop Absalon,
the city's founder.

Main
entrance

Jens Olsen spent 27 years
building this clock. One of its many
functions is to provide a calendar
for the next 570,000 years.

EXPERIENCE MORE

↑ The red-brick exterior of Copenhagen's municipal Rådhus

The stately rooms on the top floors are reached by graceful stairs with marble balustrades.

⑥ Rådhuspladsen

☑ C5 ⑤ Central Station
🚌 6A, 11, 26, 29, 33

This open space is the second-biggest square in the Danish capital (after Kongens Nytorv). City Hall Square was established in the second half of the 19th century, following the dismantling of the western gate that stood on this site, and the levelling of the defensive embankments. Soon afterwards it was decided to build the present city hall, providing further impetus to the development of the surrounding area. The square has been pedestrianized since 1994 and is popular with sightseers. It is also a gathering point for revellers on New Year's Eve.

A number of monuments in Rådhuspladsen are worthy of note. Standing immediately by the entrance to the city hall is the Dragon's Leap Fountain, erected in 1923. A little to one side, by Rådhus's tower, is a tall column, unveiled in 1914, featuring two bronze figures of Vikings blowing bronze horns. Legend has it that the figures will blow their horns when a virgin passes underneath.

> **Did You Know?**
>
> In the Danish edition of Monopoly (Matador), Rådhuspladsen is the most expensive location.

Close by, on Hans Christian Andersens Boulevard, is a lovely and very photogenic sitting figure of Andersen that faces Tivoli. Another curiosity is an unusual barometer hanging on a building that is covered with advertisements, located at the corner of Vesterbrogade and H C Andersens Boulevard. The barometer includes a figure of a girl who rides a bicycle in fine weather and opens her umbrella when it rains. A nearby thermometer gives a daily temperature reading.

> **The barometer includes a figure of a girl who rides a bicycle in fine weather and opens her umbrella when it rains.**

↑ City Hall, or Rådhus, located in Rådhuspladsen

→ Two horn-playing Vikings atop a column in Rådhuspladsen

7 🍴 🖼

Nyhavn

📍 F4

Lined with colourful houses on both sides, this short canal, known as the New Harbour, was dug by soldiers between 1671 and 1673. It was intended to enable smaller ships loaded with merchandise to sail into the centre of Copenhagen, but today it is one of the city's most iconic and attractive spots, with stylish yachts and old wooden boats moored along its quays.

In Hans Christian Andersen's time, the area just north of the canal was a notorious red-light district with a rather seedy reputation thanks to its cheap bars, rough-and-ready hotels, tattoo parlours and numerous brothels. Since then Nyhavn has gentrified and is now one of the city's best-known and most-loved districts. The boozy joints packed with sailors are long gone and have been replaced with bars, cafés and restaurants targeting a more prosperous clientele, but it is also a good spot to take a stroll or pick up a canal tour. The area is especially popular on warm evenings, and many of the restaurants and bars can fill up quickly, particularly on the north side of the harbour. The long-awaited Inderhavnsbroen (Inner Harbour Bridge) opened here in 2016, connecting pedestrians and cyclists to the neighbourhoods of Christianshavn and Holmen.

1989

Thomas Olsen sets the record for racing up and down the Rundetaarn on a unicycle (in 1 min, 48.7 secs).

ANDERSEN'S HOUSES IN NYHAVN

Hans Christian Andersen arrived in Copenhagen in 1819 at the age of 14. After he failed to make it as an actor, he attended Slagelse Grammar School and returned to the capital in 1827. Andersen spent most of his life in the busy port of Nyhavn, where he wrote his first fairy tales. He spent four years in No 20, where he penned *The Tinderbox, Little Claus and Big Claus* and *The Princess and the Pea*. He lived a further 20 years in No 67 and two years in No 18.

8

Charlottenborg Slot and Kunsthal Charlottenborg

📍 F4 **🏛 Kongens Nytorv 1** **Ⓜ Kongens Nytorv** **🚌 1A, 15, 19, 26, 350S** **🕐 Noon–8pm Tue-Fri, 11am-5pm Sat & Sun** **🌐 kunsthal charlottenborg.dk**

This Baroque palace was built between 1672 and 1683 for Queen Charlotte Amalie (wife of Christian V) and was named after her. In the 18th century King

← Sun setting over the vibrantly coloured waterfront of Nyhavn

STAY

Hotel Nobis
In a prime location right beside Tivoli Gardens and Ny Carlsberg Glyptotek, the five-star Hotel Nobis is synonymous with restrained opulence.

D6 Niels Brocks Gade 1 nobishotel.dk

Ⓚ Ⓚ Ⓚ

Hotel Nimb
It's near impossible to surpass the charming fairy-tale appeal of this exclusive boutique hotel in the white and gold Moorish palace at Tivoli Gardens.

C6 Bernstorffsgade 5 nimb.dk

Ⓚ Ⓚ Ⓚ

Hotel D'Angleterre
Built in 1755, some of the 92 spacious rooms are named after some of the famous guests who have stayed here. The champagne bar stocks 160 types of bubbly.

E4 Kongens Nytorv 34 dangleterre.com

Ⓚ Ⓚ Ⓚ

Frederik V handed over the palace to the newly created Royal Academy of Fine Arts. An adjacent building holds both Kunsthal Charlottenborg and the Danish Art Library.

9

Rundetaarn

D4 Købmagergade 52A May-Sep: 10am-8pm daily; Oct-Apr: 10am-6pm daily (to 9pm Tue & Wed) rundetaarn.dk

The Rundetaarn (Round Tower) provides an excellent vantage point from which to view the city. Access to the top is via a cobbled spiral ramp, which winds seven and a half times round to the top.

The tower was erected in 1642 as a platform for the university observatory. It was built on the orders of Christian IV, who sketched the famous golden rebus on the front of the tower. The observatory is still in use, making it the oldest working observatory in Europe. The tower was

damaged by the Great Fire of 1728, resulting in the observatory being rebuilt in the 18th century and several times since then. In 1716, the Tsar of Russia, Peter the Great, rode his horse up the spiral staircase to the top, followed by his wife Tsarina Catherine I who, as legend has it, rode up in a coach drawn by six horses.

The modern-day equivalent is the annual unicycle race. The winner is the person who cycles to the top of the tower and back again in the fastest time, without dismounting or falling off.

← Copenhagen's historic Round Tower, the Rundetaarn, soaring above the city

⑩ Det Kongelige Teater

📍 F4 🏛 August Bournonvilles Passage, Kongens Nytorv
🌐 kglteater.dk

Visit the area around Kongens Nytorv and you'll be struck by the sight of the Royal Theatre, a vast Neo-Renaissance building that has been the main arts venue in Denmark since it was founded in 1748. The present building, which occupies the original site, dates from 1874. For many years, this theatre set itself apart by putting on ballet, opera and theatre in the same space. The complex includes two theatres – Gamle Scene (Old Stage) and Nye Scene (New Stage), the latter built in 1931 and popularly known as Stærekassen. Since the opening of Operaen (*p123*), the striking opera house across the harbour from Amalienborg Slot, the Old Stage primarily hosts ballet, while drama is staged at Skuespilhuset.

The statues at the front of the theatre celebrate two distinguished Danes who made contributions to the development of theatre and the arts. One is the playwright

Ludvig Holberg, often hailed as the father of modern Danish theatre, the other is the poet Adam Oehlenschläger, who introduced Romanticism into Danish literature.

---

⑪ Kongens Nytorv

📍 F4

King's New Square was created more than 300 years ago. This is one of Copenhagen's central points and the location of Det Kongelige Teater (The Royal Theatre) and Charlottenborg Slot. As well as marking the end of Nyhavn, it is also a good starting point for exploring Strøget, Copenhagen's famous walkway, which is lined with shops and restaurants.

At the centre of this oval square is an equestrian statue of Christian V, for whom the square was built. The original sculpture was made in 1688 by a French artist. With time, however, the heavy lead monument, which depicts the king as a sombre Roman general, began to sink, distorting the proportions of the figure. In 1946 the monument had to be recast in bronze. In June

each year, new high school graduates descend upon the square to dance around the statue as part of a traditional matriculation ceremony.

Kongens Nytorv was once filled with elm trees, planted in the 19th century. Sadly, these fell prey to disease in 1998 and the square has since been replanted. Construction of the city's new circular metro (*Cityringen*) will affect access until mid-2019, especially near Strøget, the Danish Royal Theatre and Nyhavn.

↑ The equestrian statue of Christian V at the centre of Kongens Nytorv

← Strikingly modern Skuespilhuset glowing on the city's waterfront

arts centre aims to encourage experimentation and innovation, furthering the dialogue between Danish and international art, taking in historical perspectives as well as the most recent trends.

Nikolaj Kunsthal presents five or six exhibitions annually. Among these, one is aimed specifically at children and young people. Another, the Fokus Video Art Festival, takes place in February, premiering works by Danish and international artists alongside Q&As and other events.

The cultural heritage of the building is incorporated into the institution's identity and often the exhibitions as well, with the large arched spaces becoming part of the works on show.

Did You Know?

Copenhagen's waterways are so clean that you can swim in them. There are designated swimming spots.

12

Skuespilhuset

G4 **Sankt Annæ Plads 36** **kglteater.dk**

Throughout the 20th century, a number of venues across the city were used to house the Royal Danish Theatre's Drama Department – with varying degrees of success. Although the need for a suitable playhouse was recognized as early as the 1880s, it was not until 2001 that the Danish government unveiled plans to build a dedicated theatre.

Skuespilhuset, the Royal Danish Playhouse, was inaugurated in 2008. The strikingly modern building offers a range of performance spaces, such as the main auditorium (Main Stage), seating 650, two small stages (Portscenen), seating 200 each, and the Studio Stage, which has seats for 100 people. There are also several open-air spaces, such as the waterfront foyer and the footbridge

terrace, which are used for a host of children's activities and other events. In addition to its seasonal repertoire of plays, the theatre hosts ballets, public lectures, concerts and Q&As with playwrights, directors and actors. Note that all drama performed here is in Danish.

The playhouse incorporates a variety of materials: the dark cladding on the external walls was created with ceramic tiles; the outside of the stage tower is covered with copper; and the footbridge linking the foyer to the harbourfront promenade is made from oak.

13

Nikolaj Kunsthal

E4 **Nikolaj Plads 10** **Nørreport** **Kongens Nytorv** **2A, 9A, 15, 19, 26, 66, 350S** **Noon–6pm Tue– Fri, 11am–5pm Sat & Sun (free on Wed)** **nikolaj kunsthal.dk**

This unique exhibition space, housed in the renovated 13th-century Sankt Nikolaj Kirke, seeks to present art that has never been seen before and to inspire public debate. The

STRØGET

The word "Strøget" ("pedestrian street") cannot be found on any of the plates bearing street names; nevertheless, all those who know the city are familiar with it. Copenhagen's main walkway runs east to west and is made up of five interconnected streets: Østergade, Amagertorv, Nygade, Vimmelskaftet and Frederiksberggade. Pedestrianized in 1962, it has since become one of the city's favourite strolling grounds. Shops here range from exclusive boutiques to souvenir and toy shops, along with numerous cafés and restaurants. There are also some pretty churches and squares and a handful of museums.

14 🍴 🚊
Gråbrødretorv

◉ D4 🚌 6A

This charming, cobblestone square is filled with the music of buskers in summer, when the restaurant tables spill out into the street. Whatever the time of year, it is an excellent place to stop for lunch. The square and its name date to 1238, when Franciscan monks the Grey Brothers built the city's first monastery here. The Great Fire of 1728 destroyed the surrounding buildings and the square was devastated once more by British bombs in 1807; its present appearance dates mainly from the early 19th century. In the late 1960s, the square became a hangout

---

🔍 HIDDEN GEM
Bo-Bi Bar

Founded by a sailor in 1917, the city's oldest bar has been pouring booze for writers and artists for over 100 years at Klareboderne 4. The decor in the tiny pub is the same as on the bar's opening day.

---

for hippies, who would gather under the large tree in the centre. It now has a slightly more laid-back atmosphere.

---

15 🎨 🎭 🚊 🛍
Kunstforeningen GL STRAND

◉ E5 🏛 Gammel Strand 48 Ⓜ Kongens Nytorv 🚌 1A, 2A, 5C, 9A, 250S, 350S ⏰ 11am–5pm Tue–Sun (to 8pm Wed) 🌐 glstrand.dk

GL STRAND was founded in 1825 by the artist and professor C W Eckersberg as a way to bridge the gap between the elitist art establishment and the viewing public, thereby making art more accessible. Its mission today is to focus on and support emerging young artists. The gallery has occupied its current premises, a building on Gammel Strand designed by the 18th-century architect Philip de Lange, since 1952. GL STRAND doesn't have a permanent collection, relying instead on temporary shows spotlighting individual artists. During the course of its history, GL STRAND has hosted many fascinating exhibitions by the

---

↑ Dusk falling over Gråbrødretorv, home to numerous pavement bars and restaurants

---

likes of Edvard Munch (1908), Asger Jorn (1953), film director and artist David Lynch (2010) and Louise Bourgeois (2011).

16
Helligåndskirken

◉ D4 🏛 Niels Hemmingsensgade 5 ⏰ Noon–4pm Mon–Fri, 11am–1pm Sat 🌐 helligaandskirken.dk

Dating originally from the early 15th century when it was an Augustinian monastery, the Church of the Holy Spirit was built on an even earlier sacred site, founded in 1238. The church, one of the oldest in the city, acquired its towers in the late 16th century and its sandstone portal, originally intended for the Børsen (Stock Exchange), in the early 17th century. The building was ravaged by the city's Great Fire in 1728, and has been largely rebuilt, although some original 14th-century walls in the right-hand wing can still be seen. Now surrounded by a park, the church still holds religious services. It is also used for art shows and exhibitions, which provide an occasion to admire its magnificent vaults.

A memorial entitled "Grave of the Unknown Concentration Camp Prisoner", a tribute to Danish victims of the holocaust, is in the churchyard.

---

17 🍴 🖥

Sankt Petri Kirke

📍 D4 🏛 Sankt Peders Stræde 2 Ⓜ Nørreport 🚌 5A, 6A, 14, 42, 43, 173E, 150S, 350S 🕐 Apr–Sep: 11am–3pm Wed–Sat 🌐 sankt-petri.dk

Saint Peter's has been the main church for Copenhagen's German-speaking community since 1586. Records of there being a church on the site, in the heart of the Latin Quarter, date to the 13th century, but parts of the present church date from the 15th century, making it one of the oldest buildings in the city. It suffered serious damage in the course of a series of fires and in the British bombardment of 1807. However, many of the bricks used in the rebuilding work are from the original structure, and the 18th-century copper-clad spire somehow survived the British attacks. Especially noteworthy is the sepulchral chapel that extends from the church, containing numerous tombs and epitaphs, mainly from the 19th century (there is an admission charge for the chapel). There are also some interesting tablets commemorating the dead, which can be seen on the outside wall.

→
The vast equestrian monument to Bishop Absalon in Højbro Plads

---

18 🛍

Højbro Plads

📍 E5

This cobbled square is one of the most enchanting places in Copenhagen. Although at first glance it looks like a single unit, it is in fact divided into Højbro Plads and Amagertorv.

Højbro Plads contains a vast monument to Bishop Absalon, who points out from his horse towards Christiansborg Slot on the other side of the canal. If you look in the opposite direction away from the canal and down the wide promenade, you will see Amagertorv. In the former city market is the striking Storkespringvandet (Stork Fountain), which was added in the 19th century. Despite the misleading name, the birds are actually herons.

The northern section of Amagertorv has an interesting twin-gabled house, built in 1616 in the style of the Dutch Renaissance. It is one of the city's oldest buildings and today houses the Royal Copenhagen Porcelain Shop. Adjacent to it is the showroom of Georg Jensen, which specializes in upmarket silverware. Here there's also a small museum devoted to the work of Jensen and containing some of his early pieces.

DRINK

Ruby
A nightlife institution, twice ranked among the world's 50 best bars.

📍 D5 🏛 Nybrogade 10 🌐 rby.dk

Den Vandrette Natural Wine Bar
High-class but low-key, an ideal spot for sharing a bottle with friends.

📍 F4 🏛 Havnegade 53A 🕐 Mon 🌐 denvandrette.dk

Ved Stranden
Stylish Scandi interior design with a rotating selection of wines.

📍 E5 🏛 Ved Stranden 10 🕐 Sun 🌐 dangleterre. com

Café Det Vide Hus
In a city with sky-high coffee standards, Vide Hus is always packed with locals in need of a caffeine and sweet fix.

📍 D3 🏛 Gothersgade 113 📞 60 61 20 02

19

Universitet

D4 ⚑ Vor Frue Plads
Ⓢ Ⓜ Nørreport 🚌 5A, 6A,
14, 42, 43, 150S, 173E, 350S
🌐 ku.dk/english

The cobbled Vor Frue Plads and university buildings that surround it are the heart of the so-called Latin Quarter, where Latin was once spoken. Despite the fact that the university was founded by Christian I in 1479, the buildings that now stand in Vor Frue Plads date from the 19th century. They house only a handful of faculties, including law; the remaining departments and staff have moved to the main campus, on the island of Amager, east of Copenhagen.

The vast, Neo-Classical university building stands opposite Vor Frue Kirke. It has an impressive entrance hall decorated with frescoes depicting scenes from Greek mythology, which are the work of Constantin Hansen.

> **The cobbled Vor Frue Plads and university buildings that surround it are the heart of the so-called Latin Quarter, where Latin was once spoken.**

Adjacent to the university building is the 19th-century library. On the library's main staircase is a glass cabinet containing fragments from a cannonball that was fired during the British bombardment in 1807. The ball struck the library and ironically hit a book entitled *The Defender of Peace*. A number of second-hand bookshops are located along Fiolstræde, which runs up to the Universitet.

20 🖐

Vor Frue Kirke

D4 ⚑ Nørregade 8
Ⓢ Ⓜ Nørreport 🚌 5A, 6A,
14, 42, 43, 150S, 173E,
350S 🕐 8am–5pm daily
🌐 koebenhavnsdomkirke.dk

Copenhagen's cathedral, Vor Frue Kirke (Church of Our Lady), has a somewhat sombre look and is the third consecutive church to be built on this site. The first, a 12th-century Gothic church, was consumed by fire in 1728, while the next was destroyed by British bombs in 1807 (the tower was a favoured target). The present structure, designed by Christian Frederik Hansen, dates from 1820. Its interior is a veritable art gallery full of sculptures by prominent Danish sculptor Bertel Thorvaldsen, who also created the relief of St John the Baptist, at the entrance.

You will sometimes see Queen Margrethe II at Sunday mass. In the past she would occupy a special royal box, but today the monarch sits in the pews with the rest of the congregation. Visitors can climb the bell tower for excellent panoramas of the city.

21

Folketinget

E5 ⌂ **Christiansborg**
🕐 **Jun–Sep: daily**

The Folketinget is the Danish parliamentary chamber. The seating for the 179 members is arranged in a semicircle with "left-wing" MPs positioned on the left and "right-wing" MPs on the right. The civil servants' offices occupy the majority of the palace. Separate offices are used by Queen Margrethe II, whose duties include chairing weekly meetings of the State Council and presiding over the annual state opening of parliament in early October.

22

Nytorv

D5

Although Nytorv looks like one big square, it is in fact made up of two separate areas – Gammeltorv (Old Square) and Nytorv (New Square), which are separated by the Nygade section of the Strøget walkway. To the northwest, Gammeltorv was a busy marketplace in the 14th century. Today, it is dominated by a fruit and veg market and stalls selling handicrafts.

At the square's centre is Caritasspringvandet (The Charity Fountain), which dates from 1609. This Renaissance treasure depicts a pregnant woman carrying one child in her arms and leading another by the hand – a symbol of charity and mercy. Water flows from the woman's breasts and from the urinating boy at her feet (the holes were blocked for reasons of decency in the 19th century). The fountain was commissioned by Christian IV to draw the public's attention to his charitable virtues.

Nytorv was established in 1606 and for a long time was used by the authorities as a place of execution. The squares were joined together and took their present form soon after the city hall was destroyed by fire in 1795. The outline of the city hall can still be seen in Nytorv's pavement.

The striking Neo-Classical Domhuset (Court House) on the south side of Nytorv was completed in 1815 to a design by Christian Frederik Hansen, who worked on rebuilding Copenhagen after a fire in 1795. The materials used to rebuild the Court House included those taken from the ruined Christiansborg Slot, and the result is redolent of an ancient temple. The building was first used as the city hall, becoming the fifth seat of the town's authorities. In the early 20th century the city hall was moved to the

↑ Statue of Christian V astride his horse, in Nytorv

Rådhus. The inscription on the front of the Domhuset quotes the opening words of the Jutland Code of 1241: "With law the land shall be built."

23

Ripley's Believe It or Not!

C5 ⌂ **Rådhuspladsen 57**
🚌 **2A, 5A, 6A, 10, 12, 14, 26, 29, 33, 67, 68, 69, 173E, 250S**
🕐 **Mid-Jun–Aug: 10am–10pm daily; Sep–mid-Jun: 10am–6pm Sun–Thu, 10am–8pm Fri–Sat** 🌐 **ripleys.com/copenhagen**

Part of an American chain founded by Robert L Ripley – a radio presenter, comic book writer and adventurer – this museum of curiosities is particularly popular with children. Visitors can marvel at a man who eats bicycles or a doll covered in 7,000 buttons, wince at medieval torture devices and shrunken voodoo heads, and so much more.

↑ Vor Frue Kirke surrounded by the rooftops of Copenhagen

← Admiring a row of classical sculptures at Thorvaldsens Museum

㉔ 🖼️ 🖼️ 🖥️ 🛍️

Thorvaldsens Museum

📍 E5 🏛️ Bertel Thorvaldsens Plads 2 ⑤ Central Ⓜ️ Nørreport, Kongens Nytorv 🚌 5C, 12, 14, 33, 150S, 350S 🕙 10am–5pm Tue–Sun 🌐 thorvaldsens museum.dk

Located behind Christiansborg Slotskirke (the Palace Church), Thorvaldsens Museum was the first art museum in Denmark, opening in 1848. The Danish sculptor Bertel Thorvaldsen (1770–1844) lived and worked in Rome for over 40 years, becoming world famous in the process, but towards the end of his life he returned to Copenhagen and bequeathed all his works and his collection of paintings to his native city. The collection, alongside other contributions from Frederik VI and Christian VI, now lives in the palace's old Coach House. The building is worth a visit in its own right, with a frieze on the outside by Jørgen Sonne and mosaic floors inside. The

Did You Know?

Denmark's national flag is the oldest in the world. It dates back to 1625.

museum's high windows are arranged to allow the light to flood the rooms in a variety of ways, depending on the time of day or year, producing a unique experience with each visit.

Despite the fact that some of Thorvaldsen's pieces took him up to 25 years to complete, his output is staggering. Works include sculptures based on classical mythology, busts of well-known contemporaries such as the English poet Lord Byron, monumental studies of Christ and a number of self-portraits. The museum also has some of Thorvaldsen's drawings and sketches on display as well as items from his private collection of Greek, Egyptian and Roman artifacts.

㉕

Børsen

📍 E5 🏛️ Slotsholmsgade 🚫 To the public 🌐 borsbygningen.dk

Copenhagen's former Stock Exchange was built between 1619 and 1623 on the orders of Christian IV, to a design by Lorenz van Steenwinckel, who died before building began and was succeeded by his brother Hans. Today, the building houses the city's Chamber of Commerce and is not open to the public, but its stunning Renaissance façade, copper roofs, numerous gables and unusual spire have made it one of Copenhagen's best-known sights. Its sleek 54 m (177 ft) spire, carved to resemble the entwined tails of four dragons, was originally built in 1625, was renovated in 1775, and is now a city landmark. Topping the spire are three crowns representing Denmark, Sweden and Norway. Trade in goods continued at Børsen until 1857, when it was bought by a private association of wholesalers who pledged to maintain the historic building.

㉖ 🖼️ 🛍️

Krigsmuseet

📍 E5 🏛️ Tøjhusgade 3 🚌 1A, 2A, 9A, 26, 66 🕙 10am–5pm Tue–Sun 🌐 warmuseum.dk

One of Christian IV's first buildings was his arsenal building from 1604, constructed as part of his new naval harbour. It continued to be used to store weapons until the late 19th

→ Sleek steel-and-glass stacks of the BLOX centre, nudging the harbourfront

century. Today it houses the Danish War Museum, depicting Danish and international war history from the 1500s until today. Its collection covers the history of artillery, from the invention of gunpowder up to the present day, with heavy weaponry and firearms on display. You'll also find an eclectic assortment of hunting knives, model planes, samurai armour, medals, sanitary appliances and posters. Upstairs, you can get a chronological overview of Danish wars, from knights in shining armour, through wars with the Swedish and English, to World War II, the Cold War and the wars in Iraq and Afghanistan.

↑ Grand interior of the gorgeous reading room at Det Konglige Bibliotek

BLOX & Danish Architecture Centre

⊙ E6 **⌂ Frederiksholms Kanal 30** **ⓦ blox.dk**

This public space on the city's harbourfront hosts creative and cultural offerings, such as the Danish Architecture Centre (DAC). The BLOX venue has transformed a former brewery and car park into a space for the people, with private homes, a fitness centre, a playground and delightful squares in the surrounding outdoor spaces. The project further connects the Folketinget (parliament) district with the canals, and brings creativity to the water's

existings cultural hub. The highlight of BLOX is DAC, which curates temporary exhibitions that showcase leading Danish and international architects, and explore urban planning and architectural wonders. DAC is also home to permanent exhibitions of Danish architecture and design history. The centre – itself based in a work of architectural art – has a regular turnover of events and weekly walking tours.

The DAC Design Shop offers lifestyle and design products from leading and upcoming Scandi brands. The DAC Café's three large rooftop terraces give you fantastic panoramas of Copenhagen's vibrant city life. Here visitors can indulge in elegant New Nordic dishes made from local and organic produce or simply drop in for a drink with a view.

Det Kongelige Bibliotek

⊙ E6 **⌂ Christians Brygge** **🚌 5C, 250S, 350S** **🚌 991, 992** **⊙ Jul & Aug: 8am-7pm Mon-Fri, 9am-7pm Sat; Sep-Jun: 8am-9pm Mon-Fri, 9am-7pm Sat** **ⓦ kb.dk**

The Royal Library stunningly merges two entirely different architectural forms. The courtyard of the 19th-century Neo-Classical building has been transformed into a garden and contains a statue of the Danish philosopher and theologian Søren Kierkegaard. Next to that is the ultra-modern Black Diamond, linked by a passage to its historic predecessor. It was built as part of the effort to reconnect Danes with their harbour in the post-industrial age. The collection includes medieval manuscripts and the Søren Kierkegaard Archive.

A SHORT WALK
AROUND KONGENS NYTORV

Distance 1.5 km (1 mile) **Time** 20 minutes
Nearest metro Kongens Nytorv

During the late 17th century, Kongens Nytorv (King's New Square) was laid out to link the medieval parts of the city with its newer districts. Today, it is Copenhagen's biggest square and makes an excellent starting point for exploring the city. To the southeast it joins the picturesque Nyhavn district, where the historic ship *Anna Møller*, part of the Nationalmuseet's collection, can be admired from a canalside café. It also marks the beginning of Strøget, which has plenty of restaurants and bars as well as specialist shops and boutiques to tempt those with kroner burning a hole in their pocket.

Hotel d'Angleterre *is one of the oldest and most exclusive hotels in Scandinavia and has hosted many celebs.*

The **Guinness World Records Museum** *has numerous curios, including a figure of the world's tallest man (2.72 m/8 ft 11 inches).*

The 13th-century **Nikolaj Kunsthal** *(p107) today houses the Copenhagen Contemporary Art Center.*

NY ADELG.

NY ØSTERGADE

HOVEDVAGTSG.

KR. BERNIKOWS G.

STERGADE

LILLE KONGENSGADE

ST. KIRKESTRAEDE

NIKOLAJGADE

BREMERHOLM

LAKSEGADE

HOLMENS KANAL

Stunning exterior of Magasin du Nord in Kongens Nytorv ↑

Magasin du Nord *is more than 100 years old and is one of Scandinavia's most exclusive department stores.*

↑ Copenhagen's most famous canal, Nyhavn, illuminated at night

Locator Map
For more detail see p92

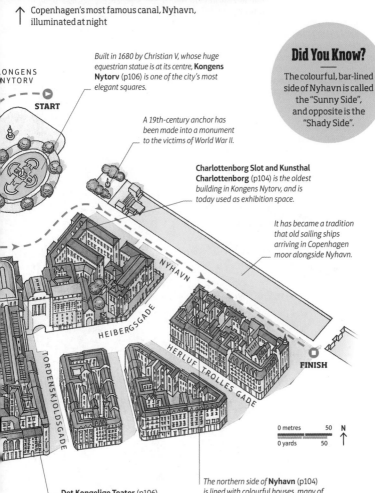

Built in 1680 by Christian V, whose huge equestrian statue is at its centre, **Kongens Nytorv** (p106) *is one of the city's most elegant squares.*

KONGENS NYTORV

START

A 19th-century anchor has been made into a monument to the victims of World War II.

Charlottenborg Slot and Kunsthal Charlottenborg (p104) *is the oldest building in Kongens Nytorv, and is today used as exhibition space.*

It has became a tradition that old sailing ships arriving in Copenhagen moor alongside Nyhavn.

NYHAVN

HEIBERGSGADE

HERLUF TROLLES GADE

TORDENSKJOLDSGADE

FINISH

Did You Know?

The colourful, bar-lined side of Nyhavn is called the "Sunny Side", and opposite is the "Shady Side".

| 0 metres | 50 | N |
| 0 yards | 50 | ↑ |

Det Kongelige Teater (p106) *is a 19th-century building and stages prominent theatre and ballet performances.*

The northern side of **Nyhavn** (p104) *is lined with colourful houses, many of which were once brothels frequented by sailors after months at sea.*

A SHORT WALK
AROUND
CHRISTIANSBORG SLOT

Distance 2 km (1.25 miles) **Time** 25 minutes **Nearest metro** Kongens Nytorv

Separated from the hub of the city by a canal is the compact islet of Slotsholmen. The island derives its name from a castle that was built on this site in 1167. The complex of historic buildings here includes Christiansborg Slot, a palace and government building that comprises a former royal coach house and stables. Opposite the palace, across the canal, is the encyclopedic Nationalmuseet. Old meets new around Christiansborg Slot thanks to a number of buildings and collections that demonstrate the best of cutting-edge Danish architecture and design, such as the "Black Diamond" extension at Det Kongelige Bibliotek.

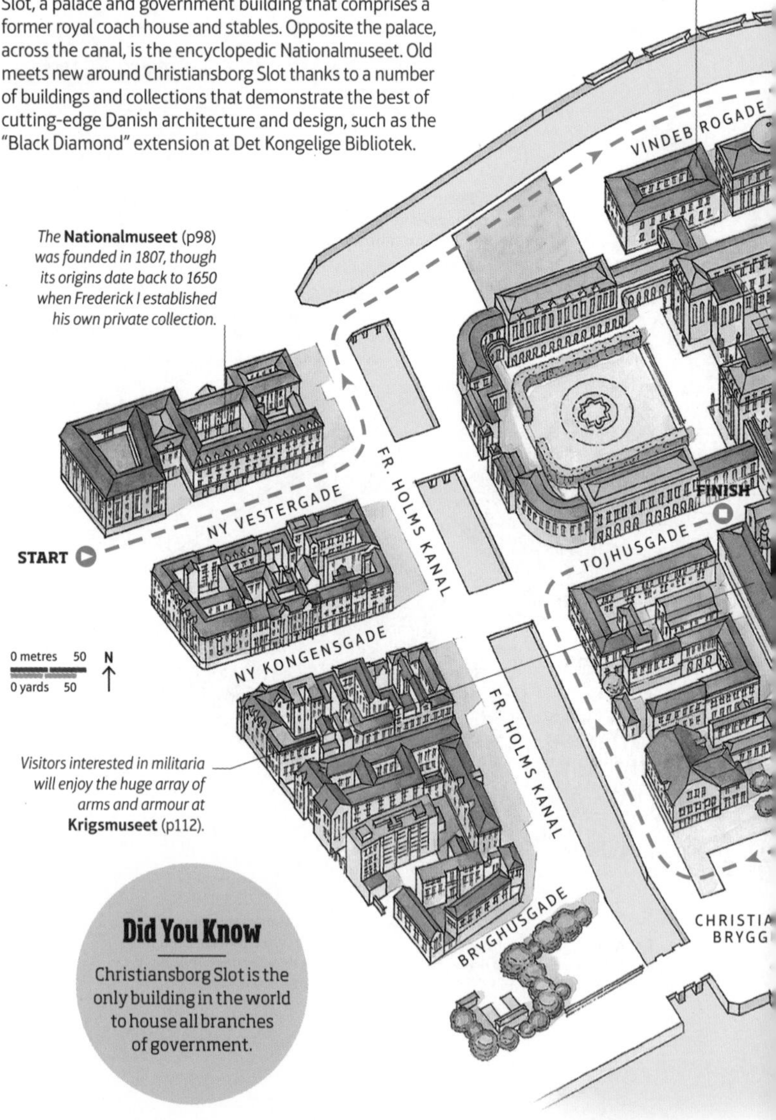

Thorvaldsens Museum (p112) confirms the genius of the Danish sculptor, whose tomb can be found in the courtyard.

*The **Nationalmuseet** (p98) was founded in 1807, though its origins date back to 1650 when Frederick I established his own private collection.*

VINDEBROGADE

FR. HOLMS KANAL

NY VESTERGADE

START

TOJHUSGADE

FINISH

0 metres 50   N
0 yards 50

NY KONGENSGADE

FR. HOLMS KANAL

*Visitors interested in militaria will enjoy the huge array of arms and armour at **Krigsmuseet** (p112).*

BRYGHUSGADE

CHRISTIA
BRYGG

Did You Know

Christiansborg Slot is the only building in the world to house all branches of government.

Locator Map
For more detail see p92

↑ The spire of Børsen, Copenhagen's old
Stock Exchange, piercing the sky

Although this has not been the home of the royal family
for more than 200 years, the rooms at **Christiansborg
Slot** (p98) are still used for grand occasions, such as
state banquets attended by Queen Margrethe II.

BØRSGADE

Folketinget (p111) *is the Danish parliament
building, and is open to visitors during the
summer, when its members are on holiday.*

Børsen (p112) *is the former Stock
Exchange. Its spire is sculpted in the
form of entwined dragon tails, a great
example of 17th-century architecture.*

BØRSGADE

CHRISTIANS BRYGGE

The key attraction of **Det Kongelige Bibliotek**
*(p113) is the library's "Black Diamond", which
utilizes black glass and granite from Zimbabwe
and is a particularly innovative building.*

INSIDER TIP
Get Sketching

Budding artists are
welcome to sketch art-
works at Thorvaldsens
Museum *(p112)*. For an
additional charge
there's also a drawing
workshop for families.
Check online for details.

CHRISTIANSHAVN AND HOLMEN

This remarkable section of Copenhagen was established by Christian IV in the 17th century and modelled on Amsterdam, with its criss-cross of canals, narrow cobbled streets and colourful, crooked houses. The area is geographically defined by Christian IV's ancient ramparts, extending north to the three islands of Holmen. Christianshavn, meanwhile, exemplifies the acceptable Scandinavian version of gentrification. Historic docks and decaying warehouses have given way to new, dynamic spaces, and African and Asian communities. Broad canals, imposing mansions and deliberately provocative modern architecture stand alongside medieval narrow lanes and remnants of Renaissance fortifications. The hippy ethos has not entirely evaporated: the "free city" of Christiania has flown the flag since 1971, despite police incursions and a current state of self-regulated decorum.

CHRISTIANSHAVN AND HOLMEN

Experience
❶ Christianshavn
❷ Vor Frelsers Kirke
❸ Operaen
❹ Christiania
❺ Krøyers Plads
❻ Inderhavnsbroen
❼ Cirkelbroen

Eat and Drink
① Restaurant 108
② Barr
③ noma
④ Kadeau
⑤ Café Wilder

Stay
⑥ Hotel CPHLIVING

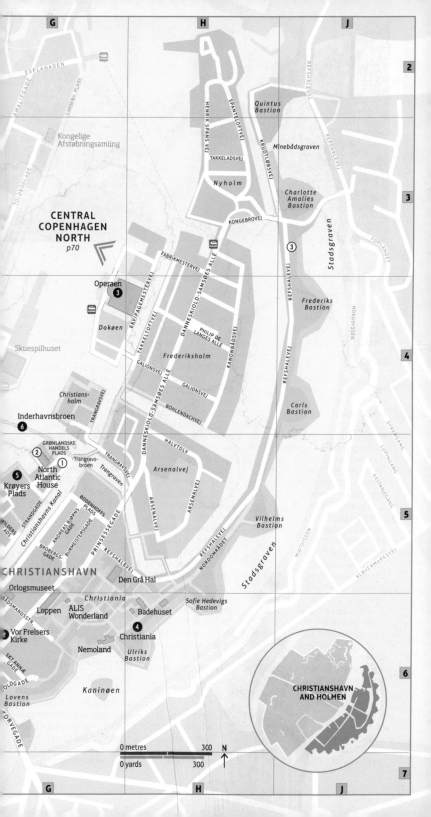

EXPERIENCE

① 🍴 🖼 🛍

Christianshavn

📍F6

This artificial island sitting snugly between Copenhagen's northern and southern halves is sometimes referred to as "Little Amsterdam" because of its many canals, which serve as a unique way of exploring the area. Built in the first half of the 17th century by Christian IV, Christianshavn was originally intended both as a fortified city and as a naval base to facilitate his maritime ambitions. The district was the site of the first boatyards established in Copenhagen, as well as warehouses belonging to major shipping lines. It is also where sailors and boatyard workers lived.

Up until the 1980s, Christianshavn was known chiefly as the site of the "Free State of Christiania" and was considered unattractive, poor and rundown. Since the 1990s, however, together with

nearby Holmen – which is a group of three small islands to the north – Christianshavn has enjoyed something of a renaissance thanks to a sustained urban redevelopment programme. With the recent addition of the Inderhavnsbroen (Inner Harbour Bridge) *(p125)*, linking Nyhavn to Christianshavn, the district has experienced an increase in foot traffic. Despite the upsurge in attention, the largely residential neighbourhood maintains an identity all of its own; locals prefer to think of themselves as Christianhavners above all else.

The old warehouses have now been transformed into trendy restaurants, stylish cafés and chic apartments, while the island's historic canal-side houses, some of which date back to the 19th century, preserve its charm and vibrancy.

←
Sightseers ascending the prominent spire of Vor Frelsers Kirke

---

⛰ **GREAT VIEW**
Vor Frelsers Kirke

Famous for its golden spiral staircase winding into the sky, this 17th-century church has one of the best panoramas in Copenhagen. Your reward for the gruelling climb is an aerial view of Christianshavn's canals and a 360-degree visual extending to Øresund Bridge, which connects Denmark and Sweden.

---

② ⛪

Vor Frelsers Kirke

📍G6 🏠 **Skt Annæ Gade 29** Ⓜ **Christianshavn** 🚌 **66, 250S, 350S** 🕐 **11am-3:30pm daily; tower: 10am-4pm Mon-Sat, 10:30am-4pm Sun & hols (late Jun-mid-Sep: to 7:30pm daily)** 🌐 **vorfrelserskirke.dk**

Our Saviour's Church is famous for its extraordinary spire, completed in 1752, accessible via a spiral staircase that runs around the exterior. Be warned: it takes considerable stamina to climb all 400 steps, not to mention a good

Boats lining the blue
waters of a pretty canal
in Christianshavn

head for heights. The spire is
one of the city's highest panoramic viewpoints, reaching a
height of 90 m (295 ft). Note
that the spire is closed in
heavy rain and strong winds.

The spire's creator was
the architect Lauritz de
Thurah, who struck upon the
idea of a spiral staircase while
visiting the church of Sant'Ivo
alla Sapienza in Rome. Legend
has it that Thurah was so
obsessed by his work that
when it was alleged that his
encircling staircase wound up
the wrong way he committed
suicide by leaping from the
top of the tower. The truth is
more prosaic, however, as the
architect died in his own bed,
poor and destitute, seven years
after completing the tower.
The tale was nevertheless
made into a movie by Danish
director Nils Vest, in 1997.

The spire aside, the church
itself is worth visiting. Vor
Frelsers Kirke was built in 1696
to a design by Lambert von
Haven, a Norwegian-Danish
architect and artist. Inside, a
Baroque altar by the Swede
Nicodemus Tessin is adorned
with cherubs. The huge three-
storey organ dates from 1698.

The organ has more than
4,000 pipes, is elaborately
carved, and is supported by
two giant elephants.

 3

Operaen

📍 G4 🏛 Ekvipagemestervej
10 🚌 9A, 66 🚌 901, 902
🕐 Foyer: 2 hrs before
performance; guided tours
in English: 2pm and 4pm
daily 🌐 kglteater.dk

The stunning Copenhagen
Opera House opened in 2005
on the Dokøen (Dock Island)
of Holmen, directly facing
Amalienborg Slot across the
harbour and Marmorkirken
just beyond it. The auditorium
was designed by the prominent
Danish architect Henning
Larsen, whose works include
the Ny Carlsberg Glyptotek
(p96) extension. No expense
was spared in the design of
this elaborate £380 million
project. The building is clad in
German limestone, the floor
of the foyer is made of Sicilian
marble and the ceiling of the
1,400-seat auditorium is
gilded in gold leaf.

Guided tours of the opera
house are available in both
English and Danish and cover
most of the building, including
the stunning auditorium and
backstage areas.

↑ Sleek and modern
interior of Copenhagen's
Opera House

EAT & DRINK

Restaurant 108
In a revamped harbour
warehouse with noma
alumni at the helm, 108
dishes up an inventive
New Nordic menu.

📍 G5 🏛 Strandgade 108
🌐 108.dk

Ⓚ Ⓚ Ⓚ

Barr
The iconic dishes of
northern Europe plus a
selection of traditional
beers, aquavit and wine.

📍 G5 🏛 Strandgade 93
🌐 restaurantbarr.com

Ⓚ Ⓚ Ⓚ

noma
Synonymous with New
Nordic cuisine, chef
René Redzepi's flavour
pairings are as striking
as the beautiful plating.

📍 J3 🏛 Refshalevej 96
🌐 noma.dk

Ⓚ Ⓚ Ⓚ

Kadeau
This two-Michelin-star
restaurant uses foraged
and farmed ingredients.

📍 F6 🏛 Wildersgade 10B
🕐 Mon, Sun, L Tue-Fri
🌐 kadeau.dk

Ⓚ Ⓚ Ⓚ

Café Wilder
Serves a sophisticated
Franco-Danish menu.
The cobbled side street,
rattan café chairs and
intimate bar evoke a
Parisian vibe.

📍 F6 🏛 Wildersgade 56
🌐 cafewilder.dk

Ⓚ Ⓚ Ⓚ

④ 🚲 🍴 🍷 🍺 🛍️

Christiania

📍H6 Ⓜ Christianshavn
🚌 5C, 9A, 66, 250S, 350S

The "Free State of Christiania" has been in existence since 13 November 1971, when a group of squatters took over some deserted military barracks to the east of Christianshavn and established a commune. The local authorities initially tried to force them out, but as the community's numbers swelled, attracting like-minded non-conformists from all over the world, the government opted to treat Christiania as a "social experiment". Today there are around 900 residents.

Christiania has its own system of government, its own infrastructure and even a kindergarten, financed in part by its cafés and restaurants and the sale of locally made handicrafts. Though it has a

salacious reputation thanks to its "alternative" lifestyle, the settlement is actually a fairly pastoral enclave defined by its homemade houses, workshops, galleries, music venues and organic eateries.

For your own safety, you should avoid filming or taking photographs in Christiania, especially in Pusher Street, which is known for drug dealing. At the entrance you will find signs indicating "do's and don'ts" in the area. You're advised to take them seriously.

📷 PICTURE PERFECT
Hued Houses

Two of the city's most photogenic row houses are in Christianshavn. No 3 Sofiegade is a crooked mint, yellow and turquoise patchwork. No 4 Overgaden Oven Vandet is ice blue with climbing roses.

---

⑤

Krøyers Plads

📍G5 🏠 Strandgade 83
Ⓜ Christianshavn 🚌 66, 9A

Krøyers Plads is one of the most recent and most controversial developments in the harbour. The area functioned as a port for nearly 200 years before a long and drawn-out battle between locals and developers ensued over the nature of the new building project. The result is a new public square and bathing pier, which has become a favourite hangout in Copenhagen. From here, you can picnic on the wooden decking while enjoying the great views over the harbour. The square was designed to complement the city's historic warehouses while reinventing its industrial traditions and is adjacent to the Michelin-starred restaurant 108 (p123) and the wine and coffee bar Corner 108.

←
Fantastic graffiti greeting visitors at the entrance to the "Free State" of Christiania

←
Cyclists and pedestrians
crossing the canal via
the Inderhavnsbroen

400

The birthday
Christianshavn
celebrated in 2018.

❻

Inderhavnsbroen

📍**G4** 🏛**Inderhavnsbroen**
Ⓜ**Kongens Nytorv** 🚌**66**

With its key location, linking
Nyhavn with Christianshavn,
Inderhavnsbroen, or Inner
Harbour Bridge, quickly became
popular among walkers and
cyclists when it opened in 2016.
The convenience of the 180 m
(590 ft) bridge has dramatically
altered the experience of visiting Christianshavn and Holmen
for the better. Functionality
aside, no matter which direction you approach from, you
can pause at the designated
platforms on the bridge to
take in the unparalleled views
of the harbour area and down
the Nyhavn Canal. Inderhavnsbroen is also known as "the
Kissing Bridge", as it somewhat
resembles a kiss because it
retracts in a graceful horizontal
gliding motion, allowing ships
to pass, and then reconnects

with itself. The bridge is the
final step of the so-called
Harbour Circle, a series of
routes for pedestrians and
cyclists to explore and enjoy
Copenhagen's offerings along
the harbourfront.

---

❼

Cirkelbroen

📍**E6** 🏛**Applebys Plads**
Ⓜ**Christianshavn** 🚌**2A,
9A, 37, 350S**

Cirkelbroen, or Circle Bridge, is
arguably the most beautiful of
the new pedestrian and cyclist
bridges revolutionizing the
city's urban design. World-
renowned and award-winning
Danish-Icelandic artist Olafur
Eliasson designed the bridge
to celebrate Christianshavn's
maritime history. The bridge
consists of five circular platforms of varying sizes, each
with its own mast held up by
steel cables, which together
come to closely resemble a
ship. Cirkelbroen makes life
easier for locals and visitors
as it straddles the canal and
connects Appelbys Plads in
the south to Christiansbro in

the north. In addition to its
functionality, the stand-out
design of the harbour's new
architectural landmark makes
for a top photo opportunity.
The wide circular platforms
are arranged in a staggered,
irregular pattern to encourage
cyclists and pedestrians to
reflect and soak up the scenery.

STAY

Hotel CPHLIVING
Float away to the
sounds of passing ships
and seagulls on this
boutique ship-cum-hotel
right on the harbour.
Designer rooms feature
views of Slotsholmen
and Den Sorte Diamant
(The Black Diamond),
and the huge rooftop
terrace has great views
of the city skyline.

📍**E6** 🏛**Langebrogade 1C**
🌐**cphliving.com**

Ⓚ Ⓚ Ⓚ

BEYOND THE CENTRE

Must Sees

❶ Fredriksberg Have
❷ ARKEN Museum

Experience More

❸ Vesterbro
❹ Østerbro
❺ Nørrebro
❻ Refshaleøen Island
❼ Experimentarium
❽ Tycho Brahe Planetarium
❾ Øresund Bridge
❿ Havnebadet Islands Brygge
⓫ Amager and Ørestad
⓬ Den Blå Planet
⓭ Dragør
⓮ Charlottenlund Slot

It is no accident that Copenhagen's outlying areas, unlike those of most capital cities, are as attractive and engaging as the centre. A deliberate plan to stretch out the fingers of culture, archi-tecture and commerce along five train routes was made in 1947, after the war. Transport is key in making Sweden's third-largest city Malmö virtually a twin city, now only 45 minutes away over the Øresund Bridge; an even faster 23-minute underground metro line is planned to open in 2035. It's outside of the city centre that visitors will find Copenhagen's coolest, most dynamic neighbourhoods – Østerbro, Vesterbro and Nørrebro – plus stand-alone attractions such as Charlottenlund Slot, Experimentarium and Den Blå Planet.

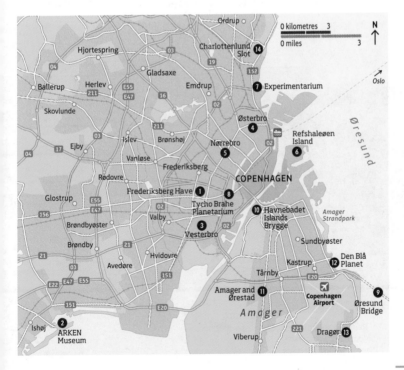

❶

FREDERIKSBERG HAVE

📍F5 🏛Roskildevej 32 🚇Valby Ⓜ Frederiksberg 🚌4A, 6A, 18, 26
🕐Daily; Zoologisk Have: times vary, check website 🌐zoo.dk

Copenhageners couldn't imagine their city without Frederiksberg Have, a romantic pleasure garden designed for a king. There is much to explore in this idyllic green space, from woodlands and waterfalls to the Chinese Pavilion. Crowning the scene is Frederiksberg Slot, King Frederik IV's summer retreat, now used by the Military Academy.

King Frederick IV had Frederiksberg Have laid out for his summer palace, the Italianate Frederiksberg Slot, erected between 1700 and 1735. The king loved the pleasure gardens, sailing on the canals in a gondola and even entertaining the Tsar of Russia here. Today a statue of the king welcomes visitors at the park's main entrance. The public received access to Frederiksberg Have in 1865 and the rambling, English-style gardens have been a favourite spot for picnickers ever since. Pathways wind throughout the bucolic landscape and take in the ornate 1799 Chinese Pavilion and Royal Horticultural Society flower gardens. Look out for the Elephant Viewpoint overlooking

Zoologisk Have's Elephant House, and the tree tied with dummies; it's a Danish tradition that parents officially take pacifiers away from their children at the age of 3 and tie them here. Frederiksberg Slot is open only for guided tours at 11am and 1pm on the last Saturday of the month (except in July and December).

> **The public received access to Frederiksberg Have in 1865 and the rambling, English-style gardens have been a favourite spot for picnickers ever since.**

Relaxing on the lawns before the king's palace, in Frederiksberg Have →

↑ Rowing on the canals of Frederiksberg Have during the summer

Zoologisk Have

Copenhagen's zoological garden was established close to Frederiksberg Slot in 1859, making it one of Europe's oldest zoos. Today it is home to a wide selection of animals, including giraffes, polar bears, hippos, elephants and lions. The Norman Foster-designed Elephant House is especially noteworthy for its stunning architecture. A tropical section houses butterflies and birds. Note that there is an entrance fee for Zoologisk Have.

Spring

▽ The park springs to life at the end of March, with trees blossoming around the canals and birds singing on their spring migration. Check out the lovely blooms at the Haveselskabets Have gardens just inside the main entrance.

Summer

The park becomes a shady respite in summer, while sun-soakers bask on the meadow and the sloping lawn in front of the palace. This is the time to see the park King Frederik's favourite way - from the water. Rent a small pleasure boat from Svendsens Bådfart.

Autumn

▽ The golden, red and orange kaleidoscope of autumn leaves is an Instagrammer's delight. Fall is also the last time. This is a good time to visit Zoologisk Have, before animals hibernate for the winter.

Winter

Winter is a magical time at Frederiksberg Have, when snow settles and trees sparkle with ice crystals. The Frederiksberg Runddel, by the garden entrance, is transformed into an ice-skating rink.

← Walking in the snowy grounds of Frederiksberg Have

2 🗺️🖼️🍴💻🛍️

ARKEN MUSEUM

📍F5 🏛️Skovvej 100, Ishøj 🚇Ishøj
🚌128 🕐10am–5pm Tue–Sun (to 9pm Wed)
🌐arken.dk

Giants of 20th- and 21st-century art await at ARKEN. Home to one of Denmark's finest collections of contemporary art, the building itself, designed to resemble a stranded ship, is perhaps ARKEN's greatest masterpiece.

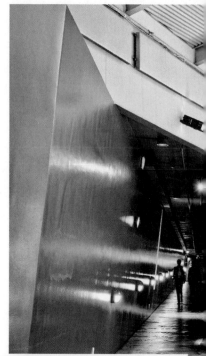

A 25-year-old architecture student called Søren Robert Lund won a competition to design this museum space, in 1988. Designed to resemble a marooned ship, the building embodies the popular Deconstructivism movement of the 1980s, and its design was regarded by many as being just as provocative as the contemporary works displayed inside. The museum is built on two axes and is character-ized by angular passageways, optical illusions and dramatic transitions from large to small spaces. Additional exhibition space has been added since the museum's official opening in 1996, some again designed by Lund.

The focus at ARKEN is cutting-edge modern art exhibitions, whether install-ations, sculpture or graphic art, and the museum plays host to excellent temporary displays.

MAKE A DAY OF IT

ARKEN makes for a great day out. The raw and angular museum building is so photogenic, and there's much to discover inside. Apart from its art collection, the chef at CAFÉ ARKEN creates exciting exhibition-themed menus using almost exclusively organic Danish ingredients. ARKEN SHOP is the area's leading design store and has a tempting mix of Nordic design, art books and gift items. Later, head to Ishøj Beach, one of Denmark's most beautiful sand beaches on ARKEN's doorstep. Gor for a dip here or a read on the beach after a morning of culture.

↑ Greenhouse installation by Thorbjørn Lausten's in ARKEN's Art Axis, and the distinct exterior of the museum *(inset)*

The museum's permanent collection holds post-1945 artworks and boasts names such as Andy Warhol, Anselm Reyle, Damien Hirst and Ai Weiwei, plus prominent Danes including Candice Breitz, Asger Jorn and Olafur Eliasson. One of ARKEN's most fascinating installations is Ai Weiwei's *Circle of Animals/Zodiac Heads*, a playful take on identity and repatriation.

Art Aside...

ARKEN Museum has much more to offer in addition to compelling contemporary art, including a brilliant design shop and the delightful ARKEN CAFÉ, with incredible panoramic views out over Køge Bay. You'll find a sandy beach right on the museum's doorstep, complete with a wooden pier and children's play area (plus a lifeguard during the summer). The area around the museum offers forests, harbour areas and a great network of paths, with excellent opportunities for cycling, running and hiking.

↑ *Love's Paradox* and, behind it, *2-Amino-5-Bromobenzotrifluoride* by Damien Hirst

EXPERIENCE MORE

3

Vesterbro

🔲 Dybbølsbro, Enghave, Valby 🚌 1A, 3A, 6A, 10, 14

In the early 2000s, Vesterbro transformed from a red-light district to the ultra-cool area it is today. Locals and visitors flock here for the trendy bars and eateries in the old meat-packing district of Kødbyen, along with the independent cafés and boutiques lining the streets of Istedgade and Værnedsvej, known as Copenhagen's Little Paris.

In the southwest corner of the neighbourhood, the Carlsberg Brewery is a key draw. It was founded in 1847 by Jacob Christian, whose father had worked at Copenhagen's king's brewery. Jacob Christian chose this site on Valby Hill for the quality of the water, and named his company Carlsberg after his son. **Visit Carlsberg** is an exhibition centre where you can learn about the history of beer and the manufacturing process during a 90-minute self-guided tour. This concludes with beer tasting in a bar overlooking the huge copper kettles used in the brewing process. In 2005, the attached Jacobsen Brewhouse opened in part of the old brewery, developing speciality beers.

The brewery itself features some striking examples of industrial architecture, and is recognized for the intriguing Elephant Gate (1901), which consists of four larger-than-life granite elephants shipped from Bornholm.

Visit Carlsberg will be closed in 2019 for major renovation works and will reopen in 2020.

1868
—
The year that Carlsberg first exported beer, specifically one barrel to Edinburgh.

Visit Carlsberg
🎟️ 🕒 🏠 Gamle Carlsberg Vej 11 Ⓜ Carlsberg 🚌 26, 8A ⏱ For renovation until 2020 🅦 visitcarlsberg.com

---

DRINK

War Pigs
Hip brew pub with craft beers and Europe's largest meat smoker.
🏠 Flæsketorvet 25
🅦 warpigs.dk

Prolog Coffee
In-demand speciality café and micro-roastery.
🏠 Høkerboderne 16
🅦 prologcoffee.com

Mikkeller & Friends
Cheerful, minimalist bar synonymous with the Danish craft beer boom.
🏠 Stefansgade 35
🅦 mikkeller.dk

Coffee Collective
The city's most popular coffee roaster and World Barista Champion.
🏠 Jægersborggade 57
🅦 coffeecollective.dk

4 🍴 🍺 🛍️

Østerbro

Ⓢ **Østerport, Nordhavn, Svanemøllen** 🚌 **1A, 3A, 4A, 6A, 350S**

The least touristy of the city's distinctive neighbourhoods, the family-friendly oasis of Østerbro is the area to see life through the eyes of a local. Famously posh and peaceful, the area is found just east of Central Copenhagen North and can be reached by crossing Fredensbro or the main artery, Østerbrogade, lined with tempting cafés and boutiques. This includes the Normann Copenhagen flagship, an exclusive Danish interior design brand located in an old cinema and packed with stylish furniture, lighting and homewares – all the hallmarks of enviable Danish design. Østerbro also boasts Geranium, the only triple-starred Michelin restaurant in Denmark. Østerberg Ice Cream is further draw, producing handmade frozen desserts popular with Copenhageners. When you've had your fill, the lush Fælledparken is Denmark's largest urban park and a favoured meet-up for sports and festivals. STAY Seaport, with its 53 spacious design apartments, offers a range of luxurious options for accommodation.

5 🍴 🍺 🛍️

Nørrebro

Ⓢ **Nørrebro** Ⓜ **Nørreport** 🚌 **3A, 5C, 12, 66, 350S**

The atmosphere in Nørrebro is that of an intimate village. Young families zip around on bikes, while effortlessly chic locals flock to the countless stylish eateries and coffee

←

Relaxing and drinking coffee outside a café in Vesterbro

↑ Friends cycling on a sunny day in Copenhagen's Nørrebro

spots. Jægersborggade remains the coolest street in Copenhagen, with galleries, workshops and a Michelin-starred restaurant. It's also worth visiting Elmegade, with its parades of boutiques, bars and cafés, and Ravnsborggade, famous for its vintage shops and markets.

Nørrebro is linked to central Copenhagen by Dronning Louises Bro, a bridge built in the 1600s and widened in 1897. Many cyclists and pedestrians cross it daily. The district has come a long way since riots in the mid-2000s, rapidly transitioning from a rundown backwater to a polished gem.

Alongside the stellar café and shopping scene, another highlight is **Assistens Kirkegård**. Conceived in 1760 as a cemetery for poor plague victims, it later came to be the final resting place of Søren Kierkegaard and Hans Christian Andersen. Today the cemetery-cum-park is busy with joggers, cyclists and sunbathers.

Assistens Kirkegård
🏠 Kapelvej 2 Ⓜ Forum
🕐 Apr-Sep: 7am-10pm daily; Oct-Mar: 7am-7pm daily;
🌐 assistens.dk

┌─────────────────────
TOP 4 SHOPS ON JÆGERS-BORGGADE

Karamelleriet
🏠 Jægersborggade 36
🌐 karamelleriet.com
The sweet smell of handmade treats lures Nørrebro shoppers.

Lady Fingers
🏠 Jægersborggade 4
🌐 ladyfingers.dk
Stylish workshop with minimalist designs and brilliant gemstones, run by a collective of six local jewellery makers.

Tricotage
🏠 Jægersborggade 15
🌐 tricotage.dk
Has its own line of cuddly, organic wool sweaters with both elegant designs and outrageous patterns.

Sneakers & Coffee
🏠 Jægersborggade 30
🌐 sneakersandcoffee.dk
The well-heeled shop at this trendy speciality shoe store and café.

Friends gathering at popular Mikkeller in Kødbyen, Vesterbro

Interacting with
exhibits at the
Experimentarium ↑

6 🍴 💻 🛍
Refshaleøen Island

🚌 9A 🚢 Holmen Nord
🌐 refshaleoen.dk

This former industrial shipyard, just north of Christianshavn, has been reinvigorated with top-rated restaurants, bars, creative spaces and festivals. Copenhagen institutions noma and Reffen (previously Street Food Copenhagen) both relocated here, making this a must-visit for foodies. Further culinary attractions include New Nordic powerhouse Amass, wine bar La Banchina and Baghaven, part of the Mikkeller family. Copenhagen

Contemporary houses art installations by modern art heavyweights, while CopenHot lures visitors with fire-heated saunas and spa cruises. In summer, music festivals Haven and Copenhell fill the island with revellers.

---

7 🛹 🍴 💻 🛍
Experimentarium

🏠 Tuborg Havnevej 7, 2900 Hellerup 🚉 Hellerup, Svanemøllen 🚌 1A 🚌 993
🕐 9:30am-5pm Mon-Fri (to 8pm Thu), 10am-5pm Sat & Sun 🚫 1 Jan, 24, 25 & 31 Dec
🌐 experimentarium.dk

This innovative centre brings science to life via interactive exploration. There's something for everyone; learn about the natural world, the human body, inventions and so much more. Kids can try their hand at guiding a cargo vessel, explore the Tunnel of Senses, and race balls through a track. The Miniverse is aimed at pre-schoolers, who can learn through play in stimulating surroundings. Adults will like the interactive rooftop with its spectacular views over the city, open from spring to autumn. All exhibits are labelled in Danish and English, and there are numerous lectures and special events.

8 🛹
Tycho Brahe Planetarium

🏠 Gl Kongevej 10
🚉 Vesterport 🚌 9A, 31
🕐 Daily; times vary, check website 🌐 planetariet.dk

Copenhagen's planetarium, the largest in western Europe, is named after the renowned Danish astronomer Tycho Brahe (1546–1601). Brahe is credited with the discovery of a new star in the constellation of Cassiopeia, in 1572, and with making important advances in our knowledge of planetary motion before the invention of the telescope.

The planetarium opened in 1989 in a cylindrical building

EAT

Geranium
This three-starred Michelin restaurant promises a truly unique meal, with 20 courses and the best ingredients. Booking is required at least 90 days in advance.

🏠 Per Henrik Lings Alle 4 🕐 Sun-Tue
🌐 geranium.dk

Ⓚ Ⓚ Ⓚ

HIDDEN GEM

Cisternerne

This forgotten reservoir under Frederiksberg Hill is now an underground art exhibition and performance space. You can also join a tour (*www.cisternerne.dk*).

designed by Knud Munk. Built from sand-coloured brick, it is at its most attractive from across Sankt Jørgens Sø (Saint George's Lake), which was created in the late 18th century by damming the local river. The planetarium sits on the Old Royal Route (Gammel Kongevej), once travelled by royal processions heading for Frederiksberg Slot.

The planetarium is the most advanced centre in Denmark for popularizing astronomy and space research, as well as promoting natural science. A huge IMAX® cinema screens films daily, including one on the wonders of space travel.

⑨ Øresund Bridge

🌐 oresundsbron.com

When Queen Margrethe II and King Carl XVI of Sweden jointly opened the Øresund Bridge in 2000, it was the first time that the Scandinavian peninsula

had been connected to mainland Europe since the Ice Age. Now the delights of Malmö, the largest city in southern Sweden, are only 35 minutes away from Copenhagen.

The bridge is the second-longest fixed-link bridge in the world, with the length stretching for 16 km (10 miles). It includes a 430-m- (1,411- ft-) long artificial peninsula, plus a tunnel measuring more than 3.5 km (2 miles) and running 10 m (35 ft) below the water. The sight of the bridge, with its huge 204-m- (670-ft-)high pylons, is truly impressive.

The bridge is a marvel of modern engineering. It has a two-level structure; the top is for motor traffic, the bottom for rail. At its highest point the bridge is suspended 57 m (187 ft) above the water. At the tunnel entrances light filters allow drivers to adjust to the dimmer conditions. About 1,000 sensors are installed along the route as part of a fire alarm system.

The bridge has proved to be popular, and over 32,000 rail passengers and 21,000 cars make the crossing every day. It also forms part of an annual marathon, the first of which took place in June 2000.

There is a toll charge for crossing the bridge, depending on the size of your vehicle. Bikes aren't allowed and there are passport control points on the Swedish side.

⑩ Havnebadet Islands Brygge

📍 Islands Brygge 14
🌐 teambade.kk.dk

Five pools, three diving towers and a sunbathing space have made these urban baths one of the most popular places on a sunny day in the city. On warm evenings locals bring wine, portable BBQs and play music while they enjoy taking a cooling dip in the harbour. Located on the east side of Sydhaven, across from Tivoli, the pool area offers a fantastic panorama of the city skyline.

Two of the pools are for children, with the shallowest just 30 cm (12 in) deep. Lifeguards are on hand at the facilities from 1 June to 30 September, but hardcore swimmers have been known to take an icy plunge in winter. The quality of the water is checked daily and has to be approved by the authorities before swimmers plunge in.

Did You Know?

Nordic Noir series *The Bridge* (2011–18) was set on and around the Øresund Bridge.

← Tycho Brahe Planetarium standing on the bank of Saint George's Lake

EXPERIENCE Beyond the Centre

⓫

Amager and Ørestad

⌂ 3 km (2 miles) southeast of the city centre

For many the island of Amager is where their exploration of Denmark really begins, particularly as Copenhagen's international airport is nearby.

Since the opening of the Øresund Bridge, Amager has become characterized by groundbreaking architecture and housing developments and the urban conglomeration of Amager, with its residential blocks, shops and restaurants, blends into the almost futuristic Ørestad. Landmarks here include the Bella Sky Comwell Hotel, whose two towers lean away from each other

HIDDEN GEM
Amager Strandpark

Southeast of the city lies urbanites' favourite summer beach, a 2-km-(1-mile-) long artificial island with a lagoon. Helgoland, on the tip of the sand bar, is a picture-perfect vintage bathing complex.

with alternating glass panels, and the DR Koncerthuset. This world-class venue and studio space sits within a giant blue cube. Its glass façade, opaque by day, projects images of the activity within at night.

Those looking for outdoor attractions can still find them here, however: Natur-center Vestamager is an oasis with play areas, pony rides and a lake.

⓬

Den Blå Planet

⌂ Jacob Fortlingsvej 1
Ⓜ Kastrup **🚌** 2A, 5C
🕙 10am–6pm daily (to 9pm Mon) **🌐** denblaaplanet.dk

Copenhagen's aquarium, Den Blå Planet (The Blue Planet), offers the chance to admire a wide variety of marine life, and plays a major role in conservation, research and education.

The aquarium contains over 90 glass tanks in five sections: the Amazon, the African Great Lakes, the Warm Ocean, Cold Water, and Evolution and Adaptation. The tanks are populated by over 300 species of fish from all over the world,

TOP 4
STREETS WITH CHARACTER

Istedgade, Vesterbro
Recently transformed artery with a heady mix of indie boutiques and hip cafés.

Jægersborggade, Nørrebro
Vibrant, colourful and young at heart, with Michelin-starred restaurants and sneaker boutiques.

Vaernedamsvej, Frederiksberg and Vesterbro
With flower stores and cosy cafés, this is perfect Instagram material.

Blågårdsgade, Nørrebro
Golden yellow buildings with stacks of bicycles hold pubs, music venues and quirky shops.

including sharks and piranha. Among the other aquatic wildlife are a giant octopus, crocodiles and an electric eel, as well as turtles and many hundreds of brightly coloured tropical fish. In the basement, kids can come close to small marine life in the touch pools.

↑ Fishermen enjoying a drink on board a boat moored in Dragør's harbour

Dragør

🏠 12 km (7 miles) southeast of the city centre

This picturesque little town to the southeast of Amager is the ideal escape from the hustle of central Copenhagen.

As far back as the Middle Ages, Dragør was central to the Baltic herring trade. Later on, its inhabitants profited by piloting the boats across the Øresund. Many of the houses in Dragør still have distinctive observation towers (known as *kikkenborg*). The biggest of these (now a museum) stands by Lodshuset, a building that houses the local pilot service headquarters, established in 1684. Surprisingly, for a long time Dragør had no proper harbour: *dragør* means a sandy or pebbly strip of land up which boats are hauled. It was not until 1520 that Dutch settlers from nearby Store Magleby built one. By the 19th century it was the third-largest port in Denmark. These traditions are kept alive by a marina overlooking nearby Sweden and the stunning bridge.

←

Gazing up at stingrays, sharks and other marine life at Den Blå Planet

The town is a pleasant place for a stroll, with cobbled streets and pretty 18th-century yellow houses decorated with flowers. The **Dragør Museum**, housed in the old town hall and a 17th-century harbour warehouse, has a collection devoted to Dragør's rich maritime past.

Dragør Museum

🔲🔲 🏠 Strandlinien 4 🕐 Jun–Sep: noon–4pm Wed–Sun 🌐 museumamager.dk

⓮
Charlottenlund Slot

🏠 Jærgesborg Allé
🚇 Charlottenlund Slot 🚌 14
🌳 Gardens: daily

Charlottenlund Slot was built between 1731 and 1733 on the orders of Princess Charlotte Amalie, who liked the place so much that it was soon named after her. She used it as her summer residence until her death in 1782.

The building was remodelled in the 19th century, when its Baroque character gave way to a Renaissance style. A number of other Danish royals have enjoyed staying here, including Frederik VIII and his beloved wife, Princess Louise. The couple are commemorated by an obelisk located at the rear of the building.

EAT & DRINK

Amass
Upscale but informal New Nordic restaurant.

🏠 Refshalevej 153
🌐 amassrestaurant.com

Ⓚ Ⓚ Ⓚ

Bæst
Mouthwatering pizzas topped with organic Danish ingredients.

🏠 Guldbergsgade 29
🌐 baest.dk

Ⓚ Ⓚ Ⓚ

Hart Bageri
Arguably the city's hottest bakery and café.

🏠 G'l Kongevej 109
🌐 hartbageri.com

Ⓚ Ⓚ Ⓚ

Ramen To Bĭiru
Warming ramen served with Mikkeller beer.

🏠 Enghavevej 58
🌐 ramentobiiru.dk

Ⓚ Ⓚ Ⓚ

Hija de Sanchez
Ranked among the world's best street food.

🏠 Slagterboderne 8
🕐 Fri 🌐 hijade sanchez.dk

Ⓚ Ⓚ Ⓚ

The palace is off limits, but you can stroll through the conifers and avenues of the gardens, with paths and ponds dating from the 18th century. The vegetable garden dates from 1826 and once grew produce for the palace kitchen. Ancient trees in the grounds include two larches at the rear – the oldest of their kind in Denmark.

EXPERIENCE
DENMARK

Cycling in woodland on Bornholm

Northwestern Zealand.................. 142

Southern Zealand
and the Islands.......................................176

Funen..194

Southern and
Central Jutland.................................... 204

Northern Jutland..............................226

Bornholm.. 242

Greenland and
the Faroe Islands................................256

NORTHWESTERN ZEALAND

Zealand is the largest of the Danish islands, covering an area of 7,500 sq km (2,895 sq miles). On its eastern shore lies Copenhagen – the country's capital and commercial centre. Wonderful Copenhagen aside, there is much to enjoy here, from mighty castles and historic towns to sandy beaches, rural villages and arcadian countryside. The island's landscape is typical of the lowland regions: idyllic meadow scenery broken here and there by beech forests and coastal fjords that cut deep into the land. Most of the port towns were once Viking settlements and reminders of the mighty Viking empire remain.

Northwestern Zealand has long played an important part in the history of Denmark. Lejre was one of the first centres of Danish administration; later this function was assumed by the city of Roskilde, which was named the capital of Denmark in 1020 (a role that lasted until 1443, when the title transferred to Copenhagen). Historically, this area has been favoured by wealthy Danes and some of the most impressive royal castles can be found here, including Kronborg, Fredensborg and Frederiksborg.

NORTHWESTERN ZEALAND

Must Sees
1. Louisiana Museum
2. Helsingør
3. Roskilde
4. Frederiksborg Slot

Experience More
5. Jægersborg Dyrehave
6. Bakken
7. Frilandsmuseet
8. Rungstedlund
9. Grønnesse Skov
10. Gilleleje
11. Hornbæk
12. Fredensborg Slot
13. Frederikssund
14. Hundested
15. Nordskoven
16. Jægerspris Slot
17. Skibby
18. Tveje Merløse Kirke
19. Ledreborg Slot
20. Lejre
21. Holbæk
22. Nørre Jernløse Mølle
23. Tårnborg
24. Sorø
25. Korsør
26. Røsnæs
27. Kalundborg
28. Selsø Slot
29. Trelleborg
30. Dragsholm Slot
31. Odsherred
32. Svinninge

1 🎨 🖼 🏛

LOUISIANA MUSEUM

📍F4 🏠Strandvej 13, Humlebæk Gl
🚉Humlebæk ⏰11am–10pm Tue–Fri,
11am–6pm Sat, Sun & hols 🌐louisiana.dk

An art powerhouse and national treasure, the Louisiana Museum is awash with modern masterpieces. Artworks line the walls at every turn and sculptures pepper the gardens, all set against the stunning backdrop of the Øresund Sound.

The striking Louisiana Museum has something for everyone. Established in 1958 to house a collection of modern Danish art, the museum's remit has expanded considerably since then. The collection concentrates on modern European and American paintings, graphic art and photography, and houses some of art's most famous contemporary names. Not only that, the location and architecture are just as impressive. Light-filled galleries form a semicircle round a 19th-century villa, and open out onto a tranquil sculpture park. This green space offers stunning views of the Øresund, blurring the lines between art, architecture and landscape. The museum shop is a great stop for prints and homewares, and Danish cakes in the café are unmissable.

Notable Artists

Alberto Giacometti (1901-66)

▽ Swiss surrealist sculptor is best known for his spindly humanoid figures.

Yayoi Kusama (1929-)

▽ Japanese-born 'outsider' artist Kusama works in a variety of media and has a cult following of fans.

Henry Moore (1898-1986)

△ English-born sculptor Moore's bronze figures were created to be seen in outdoor settings.

Asger Jorn (1914-73)

△ Abstract painter and ceramicist Jorn was a leading light of the Copenhagen-Brussels-Amsterdam group.

↑ Admiring artworks in the airy gallery space of the Louisiana Museum *(inset)*

GALLERY GUIDE

The museum's single-storey galleries are connected by a corridor to the south wing and underground galleries. Note that works are on rotation apart from a room specifically devoted to Giacometti and Henry Moore *(inset)*. A child-ren's wing offers workshops, art materials and computers for kids and their families.

↑ *Han*, a sculpture by Elmgreen & Dragset in the city's Culture Harbour

2

HELSINGØR

F4 **Helsingør** **Havnepladsen 3; www.visit northsealand.com**

Helsingør is famous for Kronborg Slot (*p150*), a 15th-century castle and the setting of Shakespeare's *Hamlet*. The city was a centre of international shipping in the 1400s, building its wealth by taxing passing ships, and was connected to Sweden via a railway line in 1864.

1

Karmeliterklosteret Sankt Mariae Kirke

Sankt Anna Gade 38
Mid-May-mid-Sep: 10am-3pm Tue-Sun; mid-Sep-mid-May: 10am-2pm Tue-Sun **sctmariae.dk**

This is considered to be one of Scandinavia's best-preserved medieval monasteries and was described by H C Andersen as "one of the most beautiful spots in Denmark". The Gothic building once belonged to the Carmelites and was erected in the second half of the 15th century. Among its features is the "Bird Room" decorated with ornithological frescoes. Christian II's mistress, Dyveke, who died in 1517, is believed to be buried in the grounds.

2

Helsingør Bymuseum

Sankt Anna Gade 36
49 28 18 00 **Noon-4pm Tue-Fri & Sun, 10am-2pm Sat**

The building that now houses the city museum was erected by friars from the neighbouring monastery, who used it as a hospital for sailors arriving at the local harbour. Some of the instruments once used by the friars in the hospital are on display, along with other exhibits relating to the city's past. Visitors to the museum can also learn about the origin of the region's name: Øresund refers to the levy demanded by Erik of Pomerania (an "øre" is a Danish penny, and "sund" is "channel" or "sound").

3

Kulturværftet

Allegade 2, 3000
Daily; check website for performances **kuto.dk**

A glittering, modern complex of geometric glass blocks based around the city's old shipyard, Helsingør's "culture yard" opened in 2010. As the name implies, it's the focus of the city's cultural scene, hosting drama and music performances, exhibitions, festivals and countless other art-based events. Inside you'll also find an interesting shipyard museum that outlines the history of shipbuilding in Helsingør from medieval times until the 19th century. As a bonus, there's a great view across the harbour to the royal ramparts of Kronborg Slot.

> **PICTURE PERFECT**
> **Little Merman**
>
> Outside Kulturværftet, check out the steel sculpture of *Han*, based on Copenhagen's *Little Mermaid*. You can get closer to *Han* than you can to his sister and he makes for cool, reflective photos.

④ 🍴 🖵

Axeltorv

Helsingør's main square is bounded by a number of restaurants and bars. On Wednesday and Saturday mornings you'll find a colourful local market here selling flowers, vegetables, fresh fish, handicrafts, cheese and souvenirs.

The statue in the centre of Axeltorv depicts Erik of Pomerania – the Polish king and nephew of Margaret I who occupied the throne of Denmark between 1397 and 1439 (*p54*). Following the break-up of the Kalmar Union and his subsequent dethronement in 1439, the ex-monarch moved to the Swedish island of Gotland. Here, he began to occupy himself with piracy and he is sometimes referred to as "the last Baltic Viking". In his old age Erik returned to Pomerania and is buried in the Polish seaside town of Darłowo. One legend has it that Darłowo's castle still contains hidden treasure plundered from Denmark.

⑤

Stengade

Helsingør's medieval quarter includes Stengade, a lovely pedestrianized street that is linked by various alleyways to Axeltorv. Many of the colourful half-timbered houses once belonged to merchants and ferrymen, and date from the 17th and 18th centuries. Oderns Gård, at Stengade 66, was built around 1460.

⑥ 🏛 🏰 🖵

Museet Sofart

🏠 Ny Kronborgvej 1 ⏰ Jul & Aug: 10am-5pm daily; Sep-Jun: 11am-5pm Tue-Sun
🖵 mfs.dk

The spectacular Maritime Museum of Denmark was built around an old dry dock in front of Kronborg Castle by

the internationally acclaimed architecture company BIG – Bjarke Ingels Group.

The old dock walls have been left untouched and the galleries are located underground, arranged in a loop around the dry dock walls. This makes the dock the centrepiece of the exhibition. Visitors can experience the scale of shipbuilding and learn the story of Denmark as one of the world's leading shipping nations.

⑦ 🏰

Sankt Olai Kirke

🏠 Sankt Anna Gade 12
☎ 49 21 04 43 ⏰ May-Aug: 10am-4pm Mon-Fri; Sep-Apr: 10am-2pm Mon-Fri

This handsome church was built in 1559 on the site of a building consecrated in around 1200. It served as a parish church for centuries and it was elevated to the rank of cathedral in 1961.

Numerous elaborate epitaphs commemorate the many rich merchants and distinguished citizens of

↑ The impressive organ overlooking the pews in Sankt Olai Kirke

Helsingør who are buried here. Its present-day appearance aside, there are also a number of furnishings that the church gained in the 16th century. Among its most precious possessions are a 15th-century Gothic crucifix, a Renaissance pulpit (1568) and a carved wooden altar. There's also a suspended cannon ball, which was fired at the city by the British a few days before the 1801 Battle of Copenhagen.

⑧ 🎿 🎭 🍴 🍷 🖥 🛍

KRONBORG SLOT

🅰F4 📍Kronborg 2C, DK 3000, Helsingør ⏰Apr, May & Oct: 11am–4pm daily; Jun–Sep: 10am–5:30pm daily; Nov–Mar: 11am–4pm Tue–Sun
🌐kongeligeslotte.dk

Regal and resplendent, Kronborg was the setting of Shakespeare's *Hamlet* and it's easy to picture the Prince of Denmark tramping the "Castle of Elsinore". Originally built in the early 15th century, today the castle is one of Denmark's most popular tourist sights.

The Play's the Thing

This kingly Renaissance palace was built by Erik of Pomerania and later remodelled by Frederik II and Christian IV. Among the most impressive rooms are the 62-m (203-ft) Great Hall and the King's Chamber. There's little escaping the castle's eerie quality – from the dungeon passages to the garden maze – which makes it perfect for productions of Shakespeare's tragic play during the summer months. From June through to August, you might even meet characters from *Hamlet* wandering the grounds during the day. Castle tours in English are optional and included in ticket costs. They take place at noon and 3pm daily.

> ### Did You Know?
>
> Banquets at Kronborg once involved 65 courses, and buckets were on hand for those who ate too much.

HAMLET

Shakespeare probably never visited Kronborg, but he set one of his best-known plays here. The prototype for the fictional Danish prince was Amleth, whose story is told by the 12th-century Danish writer Saxo Grammaticus in his *Historia Danica*. Shakespeare might have read the tale of murder and revenge via François de Belleforest's *Histoires Tragiques* (1570).

Trumpeter's Tower

Once the longest hall in northern Europe, the Great Hall was completed in 1582 and is decorated with paintings from Rosenborg Slot (p78).

Kronborg Slot, the jewel in Helsingør's crown ↑

Helsingør's Kronborg Slot, home to
stately interiors such as the
vast Great Hall *(inset)* ↑

King's Tower, built from 1584–5, was also
known as the "Turner's Tower" because
one of its rooms housed Frederick II's
turnery, containing lathes.

The North Wing
was completed in
1585. Its western
section contained
the castle offices.

At the corner of the
North Wing, the
Queen's Chamber
had direct access to
the chapel, via the
east wing.

The Royal Chambers
contain ornate ceiling
decorations and marble
fireplaces. At one time
the walls would have
been lined with gold-
embossed leather.

The Pigeon Tower
housed birds that
were used for
sending important
royal messages.

A beautiful altar, oak benches with intricately carved
ends, a royal balcony and an organ dating from the
early 18th century fill the Chapel.

Dramatic skies looming over the courtyard of Kronborg Slot

→

Stændertorvet market square and the striking town hall in Roskilde

③

ROSKILDE

⚐ F5 🚉 Roskilde 🛈 Stændertorvet 1; www.visitroskilde.com

Founded in the 10th century, Roskilde was Denmark's first capital and Harald I (Bluetooth) built Zealand's first church here. Still a thriving city, it is popular for its cathedral and Viking ships, as well as the summer rock festival and museum of rock and pop culture.

①

Stændertrovet

This small square situated by the town's main promenade has for centuries been the heart of Roskilde. In the Middle Ages it was the site of local fairs. In the 16th century, the Romanesque Sankt Laurence church was demolished to provide more space for the growing market. A few

130,000

The number of music lovers that head here for the annual Roskilde Festival at the end of June.

remaining parts of the church can be seen today, including the tower, which adorns the town hall (built in 1884). What remains of the church foundations are based in the town hall's vaults. In the square is a monument depicting King Roar – who is often credited with the founding of Roskilde – and his brother Helge.

②

Roskilde Museum

⚐ Sankt Ols Gade 18
🕓 11am-4pm Tue-Sun (to 9pm Wed) 🌐 roskilde museum.dk

The municipal museum in Roskilde is an excellent place to get a handle on the city's fascinating history. The museum has a permanent collection and also mounts changing exhibits. There is also a further museum building in Ringstedgade, which is furnished in the style of a 19th-century shop.

③

Roskilde Palace and the Museum of Contemporary Art

⚐ Stændertorvet 3
🕓 Museum: noon-4pm Tue-Fri (to 8pm Wed), 11am-4pm Sat & Sun
🌐 samtidskunst.dk

Built in 1733, this yellow Baroque palace is the former seat of Roskilde's bishops, linked to the neighbouring cathedral by the Arch of Absalon. Part of the palace houses the Museum of Contemporary Art (Museet for Samtidskunst), which organizes temporary exhibitions.

④

Grabodre Kirkegard

The city's former cemetery, where prominent and wealthy citizens were laid to rest during the Middle Ages, is now used as a park, which can be located not far from the railway station. The station was built in 1847 to serve the Copenhagen–Roskilde line and is one of the oldest train stations in Denmark.

---

⑤
Hestetorvet

The landmarks of the market square, used in medieval times for horse trading, are the three 5-m- (16-ft)- tall jars. Engraved on one of these are verses from a poem written by Henrik Nordbrandt, dedicated to Roskilde and to Margaret I. The jars' creator, Peter Brandes, intended them to symbolize life and death.

---

⑥ 🛉 🛉
Roskilde Kloster

🏠 Sankt Peder Stræde 8
🕐 Times vary, check website
🌐 roskildekloster.dk

This brick-built monastery, which stands in its own grounds, was built in 1560 and, in 1699, became Denmark's first refuge for unmarried mothers from

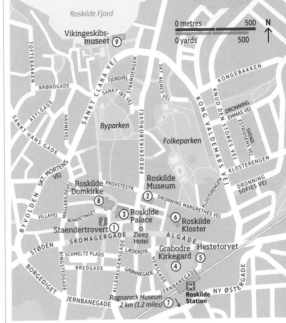

well-to-do families. It has some fine interiors, including a chapel and a banquet hall.

---

⑦ 🛉
Ragnarock Museum for Pop, Rock & Youth Culture

🏠 Rabalderstræde 16, Musicon 🕐 10am–5pm Tue–Sun (to 9pm Wed)
🌐 museumragnarock.dk

Denmark's national rock museum opened in 2015 and is based in the Musicon quarter, a cultural district that also includes a skate park, café and a modern dance theatre. Set in a striking gold cube, the museum is entered via a long red carpet, giving visitors a feeling of celebrity. The museum's range of interactive exhibits chart

music's influence on culture from the 1950s onwards. Alongside temporary exhibits, the museum hosts permanent shows that explore fan cultures and music genres, as well as the creation of dance music. Visitors are also invited to participate in a digital choir.

← Stunning jars by Peter Brandes, standing at 5 m (16 ft) each, in Hestetorvet

---

STAY

Zleep Hotel Roskilde

Rooms in this hotel are Scandi-modern and have all mod cons, belying the gracious Rococo exterior of the 300-year-old building. All Roskilde's key sights are within walking distance.

🏠 Algade 13
🌐 zleephotels.com

Ⓚ Ⓚ Ⓚ

⑧ ⟨🚇⟩

ROSKILDE DOMKIRKE

⌂ Domkirkestræde 1 ◷ May-Sep: 10am-5pm Mon-Sat (Jun-Aug: to 6pm), 1-4pm Sun; Oct-Apr: 10am-4pm Mon-Sat, 1-4pm Sun ⓦ roskildedomkirke.dk

This magnificent house of worship, with its brick twin towers, is a landmark of the city, and is perhaps Denmark's most loved cathedral. It showcases some 850 years of Danish architectural styles and a number of monarchs have been laid to rest here.

Begun in the 12th century on the orders of Bishop Absalon, the cathedral has been tinkered with across the centuries and is today listed as a UNESCO World Heritage Site. It was used as the burial site of Danish monarchs, and it is said that the remains of Harald I (Bluetooth), a 10th-century Viking king, are inside one of the columns to the side of the main altar. The cathedral holds free concerts on on Thursday evenings in summer.

Christian IV supervised the construction of his own chapel. The grand chapel contains a painting of the king in combat and a bronze statue by Bertel Thorvaldsen.

↑ The brick twin towers of Roskilde Domkirke piercing the sky

The storm bell is the oldest medieval bell in Denmark.

A unique clock with tiny moving figures in the South Tower includes one of St Jørgen chasing a dragon.

Main entrance

Exterior of ↑
Roskilde Domkirke,
a city landmark

↑ The elaborately decorated Chapel of King Christian IV in Roskilde Cathedral

Margrete's Spire replaced a tower destroyed by fire in 1968.

Set near the altar these wooden pews are beautiful examples of Gothic carving.

Depicting scenes from the life of Christ, the altar was produced in Antwerp in the 1500s.

The sarcophagus bearing an alabaster effigy of Margrete I as a young girl is considered to be the most beautiful sculpture in the cathedral.

The Chapter House contains a crucifix made from two bells that melted in the fire.

The cathedral has been rebuilt several times, acquiring features typical of the styles that were then in fashion. The last major works were carried out following a fire in 1968.

The Royal Column indicates the height of several kings. Christian I is recorded as 2.19 m (7 ft 2 inches), although his skeleton is 1.88 m (6 ft 2 inches).

This pulpit was ordered by Christian IV in 1610. Its ornate carvings in marble, alabaster and sandstone were made by Hans Brokman of Copenhagen.

⑨ ⬡ ⬡ ▭ ⬡

ROSKILDE VIKINGESKIBSMUSEET

🅰 F5 **⬡ Vindeboder 12** **⬡ Jul-Aug: 10am-5pm daily; Sep-Jun: 10am-4pm daily**
🆆 vikingeskibsmuseet.dk

Step back in time at Roskilde's Vikingeskibsmuseet, home to five original Viking ships discovered at the bottom of Roskilde Fjord. After you've taken your fill of history, sail out from the musuem's harbour on a reconstructed Viking ship.

Roskilde's mid-11th-century inhabitants built five mighty Viking longboats in the narrow channel north of their city and heaped them with stones, forming a fortification. Much later, in 1962, archaeologists used modern technology to excavate the boats – called the Skuldelev ships – and the fragments were carefully reconstructed. Today, the skeleton ships are mounted in the museum's main hall and provide a unique perspective of Viking maritime capabilities, which formed the foundation of the Viking empire.

A further nine Viking ships were unearthed during renovation work in the 1990s. This was the largest discovery of Viking ships in northern Europe, and included the longest Viking warship ever found. Excavation work on the 36-m- (118-ft-) long Roskilde 6 ship is not yet complete and the Skuldelev Viking ships form the main focus of the museum, but there is a small exhibition about the Roskilde ships.

Museumsø

Outside the museum is the Museumsø area, where five reconstructed longboats can be sailed from the harbour (booking essential). Here you'll also find a number of workshops and continuing excavation work.

> Ships are mounted in the museum's main hall and provide a unique perspective of Viking maritime capabilities, which formed the foundation of the Viking empire.

Did You Know?

Ironically nine Viking longships were found under the museum during renovations.

→

An impressive original Skuldelev longboat displayed in the Vikingeskibsmuseet's main hall, and a reconstructed sailing longboat *(inset)*

MUSEUMSØ

This museum doesn't stop at Viking ships. There are a number of special events and re-enactment workshops, running from April to October. These cover everything from painting Viking shields, shadowing a blacksmith and chatting to ropemakers, to carving Viking symbols into wood, visiting the jewelery workshop and even sailing on a Viking vessel.

↑ The attractive harbour and traditional drawbridge at the Vikingeskibsmuseet

FREDERIKSBORG SLOT

⬛F4 🏠3400 Hillerød, Slotsgade 1 🕐Apr-Oct: 10am-5pm daily; Nov-Mar: 11am-3pm daily; gardens: 10am-sunset daily 🌐frederiksborgmuseum.com

Denmark's first royal residence is a stunner. Set in beautiful Baroque gardens, and bursting with history, this makes for a great day outside of the capital.

Frederiksborg Slot was constructed on this site by Frederick II in 1560. A fire in 1859 destroyed most of the castle, which may well have remained a ruin were it not for Carlsberg boss J C Jacobsen, who restored the building and helped found a national history museum here. Jacobsen also donated many of his own paintings which, along with others, are chart Denmark's history. Period furnishings and magnificent architecture help to conjure up a feel for the past.

During the reign of Christian IV this room was used by the king's mother. When the palace became a museum, it was hung with paintings associated with Frederick III.

The Audience Chamber (Audienssalen) was completed in 1688. Among its paintings is a portrait of a proud-looking Christian V, depicted as a Roman emperor.

The Knights' Hall (Riddersalen) has a carved wooden ceiling. The ornaments, marble fireplace and tapestries add to the splendour.

The chapel's oak door, set within a portal in the shape of a triumphal arch, survived the fire and looks as it would have in Christian IV's day.

← Beautifully carved ceilings and ornamentation in the Knight's Hall

The Royal Wing has a gallery of statues symbolizing the influence of planets on human life and is an excellent example of Dutch Mannerism.

↑ The impressive Fredriksborg Slot overlooking its moat and intricate maze gardens

Room 42 is an example of over-blown Baroque style and is typical of the taste associated with Denmark's era of absolute monarchy (p54). The bed with silk draperies was made in France in 1724.

All the items in Room 46, such as the wall clock, are in perfect accord with the Rococo excess of the overall design.

↑ Baroque Frederiksborg Slot in Northwestern Zealand

💬 INSIDER TIP
History for Children

Kids can time travel by dresssing up in Renaissance attire and try their hand at writing with a feather quill and ink. Children might also like to chat to the castle hosts, who wear costumes based on portraits in the castle.

EXPERIENCE MORE

⑤

Jægersborg Dyrehave

▲F5 **▲**13 km (8 miles) north of Copenhagen city centre **Ⓢ**Klampenborg **ⓦ**naturstyrelsen.dk

The beautiful beech forests and parkland that cover the area between the motorway running from Copenhagen to Helsingør and the shore of the Øresund are popular for weekend forays out of Copenhagen. This lovely woodland area, which is criss-crossed with paths and cycle routes, was established as a royal hunting ground in 1669. The park still supports a herd of some 2,000 deer. A good vantage point from which to view them is the Ermitagen hunting lodge at the centre of the park, which was built in 1736 for Christian VI.

Bakken amusement park is based in the park, as is Kirsten Pils Kilde, a holy spring that was a pilgrimage destination in the 16th century. Nearby, Bellevue is undeniably one of the best beaches in the area. Horse-drawn carriages offer rides through the park and there is also a golf course and a horse-racing track just to the south of Dyrehaven.

⑥ 🚲 🖥

Bakken

▲F5 **▲**Dyrehavevej 62 **Ⓢ**Klampenborg **◎**Apr-Aug: Dec: Sat & Sun (times vary, check website) **ⓦ**bakken.dk

Bakken (which translates as "The Hill") was founded in 1583 and is considered to be the world's oldest amusement park. It is located just a short way out of Copenhagen, on the edge of Jægersborg Dyrehave.

The park has 30 or so rides, including roller coasters, merry-go-rounds, bumper cars and a ghost train, as well as circus shows with the park's mascot, Pjerrot the Clown, and cabaret-style revues. There are countless cafés, fast-food restaurants and ice-cream parlours on site, but you may bring your own supplies for a picnic. Entrance to the park is free, though rides must be paid for and vary in price. Bakken opens in the spring and closes at the end of the summer; on both occasions, a huge parade of motorcycles travels up to the park from north Copenhagen. During December the park opens at weekends with a Christmas theme and market.

> Over 100 buildings at Frilandsmuseet are arranged into groups and include examples of rural architecture, from cottages to grand manor houses.

⑦ 🚲 🖥 🛍

Frilandsmuseet

▲F5 **▲**Kongevejen 100, 2800 Lyngby **Ⓡ**🚌 **◎**May-Oct: 10am-4pm Tue-Sun (Jul-mid-Aug: to 5pm) **ⓦ**natmus.dk/frilands museet

Founded in 1897, this open-air museum contains virtually every kind of Danish country dwelling imaginable. Originally situated near Rosenberg Slot in Copenhagen, it was relocated to its present site in 1901 and is now run as part of the Nationalmuseet. Over 100 buildings at Frilandsmuseet are arranged into groups and include examples of rural architecture, from cottages to grand manor houses, many of which are furnished and decorated in keeping with the period in which they were

← Fallow deer crossing a path near the Ermitagen lodge, Jægersborg Dyrehave

built. Visitors should allow a day to look round the collection, which includes windmills, fishermen's cottages, peasant huts, a post mill (with working sails) and a smithy (kitted out with irons and a hearth). Some staff dress in traditional costume and demonstrate pottery and cloth weaving. The ticket also allows entry to Brede Værk, by the northern entrance of Frilandsmuseet. This textile mill, which closed in 1956, is preserved as an industrial village, complete with cottages and a school.

⑧ Rungstedlund

⚠F5 **🏠Rungsted Strandvej 111** **🚉Rungsted Kyst** **🚌388** **🕐May-Sep: 10am-5pm Tue-Sun; Oct-Apr: 1-4pm Wed-Fri, 11am-4pm Sat & Sun** **🌐blixen.dk**

Made famous by Karen Blixen, author of *Out of Africa*, this plush country house is the author's birthplace and was where she wrote most of her works under the pseudonym Isak Dinesen.

The house was built around 1500 and was first used as an inn. In 1879 her father bought the property. It is now maintained by a foundation established by the writer, and in 1991 was converted into a museum devoted to her life

↑ The gardens and the attractive exterior and interior *(inset)* of Rungstedlund, the charming home of Karen Blixen

and work. The rooms remain little changed, and there are photographs and personal items on display. Blixen's grave is in the surrounding park.

⑨ Grønnesse Skov

⚠F4

This ancient forest sits beside Roskilde Fjord, and archaeological digs have indicated that during the Neolithic era Grønnesse Skov was one of the more

important sites of early culture in Zealand. One of the most important relics of Denmark's Neolithic past is an extraordinary burial chamber known as a dolmen, consisting of a huge flat stone resting on three chunky pillars. The dolmen is referred to by locals as Carlssten (Carl's Stone) and is one of the biggest and best preserved of its type in Denmark. It must be reached on foot but the forest car park is only a short distance away.

↑ Cycling past the Nakkehoved Østre Fyr lighthouse in Gilleleje

⑩ Gilleleje

🅰F4 🚊 ℹ Peter Fjelstrup Vej 12; www.visitnorth sealand.com

The northernmost town in Zealand is also one of the oldest Danish fishing ports and has the island's largest harbour. Historical records show that the local inhabitants were fishing here as early as the mid-14th century. Today, Gilleleje is an attractive town with thatched houses, a busy harbourside fishing auction and a colourful

main street that has been turned into a promenade. Rising above the cottages is Gilleleje Kirke. During German occupation locals used the church as a hiding place for Danish Jews, who were then smuggled into Sweden aboard fishing boats under cover of darkness.

At Skibshallerne, fishing boats from several different periods are on display; in the same building is **Det Gamle Hus**, an old fisherman's house that illustrates the realities of everyday life for a mid-19th-century fishing family. A coastal trail from the town centre leads east to the Nakkehoved Østre Fyr lighthouse. Built in 1772, it is one of the few surviving coal-fuelled light-houses in the world. The Gilbjergstien is a 2.5-km (1.5-mile) path leading from Vesterbrogade, in Gilleleje, all the way to Gilbjergshoved, Zealand's northernmost point. The path offers splendid views across the water to Sweden from the cliffs. En route you can admire the Gilbjergstenen rock, which has a natural seat and back support, and a monument to the Danish philosopher Søren Kirkegaard.

Det Gamle Hus

⊗ 🏠Hovedgade 49 📞7217 02 40 ⏰Mid-May–mid-Oct: 11am–4pm Tue–Sun; ticket includes the lighthouse

⑪ Hornbæk

🅰F4 🚊🚌 ℹ Vestre Stejle-bakke 2A; www.visitnorth sealand.com

The northern shore of Zealand is famous for its neat sandy beaches, clean water and the small resort town of Hornbæk. A large number of visitors come from Copenhagen, many of whom have built holiday homes here. In summer the resort fills with holiday-makers enjoying various outdoor pursuits, such as sailing and swimming. Esrum, situated southwest of Hornbæk, is famous for its Cistercian monastery, Esrum Kloster. Founded in 1151, it was regarded as one of the most important monasteries in Denmark in the Middle Ages. Even the fires that plagued the building in 1194 and 1204 did not stop it from becoming one of the largest in Scandinavia. During the Lutheran Reformation in the 16th century, much of the church was demolished and the materials were used to build Kronborg Slot (p150).

The remaining buildings were used first as a hunting base and later as warehouses before being turned into army barracks. In the 20th century they were used as offices, as a post office and then as an orphanage. During World War II they became air-raid shelters and a fireproof store for documents brought from the National Archives, and for the Royal Library collection.

This chequered history came to an end when the ancient walls were renovated, and in 1997 the monastery opened to visitors. The main building now houses an exhibition on the Cistercian order, and the vaults have been transformed into a café. Also open to visitors is the herb garden, some of

the plants from which are used to produce a flavoured beverage, on sale in the shop.

---

12 ✦ ✦

Fredensborg Slot

F4 **Jul–early Aug: 12:30–4:30pm daily; gardens: 9am–5pm daily** **kongeligeslotte.dk**

Frederick IV built Fredensborg Castle in order to commemorate the 1720 peace treaty between Denmark and Sweden at the end of the Nordic Wars (Fredensborg means "Palace of Peace"). The building was originally used as a hunting lodge. Nowadays the castle is one of the main residences of the Danish royal family and is often used to receive VIPs from all over the world. According to tradition, guests who spend the night at the palace must sign their name on a glass pane using a diamond pen.

The castle's original design was modelled on similar ones found in France and Italy. The present-day complex consists of 28 separate buildings. At its centre is Kuppelsalen (the

Dome Hall), surmounted by a dome crowned with a lantern. This magnificent room is encircled by a gallery, which divides the hall into two levels and is used for royal events and for entertaining special guests.

The most interesting room in the palace is Havesalen (the Garden Room), which features a wide door leading towards the castle gardens. Its ceiling is decorated with a painting by Hendrik Krock depicting Denmark and Norway begging the Olympian gods for help against Sweden.

Another notable room is the ornate Kinesisk Spisesalon (Chinese Dining Room), which is decorated in yellow and red and houses a collection of rare Chinese porcelain.

The palace's gardens were established in the 1760s and contain a lane decorated with a sculpted group of 70 figures, created by J G Grund, of fishermen and farmers from Norway and the Faroe Islands. Plants sensitive to cold, including a 250-year-old myrtle shrub, are shielded from the freezing temperatures in a greenhouse built in 1995.

Note that the palace, orangery and herb garden are reserved for the royal family. As a result they are only open in July and early August. It is compulsory to join a tour; they run every 15 minutes and last for 35 minutes.

←

Fredensborg Slot rising above the immaculately maintained palace gardens

Hundested harbour, studded with boats and fishing warehouses ↑

13
Frederikssund

🅰F5 🚉 𝒊Havnegade 5A; www.visitfrederikssund.dk

This town was founded in 1655 on the orders of Frederick III. The choice of site was not accidental; it overlooks the narrowest part of the Roskilde Fjord, used for many years to cross to the other side by boat.

In the town centre is the **J F Willumsens Museum**. Jens Ferdinand Willumsen (1863–1958), a prominent Danish Symbolist painter, donated his paintings, sculptures and drawings to Frederikssund on the condition that a suitable building be erected to display

them. The museum also keeps works by other artists that were collected by Willumsen.

Frederikssund is primarily known, however, for its reconstructed Viking Village, located near the town's harbour. The village is open to visitors from April to October, but the best time to visit is around the summer solstice, during the annual Viking Festival. The most popular events are the evening Viking plays that can feature hundreds of actors, many of them local residents and children; the final night is marked by a grand banquet.

J F Willumsens Museum
⊛ 🅳Jenriksvej 4 🕙10am–5pm Tue–Sun 🅦jfwillumsensmuseum.dk

14
Hundested

🅰F4 🚉 𝒊Havnegade 20; www.visitnorthsealand.com

The small town of Hundested lies on a slender peninsula. Its name translates literally as "Dog's Place" and derives from a local species of seal known as a sea dog because of its uncannily canine-like barking. The main reason to come here is to take a look around **Knud Rasmussens Hus**, which is situated on a high cliff close to Spodsbjerg lighthouse. The house was built in 1917 by the intrepid Arctic explorer Knud Rasmussen and now houses a museum devoted to his life and travels. Close by is a monument to him erected in 1936, made of stones brought over from Greenland.

A short way to the northeast is Kikhavn, the oldest fishing village on the Halsnæs peninsula, which dates back to the 13th century. There

KNUD RASMUSSEN

Born in 1879, Rasmussen was part Inuit; he was fascinated by Inuit culture and resolved to become a polar explorer. From 1921 to 1924 Rasmussen voyaged from Greenland to the Bering Strait, covering 18,000 km (11,815 miles) by dog sleigh. The explorer brought back many artifacts from his travels, now displayed in the capital's Nationalmuseet *(p100)*. He died in 1933, aged 54.

KNUD RASMUSSEN

→
Grand exterior of Jægerspris Slot, watched over by a bronze deer statue

were many small farms here in the 18th century, some of which were partly destroyed by a fire in 1793. The remaining farms and buildings have been preserved, and form a picturesque village. Kikhavn is also the starting point of a footpath named Halsnæsstien that links the shores of Isefjord and Kattegat.

Also worth a visit is Lynæs, just south of Hundested. The local church, built in 1901 from granite blocks, serves as a guide for returning fishermen. A monument standing by the church commemorates those who lost their lives at sea.

Knud Rasmussens Hus

◈ ⬚ Knud Rasmussensvej 9
⊙ Easter-Oct: 11am-4pm
Tue-Sun ⬚ knudrasmus.dk

15

Nordskoven

⬚ F5

The peninsula that separates Roskilde Fjord from Isefjord contains one of Denmark's most beautiful beech forests. The forest has two sections, known as Fællesskoven and Studehaven. Running between them is a 15-km- (9-mile-) long bicycle trail with views over Roskilde Fjord. At its highest point, called Frederikshøj, is a hunting pavilion built by Frederick VII in 1875. A number of ancient

trees can be found in the forest, including three famous oaks: Kongeegen, Storkeegen and Snoegen, which have inspired many artists. Kongeegen, the most ancient of the three trees, is believed to be 1,500–1,900 years old. In 1973 its last bough broke away, leaving only the vast trunk, which has a circumference of 14 m (46 ft).

---

16 ◈

Jægerspris Slot

⬚ F5 ⬚ Slotsgården 20
⊙ Easter-Oct: 11am-4pm
Tue-Sun; park: all year
round ⬚ kongfrederik.dk

This medieval castle, situated about 6 km (4 miles) west of Frederikssund, has been used by Danish royalty since the early 14th century and is open to the public. The first royal building, Abrahamstrup, still exists, although it has been swallowed by the north wing of the present complex. A lifesize statue of a deer standing before the entrance to the castle is by Adelgund Vogt, a pupil of the preeminent Danish sculptor Bertel Thorvaldsen.

In the mid-19th century Frederick VII made the palace his summer residence. After his death in 1863, the monarch's widow, Countess Danner, turned part of the palace into a refuge for poor and

unwanted girls. The centre became the first children's home in Denmark. A special exhibition depicts the austere way of life in an early 20th-century Danish orphanage.

Much of the house retains its royal character, and visitors can take a look at grand rooms arranged by Frederick VII himself. There is also an exhibition of archaeological finds reflecting one of Frederick VII's abiding passions.

The gardens stretching to the rear include Zealand's largest collection of rhododendrons; standing among them are 54 obelisks with busts of famous Danes. The forests around Jægerspris offer great walking and cycling opportunities.

⑰ Skibby

🅰F5 🚌 ℹ Havnegade 5A, 3600 Frederikssund; www.visitfrederikssund.dk

Skibby is known mainly for its early 12th-century church, which is decorated with some well-preserved frescoes. The oldest of these, found in 1855 in the Romanesque apses, date from the late 12th century. In 1650 a Latin manuscript, known as the *Skibby Chronicle*, was found buried behind the altar. The work recounts the history of Denmark between 1046 and 1534, and has provoked much debate as to the identity and fate of its author. Northeast of Skibby, in the harbour town of Skuldelev, is a doll museum with a 6,000-strong collection (open from March to October).

💬 INSIDER TIP
Fjordstien

The Fjord Path is a 275-km (171-mile) path of great natural beauty, passing through rolling fields, quaint villages and larger cities like Roskilde *(p154)*. The most beautiful stretch circles the island of Orø.

> Elegant on the outside, opulent on the inside, Ledreborg Slot is one of the foremost examples of Baroque architecture in northern Europe.

⑱ Tveje Merløse Kirke

🅰E5 ℹ Holbæk, Tveje Merløse 14 🕐 8am–3:30pm daily 🌐 tvejemerloese kirke.dk

Albeit a miniature version of Roskilde's original 12th-century cathedral *(p156)*, the church in Tveje Merløse, south of Holbæk, is one of the most interesting Romanesque sacred buildings in Denmark. Its most distinctive features are the two near-identical square towers. The history of the site as a place of worship is believed to date back to the Viking era; some records suggest it was used for worship in the 3rd century.

At one time the church contained some colourful 13th-century frescoes

Romanesque Tveje Merløse Kirke with its simple interior (inset) and pretty gardens ↓

depicting, among other things, the devil and the motif of God's Majesty, a common medieval theme found particularly in the region of Øresund. These have now been removed and are on display in the Nationalmuseet in Copenhagen *(p100)*.

---

⑲ Ledreborg Slot

🅰F5 🚗 Ledreborg Alle 2, 4320 Lejre 🕐 Park: 11am–4pm daily; palace: closed to the public 🌐 ledreborg.dk

Elegant on the outside, and opulent on the inside, Ledreborg Slot is one of the foremost examples

→ Living like a Viking at Sagnlandet Lejre, an open-air museum

of Baroque architecture in northern Europe. The palace itself is closed to the public, but the gardens are open and house Scandinavia's longest zipline course. The neatly trimmed hedges make this one of the most enchanting Baroque gardens in Scandinavia. The grounds host a lifestyle exhibition in May and an outdoor chamber music concert in August.

⑳ Lejre

F5 ⬛ 8 km (5 miles) southwest of Roskilde

The main attraction of Lejre is **Sagnlandet Lejre** ("Land of Legends"), an authentic open-air museum dedicated to the Stone Age, the Iron Age and the Viking era, where museum staff in period clothing show visitors how to use traditional tools, chop firewood and make clay pots. The village is popular with children, especially in summer, when they can try out activities such as archery, clothes dying and canoeing. There is also a 19th-century cottage farm that re-creates the lives of Danish farmers of the period.

Lejre was one of the country's earliest centres of government. Legend has it that it was the seat of a royal Stone Age clan, the Skjoldungs. It is quite likely that the nearby grave mound dates from the Stone Age period. The **Lejre Museum** has displays on the Skjoldung clan and artifacts from Viking times, as well as from the Stone and Iron ages.

Sagnlandet Lejre
⊘ ⬛ Slangealleen 2
🕐 Times vary, check website
🌐 sagnlandet.dk

Lejre Museum
⊘ ⬛ Orehøjvej 4B 📞 45 46 31 65 30 🕐 11am–4pm Tue–Sun (Nov–Mar: Sun only)

㉑ Holbæk

F5 ⬛ ℹ Ahlgade 1C; www.visitholbaek.com

A vital port, Holbæk is also the main commercial town for the area. It serves as a good starting point for visiting Ørø island, just 7 km (4 miles) away. The area has several trails, and the town is popular with cyclists.

Holbæk was made a municipality in the late 13th century, making it one of the oldest of Zealand's towns. At that time it was the site of a Dominican monastery; the oldest remains, however, are from a Franciscan monastery, next to the Neo-Gothic Sankt Nicolaj Kirke in the medieval part of town.

Not far from this church is the **Holbæk Museum**, which consists of a dozen or so period houses dating from 1660 to 1867. Their interiors include typical 17th- and 18th-century items and furnishings. The tiny market square between the houses hosts numerous events in the summer, which often feature people dressed in period costumes.

Holbæk has some good parks, such as Østre Anlæg and Bysøparken. Just outside the city is **Andelslandsbyen Nyvang**, an open-air museum that re-creates country life from the 1870s to the 1950s.

Holbæk Museum
⊘ ⬛ Klosterstræde 18
🕐 10am–4pm Tue–Fri, noon–4pm Sun 🚫 Jan 🌐 vest museum.dk

Andelslandsbyen Nyvang
⊘ ⊘ ⬛ Oldvejen 25 🕐 Mid-Apr–mid-Oct: 10am–4pm Tue–Thu, Sat & Sun 🌐 adlbn.dk

---

DANISH WINE

Denmark's budding wine industry is often overlooked. The sunny, temperate climate on the Danish Riviera in North Zealand is conducive to growing grapes such as Rondo for reds and Solaris for whites. The first commercial Danish Winery approved by the government, Domaine Aalsgaard, is situated between Helsingør and Horbæk (*www.domain aalsgaard.dk*) and open for tastings. Vexebo Vin delivers to various Michelin restaurants (*www.vexebovin.dk*).

←
Charming 19th-century windmill, Nørre Jernløse Mølle

22
Nørre Jernløse Mølle

🅐E5 🅐Møllebakken 2, Regstrup 🅒Apr–Oct: 2–4pm 1st Sun of the month 🅦nrjernlosemolle.dk

The small village of Nørre Jernløse, located some 25 km (16 miles) west of Roskilde, has a 12th-century church containing 16th-century frescoes. The town is best known, however, for its 19th-century windmill, which is set on a sturdy octagonal base ringed by a distinctive gallery.

The Dutch-style windmill was built in 1853 in Nørrevold, near Copenhagen, where it was known as Sankt Peders Mølle. When financial difficulties forced its owners to sell the mill it was bought by Niels Peter Rasmussen, a miller, who dismantled it and transported it in pieces on a horse cart to Jernløse, 70 km (43 miles) away. In 1899 it was bought by Ole Martin Nielsen, whose family used and maintained it for the next 60 years. Finally, in 1979

the windmill was handed over to the parish of Jernløse. Built using stone and timber, the mill has a shingled roof with a wooden, onion-shaped cupola. Its sails were once covered with cloth and could be operated directly from the gallery. The mill has an information centre where visitors can learn about its history and early methods of flour production.

23
Tårnborg

🅐E6

This ancient parish on the shores of Korsør Bay, with the rising outline of a 13th-century church, was once occupied by a castle and a settlement. It is likely that a stronghold existed here from at least the 12th century, and together with the forts at Nyborg and Sprogø, it controlled the passage across the Store Bælt (p173). From the 13th century it was also a major centre of commerce, and in the 14th century Tårnborg united

with neighbouring estates to intensify foreign trade. The castle was demolished in the 15th century following a financial crisis.

24
Sorø

🅐E6 🚺Storgade 7; www. visitwestzealand.com

Located on the banks of the Tuel and Sorø lakes, Sorø is one of the most beautiful towns in Zealand. In 1142 Bishop Absalon, the founder of Copenhagen, began to build a monastery here. When it was complete, the Klosterkirke was the largest building of its kind in Scandinavia and one of the first brick structures ever to be built in Denmark. This 70-m (230-ft)- long Romanesque-Gothic church contains the remains of Bishop Absalon in a tomb at the rear of the main altar. The church also contains the sarcophagi of Christian II, Valdemar IV and Oluf III.

Attractions in Sorø include the **Museum Vestsjælland** (Museum of West Zealand), which displays exhibits from the Stone Age right up to the present. Next to the museum is the Bursers Apotekerhave (Apothecary Garden), with plants from the herbarium of Joachim Burser, the royal pharmacist in the 1600s.

Sorø is perhaps best known for its Akademiet, which is set in a picturesque spot on Lake Sorø. Dedicated to the education of the sons of the nobility, it was founded in 1623 by Christian IV in the monastery buildings left empty after the

→

Evening light falling across the tower of Korsør Fæstning

406

The number of islands in Denmark. Only 72 are inhabited.

Reformation. The Akademiet is surrounded by a park which contains a monument to the writer Ludwig Holberg, who bequeathed his considerable fortune to the school in 1754.

Tystrup-Bavelse is a national wildlife reserve 17 km (11 miles) south of Sorø with two inter-connected freshwater lakes that attract a variety of birds. The forests contain many prehistoric grave mounds, including Kellerøddysen, Zealand's largest megalithic stone formation. Bjernede, near Sorø, has the only surviving round church in Zealand. Constructed from stone and brick, it is distinct from the round churches in Bornholm and was built in 1175 by Sune Ebbesøn, a governor to Valdemar I.

Museum Vestsjælland

🖼🏛 🅰 Storgade 17 🕐 1–4pm Tue–Thu, 11am–2pm Sat & Sun 🌐 vestmuseum.dk

25 Korsør

🅰 E6 🌐 visitwestzealand.com

The most prominent building in Korsør is its 13th-century fortress (Korsør Fæstning), which played a crucial role in the town gaining control of the Store Bælt. In 1658 it was captured by the Swedes, but returned to Danish control a year later. Its imposing tower now houses the **Korsør By-og Overfartsmuseet** (Town and Ferry Service Museum), whose collection includes models of ships that once sailed across the Store Bælt.

Clusters of 18th-century buildings can be seen around Algade, Slottensgade and Gavnegade. The Rococo-style mansion at No 25 Algade dates from 1761 and was originally used as an inn for sailors waiting to cross the Store Bælt. Its front is adorned with allegories of the four seasons. Inside is a small museum with sculptures by the artist Harald Isenstein, who died in 1980.

Korsør By-og Overfartsmuseet

🖼 🅰 Søbatteriet 7 🕐 Easter–Nov: 11am–4pm Tue–Sun 🌐 byogoverfartsmuseet.dk

STAY

Skovshoved Hotel
This coaching inn dates from 1660 and retains an old-world feel. Found on the Øresund coastal road, it features an upmarket restaurant and offers sea views from many of its rooms.

🅰 F5 🅰 Strandvejen 267, Charlottenlund 🌐 skovshovedhotel.com

Ⓚ Ⓚ Ⓚ

Hornbækhus
Unashamedly romantic, Hornbækhus was a popular rural retreat for Copenhageners in the 1920s and 1930s. It is tastefully furnished, with pops of colour and pattern, and guests can relax with a drink in the hotel's elegant living room, which opens onto an idyllic garden.

🅰 F4 🅰 Skovvej 7, Hornbæk 🌐 hornbaekhus.com

Ⓚ Ⓚ Ⓚ

26

Røsnæs

 E5 ⓘ Kalundborg

Some 20,000 years ago a continental glacier formed the Røsnæs peninsula, as well as the Asnæs peninsula that flanks the Kalundborg Fjord on the other side. In the Middle Ages the Røsnæs peninsula, which thrusts into the Store Bælt, was covered with thick forest, making it a favourite spot for royal hunts. A hunt in 1231 ended in tragedy when a stray arrow killed the son of Valdemar the Victorious.

The peninsula's tip is the westernmost point of Zealand and is marked by a lighthouse erected in 1845. The light from its lantern can be seen up to 40 km (25 miles) away. Just before the lighthouse, in the village of Ulstrup, is a Dutch-style windmill built in 1894.

At the base of the Asnæs peninsula is Lerchenborg Slot, a Baroque castle built in 1753 by General Christian Lerche. Hans Christian Andersen

Did You Know?

Sprogø Island, in the middle of the Store Bælt, served as a home for unmarried mothers from 1922 to 1961.

> In the Middle Ages the Røsnæs peninsula, which thrusts into the Store Bælt, was covered with thick forest, making it a favourite spot for royal hunts.

stayed here in 1862 and some of the rooms contain items relating to the famous writer.

27

Kalundborg

 E5 🚉 ⓘ Klosterparkvej; www.visitwestzealand.com

Kalundborg is one of Zealand's oldest towns and was populated by the Vikings as early as the 9th century. The town was also once used as a base by pirates, but in 1168 a castle was built and the crown assumed control of the fjord's waters.

The ruins in Volden square are all that remains of the castle. Its builder was Esbern Snare, the brother of Bishop Absalon. Snare was also the creator of the well-preserved 12th-century Vor Frue Kirke (Church of Our Lady), which has five octagonal towers and a Byzantine design based on a Greek crucifix.

Kalundborg's medieval quarter surrounds the church and includes cobbled streets and 16th-century buildings. One of these houses the

Kalundborg Museum. Most of the exhibits are devoted to local history and include a collection of costumes and the skeletons of two beheaded Vikings. Standing in the museum courtyard is a model of Kalundborg, providing a view of the town's 17th-century layout.

Kalundborg Museum
◈ 🏛 Adelgade 23 📞 59 51 21 41 🕐 10:30am–4pm Tue–Sun

28 ⟨⟩

Selsø Slot

🔺 F5 🏛 Selsøvej 30A, Skibby 🕐 May–mid-Sep: 11am–4pm Tue–Sun
ⓦ selsoe.dk

The history of this estate dates back to the 12th century. According to records, Bishop Absalon became interested in the site in about 1170 and by 1228 a sumptuous residence had been built here. The manor house was built in 1578 and reworked in 1734; much

STOREBÆLT BRIDGE

Until the late 20th century, the only way of travelling to Zealand was by air or ferry across the Store Bælt (Great Belt). In 1998, after 10 years of construction work, the two biggest Danish islands - Zealand and Funen - were joined together in the largest construction project in Danish history. The link consists of a tunnel and two bridges with Sprogø Island in between (which quadrupled in size with the excavated material from the tunnel) and has cut the journey time to 10 minutes. Of the two bridges, the Østbro (Eastern) suspension bridge is the most impressive, and remains one of the most ambitious engineering projects ever. The bridge is open 24 hours a day, weather permitting. A toll charge of around 245-365 Dkr, depending on the size of your vehicle, is payable at the toll station on the Zealand side.

of its original Renaissance style was replaced with Baroque details. The house was abandoned in 1829 and was left uninhabited (but for the dogs, birds and bees kept there by a game keeper) for 144 years. It now acts as a museum and gives visitors an idea of what aristocratic life was like in the early 1800s. The castle's stern, simple exterior hides a richer interior, particularly the Grand Ballroom. With original marble panels and a richly decorated ceiling, it is often used as a venue for classical music concerts. Historical events are also celebrated in the castle vaults.

The property owes much of its charm to its proximity to Roskilde Fjord and Selsø Lake. A wildlife reserve was established at the lake and is one of the premium places for birdwatching in Denmark. A viewing tower was built by the lake specifically for this purpose.

←

Soaring octagonal towers of Vor Frue Kirke in Kalundborg

29

Trelleborg

🅰E6 🏛Trelleborg Allé 4, Slagelse 🕐Apr-May & Sep-Oct: 10am-4pm Tue-Sun; Jun-Aug: 10am-5pm Tue-Sun 🌐natmus.dk

The most well-preserved of Denmark's Viking fortresses was built in the 10th century by Harald I (commonly known as Bluetooth). At the height of its power it was manned by an estimated 1,000 warriors. Of the reconstructed buildings, the longhouse is the most impressive. It is built of rough oak beams and furnished with benches on which the Vikings slept.

Originally, there were 16 buildings in the main section of the fortress. Outside was a small cemetery, where archaeologists have counted about 150 graves.

In summer visitors can take part in a variety of activities. Staff dressed in Viking costume are on hand to demonstrate such workaday jobs as grinding corn and sharpening tools. Daily workshops provide children with the opportunity to try their hand at archery and even dress up as Vikings.

The museum exhibits interesting finds excavated from the grounds, such as jewellery and pottery.

↑ Carving demonstration at the open-air Viking museum in Trelleborg

30 🏃 Ⓜ 🍴

Dragsholm Slot

🅰E5 🏛Dragsholm Allé, Hørve 🌐dragsholm-slot.dk

The castle in Dragsholm was once a fortress and later a royal residence. These days it is used as a luxurious hotel and restaurant, but has lost none of its historical grandeur. Tours can be arranged by advance booking (English and German).

Situated on the shores of Nekselø Bay, at the foot of Vejrhøj (Zealand's third-highest hill), Dragsholm Slot is one of Denmark's oldest castles. Its origins date back to the beginning of the 13th century, when the Bishop of Roskilde decided to build a palace, which would also serve as a military fortress. The bishops owned the castle until 1536, when the king took possession of it following the Reformation. The king established a prison at the castle. The most famous prisoner was James Hepburn, the 4th

Earl of Bothwell. He was married to the Scottish queen, Mary Stuart, but had to flee from Scotland. He was captured in Bergen and later sent to Dragsholm, where he was imprisoned for five years. Hepburn died in 1578, and his mummified body is located in the church in Fårevejle.

In 1657 Denmark declared war on Sweden. When Sweden won, the Swedish soldiers blew up parts of the castle. It was then given to Henrik Müller, who rebuilt the southern wing in 1675. In 1694 the castle was bought by Frederik Christian Adeler and his wife Henriette Margrethe von Lente. They rebuilt the rest of the castle as the Baroque building seen today. The Adeler family owned the castle until 1932, when the state had to take over.

Since 1937 the property has been owned by the Bøttger family, who today run it as an upmarket hotel with a spa and two restaurants. The castle's

↑ Looking up at the formidable Dragsholm Slot, the interiors of which are more welcoming (inset)

rooms all have unique and beautiful furnishings. Some rooms overlook the park, with others offering views of the fields, moat or beautiful cobblestone castle yard. The thick walls, high ceilings and sumptuous decor enhance the historic aura of the place. The most interesting rooms include the magnificent Banqueting Hall (Riddersalen) and Hunting Room (Jagtværelset).

The castle and its moat are surrounded by a large expanse of parkland with a collection of rhododendrons. Like all great castles, Dragsholm is reputed to be haunted. Its three resident ghosts are the White Lady, the Grey Lady and, of course, Lord Bothwell.

> Like all great castles, Dragsholm is reputed to be haunted. Its three resident ghosts are the White Lady, the Grey Lady and, of course, Lord Bothwell.

Gniben

The needle point of Odsherred has wide sandy beaches and affords magnificent views of the Kattegat sea. It is popular for sunbathing and fishing. It is closed when the nearby naval base uses it for military exercises.

31

Odsherred

🅰 E4 🎫 Holtets Plads 1; www.visitodsherred.com

Surrounded by the waters of the Kattegat, Isefjord and Sejerø Bay, the Odsherred peninsula is one of the most popular holiday destinations in Denmark, visited annually by sun-seekers and watersport enthusiasts. Its wide sandy beaches, the lure of the sea and the varied landscape also make this region popular with artists, some of whom have established galleries here.

The interior of the local church in Højby is decorated with frescoes depicting, among others, Sankt Jørgen. The banks of Højby Sø, meanwhile, are inhabited by a wide variety of birds while the lake is also popular with anglers.

The **Sommerland Sjælland** amusement park has many playful attractions, including a mini-train, roller coaster and giant water slides. It's a good day out for families with kids.

The restored Lumsås Mølle windmill dates from the 19th century, and you can even buy flour ground on site.

Finally, the small fishing village of Havnebyen makes for a memorable visit thanks to its local smokehouses, the aromas of which are prevalent.

Sommerland Sjælland

⊛ 🅰 Gl Nykøbingvej 169, 4572 Nørre Asmindrup ⏱ Mid-May–Sep: times vary, check website 🆆 sommerlandsj.dk

---

32

Svinninge

🅰 E5 📞 59 91 08 88 🚉

The main reason people come to this town, located at the base of the Odsherred peninsula, is to visit its electric model railway, which is one of the longest in Europe. **Svinninge Modeljernbane** has over 550 model railway coaches and nearly 90 locomotives. All of the rolling stock, as well as the reconstructions of well-known Danish stations (including Svinninge, Hilbæk, and Egaa), are built to a scale of 1:87. The creators have meticulously re-created entire railway routes, including the link from Holbæk to Oxneholm. The railway was opened to the public after it was donated to the town by its original creator. The display was built by many skilled people, including model makers, carpenters, and electricians. More than 80 m (262 ft) of cable was laid in order to supply current to over 2 km (1.3 miles) of track. The display continues to grow, with new sections of track and loco-motives added yearly.

Svinninge Modeljernbane

⊛ 🅰 Stationen 2, 4520 Svinninge ⏱ End Apr–end Oct: 10am–4pm Fri–Sun 🆆 svmjk.dk

EAT & STAY

Dragsholm Hotel

The starkly beautiful Dragsholm radiates old-world charm. Its 34 luxurious, period-furnished rooms look out onto the surrounding countryside, designated a Geopark by UNESCO. Its two award-winning restaurants are world class, and the food is as dramatic as the setting. The gourmet restaurant Slotskøkkenet and its sister bistro Spisehuset have attracted some of Denmark's best chefs. The atmospheric decor and elite Scandinavian gastronomy highlight its history and location. Reservations are a must.

🅰 E5 🅰 Dragsholm Allé, Hørve 🆆 dragsholm-slot.dk

Ⓚ Ⓚ Ⓚ

↑ A rowing boat basking in sunshine on a shoreline in Odsherred

SOUTHERN ZEALAND AND THE ISLANDS

Southern Zealand (Sjælland) is an important region for the Danes. Vordingborg was the capital of the Valdemar dynasty and, in the 12th century, was used by Bishop Absalon as a staging post for his military expeditions to eastern Germany. The market town of Ringsted, in central Zealand, was for many years the venue of the *landsting*, a regional government assembly that formed the basis of the present-day parliament. In 1677, Køge Bay was the scene of a major naval engagement in which the Danish Admiral Niels Juel became a national hero when he dealt a crushing blow to the Swedish fleet.

The lowlands of southern Zealand are characterized by cultivated fields and beautiful lakes. Many visitors see only Vordingborg and Køge, two towns that have played a significant part in Denmark's history, but the islands of Lolland, Falster and Møn to the south are more rural in character and are attractive holiday destinations. They offer miles of sandy beaches, woodland and awe-inspiring views of coastal cliffs.

SOUTHERN ZEALAND AND THE ISLANDS

Must See

① Stevns Klint

Experience More

② Agersø
③ BonBon-Land
④ Ringsted
⑤ Suså
⑥ Næstved
⑦ Gavnø Slot
⑧ Knudshoved Odde
⑨ Vordingborg
⑩ Sakskøbing
⑪ Maribo
⑫ Nakskov
⑬ Lalandia
⑭ Fejø and Femø
⑮ Tågerup
⑯ Nysted
⑰ Fanefjord Kirke
⑱ Nykøbing F
⑲ Eskilstrup
⑳ Marielyst
㉑ Fuglsang Kunstmuseum
㉒ Liselund Slot
㉓ Elmelunde
㉔ Kong Asgers Høj
㉕ Møns Klint
㉖ Middelaldercentret
㉗ Knuthenborg Safari Park
㉘ Stege
㉙ Vallø Slot
㉚ Fakse
㉛ Nyord
㉜ Køge

Tissø

Gørlev

Dianalund

Slagelse

Sørbymagle

STOREBÆLTSBROEN

Tårnborg

Fuglebjerg

Halsskov

Dalmose

Skælskør

Snadved

Tornemark

Rude

AGERSØ ②

Agersø By

Stigsnæs

Bisserup

Gisøen

Kirkehavn

Omø

Smålandsfarvandet

Vejrø

FUNEN
p194

Rågø Skalø

FEJØ
⑭

Horslunde

Lilleø
Askø

Tårs

Birket

Bandholm

NAKSKOV
⑫

Søllested

**KNUTHENBORG
SAFARI PARK**

Enehøje

Langø

MARIBO

Lolland

Dannemare

Holeby

Rødby

LALANDIA ⑬

Rødbyhavn

TÅGERUP ⑮

Baltic Sea

0 kilometres   10
0 miles   10

N ↑

Fehman ↙

❶

STEVNS KLINT

⬛F6 🏠Rødvig, Havnevej 21 🚉Rødvig 🚌252
🌐cphcoastandcountryside.com

The dramatic white cliffs of Stevns Klint are one of the world's most important fossil records, as confirmed by UNESCO in 2014. Thanks to the crashing waves of the Baltic Sea eroding the cliff face, here you can witness 65 million years of Mother Earth's history.

Stretching for 20 km (12 miles) along Køge Bay (Køge Bugt), Stevns Klint connects the Øresund to the Baltic Sea. A coastal path follows the cliff side from the town of Rødvig to Bøgeskov Harbour. The cliffs reach a height of 41 m (135 ft) and stop with an abrupt drop-off. Dizzying though this might be, the views from the cliff edge are utterly stunning. On a clear day, the impressive Øresund Bridge (p137) and even Sweden's coastline can be seen. The chalk sea floor colours the water stunning shades of turquoise and the white chalk surface of the cliffs glints when the sun shines. Højerup's Romanesque style church, built in 1250, stands on the very edge of the cliff.

The area around Stevns Klint was for centuries known for its limestone quarries, which supplied material for the first castles of Copenhagen. Large-scale limestone quarrying was abandoned in the 1940s.

> 💬 **INSIDER TIP**
> **Observe the Clay**
>
> The best place to see the 10-cm- (4-in-) layer of grey clay in the cliff face is to climb down the cliff side staircase beside the old limestone church in Højerup. This clay is believed to prove that a meteorite contributed to the mass extinction of the dinosaurs.

1928

The year a presbytery collapsed and crashed into the water due to erosion.

STAY

Stevns Klint Beach House
Lovely beachside inn, right next to Stevns Klint, with ten bright and minimal rooms, many boasting a sea view. Kayaks and electric bicycles are available for rent.

🏠 Klintevej 28, 4673 Rødvig Stevns
🌐 strandpension.dk

Ⓚ Ⓚ Ⓚ

Rødvig Inn & Seaside Hotel
This charming, white *badehotel* – or bathing hotel – is a family operation with many rooms offering panoramas of Stevns Klint. The cosy restaurant is the definition of *hygge* while the kitchen concocts comforting lunches and dinners using seasonal and local ingredients.

🏠 Østersøvej 8, 4673 Rødvig Stevns
🌐 roedvigkro.dk

Ⓚ Ⓚ Ⓚ

↑ The scenic and chalky edge of the gorgeous Stevns Klint on a sunny day

Science Behind Stevns Klint

The animal fossils on the lower parts of the chalky cliffs suggest that Stevns Klint formed 65 million years ago. Geo museum Faxe *(p193)* has exhibits on fossils found here. The upper parts of the cliffs, meanwhile, are limestone but also have a narrow layer of grey clay. This clay supports a theory that a giant meteorite hit Earth and contributed to the mass extinction of the dinosaurs.

→ Staircases descending Stevns Klint's cliff side and leading to the shore

←
Patterned ceilings arching over the nave of Sankt Bendts Kirke, Ringsted

plenty of options for toddlers too. Queues lengthen for the water slides and white-water rapids in warm weather.

BonBon-Land is attractively situated in woodland a short walk from Holme-Ostrup train station. There are a number of picnic benches, so visitors can bring lunch into the amusement park. Otherwise, expect queues at the snack bars.

④ Ringsted

🅰 F6 🚉 ℹ Tvær Allé 1-3; www.visitringsted.dk

Ringsted was once an important market town as well as the venue for regional assemblies – the *landsting*. Three stones standing in the market square were used hundreds of years ago by its members.

Ringsted gained notoriety in 1131 when Knud (Canute) Laward, duke of southern Zealand, was murdered in the neighbouring woods by his jealous cousin Magnus. He is buried in Ringsted's Sankt Bendts Kirke (St Benedict's Church) along with a number of Danish kings and queens. Items recovered from their coffins in the 17th century are displayed in one of the chapels. Sankt Bendts Kirke was erected in 1170 and is believed to be the oldest brick-built church in Scandinavia. Its baptismal font is believed to be from the 12th century and was for a time used as a flower pot until it was discovered quite by chance. The church's splendid frescoes were painted around 1300 and include a series on Erik IV.

EXPERIENCE MORE

② Agersø

🅰 E6 🚢 🌐 agersoe.com

The lovely island of Agersø is accessible via a 15-minute ferry trip from Stigsnæs, a small port an hour's drive from Næstved. Despite its small size, Agersø has a lot to offer, starting with the harbour, which plays host to all manner of vessels, from ferries and yachts to fishing boats. There is also a comprehensive network of walking and cycling routes starting from the harbour and covering 20 km (12 miles). The north of the island features several unspoiled beaches with good bathing opportunities.

The island's main attraction, however, is **Agersø Mølle**, a windmill built in 1892. The structure was in use until 1959, when its owner, a

baker called Erik Thomsen, bequeathed it to the people of Agersø. A bench was placed next to the windmill in his honour.

Agersø Mølle

⊛ 🅰 Agersø Møllevej 17 🕐 Jul–early Aug: 2–4pm Fri–Sun 🌐 agersoe-moelle.dk

③

BonBon-Land

🅰 F6 🅰 Holme-Ostrup, Gartnervej 2 🕐 End Apr–late Oct: times vary, check website 🌐 bonbonland.dk

This nostalgic amusement park is a huge draw in summer. Of the 100 or so attractions, the greatest thrill is undoubtedly the giant roller coaster. Gentler rides for younger kids can be had on merry-go-rounds or mini-racetracks, and there are

→
Canoeing down the peaceful waters of the Suså river

Near Haslev, 18 km (11 miles) southeast of Ringsted, is the magnificent **Gisselfeld Kloster**, one of the finest Renaissance castles in northern Europe. The name Gisselfeld can be traced back to 1370, but the red building as it appears today was completed in 1575. There has been a garden park around the castle since then. The present English landscape garden, with its beautiful oases and botanic rarities, is worth a visit.

Bregentved Slot, on the outskirts of Haslev, was erected in the 1650s and substantially modified in the New Rococo style in the late 1880s.

Gisselfeld Kloster

 Godskontoret, Gisselfeldvej 12 A, Haslev ⏱ Times vary, check website 🌐 gisselfeld-kloster.dk

---

5

Suså

A F6

At nearly 90 km (56 miles) long, the Suså is one of the longest rivers in Denmark. From its source near Rønnede it flows through two lakes, Tystrup Sø and Bavelse Sø, ending its journey in Karrebæk Bay, near Næstved. The picturesque surroundings and slow-flowing current make the river particularly popular with canoeists. Trips are usually taken over the final stretch of the river, where a canoe or a kayak can be hired for an hour or two. River traffic gets quite busy in summer, and many families enjoy picnicking along the riverbanks.

6

Næstved

A F6 🏛 🛈 St Peders K'plads 4; www.visitsouthzealandmon.com

Southern Zealand's largest town has been a vital centre of trade since medieval times. The 15th-century town hall in Axeltorv, the main square, is one of the oldest in Denmark. The town has two Gothic churches. The 14th-century Sankt Peder Kirke (St Peter's Church) and the 13th-century Sankt Mortens.

Other notable buildings include Kompagnihuset, a half-timbered guildhall (1493) and Apostelhuset (Apostles' House), built in the early 16th century. Its name derives

from the figures of Christ and his 12 disciples placed between the windows.

Næstved's oldest building is Helligåndshuset (House of the Holy Spirit), which dates from the 1300s and was used as a hospital and almshouse. It now houses part of the **Næstved Museum**, which boasts a fine collection of medieval and contemporary woodcarvings. An annex of the museum displays local handicrafts from the Holmegaard glass factory and nearby potteries. The Løveapoteket (Pharmacy) on Axeltorv dates back to 1640 and has a herb garden in the courtyard. Munkebakken Park (not far from Axeltorv) contains statues of seven monks carved out of tree trunks.

Næstved Museum

 🏛 Ringstedgade 4 📞 70 70 12 36 ⏱ 11am–4pm Tue–Fri, 10am–3pm Sat & Sun

⑦

Gavnø Slot

🅰E6 🅰Gavnø 🕑Late Apr-
Sep: 10am–4pm daily
🌐gavnoe.dk

Located a little way from
Næstved, Gavnø Slot is one
of Denmark's finest Rococo
castles and houses the largest
privately owned collection of
paintings in Scandinavia. Highlights include the Great Dining
Room, with its stunning
French chandelier, and the
guest rooms dating from the
1750s. The rooms are still used
on special occasions.

The castle garden is thought
by some to be the most beautiful in all of Denmark. There's
no denying that the grounds
look spectacular in spring when
the tulips and narcissi are in
full bloom. The floral splendour
continues into the autumn with
a succession of rhododendrons,
begonias, lilies and roses. In
the centre of the garden is the
"Skjærsommer" playhouse,
which was built for the little
Baroness Julie Reedtz-Thott in
1846. A part of her private doll
collection is exhibited here. The
gardens also have a butterfly
house, a pirate-themed playground and a treasure hunt
for both children and adults.

Did You Know?

Gavnø Slot has served
as both a pirate lair and
convent for unmarried
noble women.

⑧

Knudshoved Odde

🅰F6

The narrow strip of this peninsula is 20 km (12 miles) long
and only 1 km (half a mile) at
its widest point, and can only
be reached by car. There are
no towns or villages here, and
the only road is closed to motor
vehicles after 10 km (6 miles).
This inaccessibility makes the
Knudshoved Odde popular
with people who wish to get
away from it all and indulge in
simple activities such as sitting
on the seashore, picking berries
and exploring the woods.

The peninsula is also known
for its Neolithic burial mounds,
one of which is close to the car
park. Excavations have found
that its ancient occupant was
provided with plenty of food
and drink for the afterlife.

⑨

Vordingborg

🅰F6 🌐visitsouthzealand-
mon.com

Vordingborg is on the strait
between Zealand and Falster
and was once the most important town in Denmark. It was
the home of Valdemar I (The
Great), who came to the throne
in 1157 and built a castle here,
ushering in a period of relative
peace. In 1241 he sanctioned
the Jutland Code here, which
gave Denmark its first written
laws. Subsequent monarchs in
the Valdemar dynasty expanded the castle over the years,
adding nine mighty towers.

Most of the towers are in
ruins but for the 14th-century
Gåsetårnet (Goose Tower),
whose name dates back to
1368, when Valdemar IV placed
a golden goose on top of the
tower as a way to make fun
of the German Hanseatic
League – their declaration of
war being no more threaten-
ing to him than the cackling
of geese. Gåsetårnet is
important as the only intact
building to remain from the
Valdemar era. Directly opposite
is the remodelled **Danmarks
Borgcenter** (Danish Castle
Centre), with displays on the

↑ Historic portraits
lining the walls of
grand Gavnø Slot

↑ Sun breaking through the trees by Goose Tower, Vordingborg

castle's history and the three kings who lived there.

Algade, Vordingborg's main thoroughfare, leads to Vor Frue Kirke (Church of Our Lady), a 15th-century church with a Baroque altarpiece dating from 1642.

Gåsetårnet and Danmarks Borgcenter

⊗ 🏠 Slotsruinen 1
⏰ Times vary, check website
🌐 danmarksborgcenter.dk

---

⑩
Sakskøbing

🅰 E7 🏠 Lolland 🛈 Torvet 4; 53 35 87 61 (Jun-Sep)

One of Lolland's oldest settlements, Sakskøbing has few historic remains other than a Romanesque church (13th century). However, the town's location on the E47, the main road linking Zealand to Falster and Lolland, makes it a popular stopping-off point. One of the town's most striking features is a water tower with a giant smiling face painted on top. A distinctive landmark in the market square is a monument erected in 1939 for local Polish field workers. The town's links with Poland date back to the late 19th century, when many Poles

came here to work. Many settled permanently, and some local Catholic churches still celebrate mass in Polish.

---

⑪
Maribo

🅰 E7 🏠 Lolland 🛈 Torvet 1, Det Gamle Rådhus; www. visitlolland-falster.com

Situated on the northern shore of Maribo Søndersø, the largest of four inland lakes, the town of Maribo is Lolland's main commercial centre. Maribo was founded in 1416 by Erik of Pomerania and soon acquired a Gothic cathedral, whose bells still toll six times a day.

Maribo has two museums, which offer separate as well as joint admission fees. The **Lolland-Falster Stiftsmuseet** has a collection of church art and displays relating to Polish workers. **Frilandsmuseet**, a short way southwest of Maribo, is an open-air museum with a number of period cottages, as well as a windmill, a school and a smithy.

Lolland-Falster Stiftsmuseet

⊗ 🏠 Banegårdspladsen 11 📞 54 84 44 00
⏰ Times vary, call ahead

Frilandsmuseet

⊗ 🏠 Meinckesvej 5
📞 54 84 44 00
⏰ May–Sep: 10am– 4pm Tue–Sun

←
The smiling water tower of Sakskøbing

← A quiet, charming street in the town of Nakskov

water slide, the Tornado. Further indoor fun includes bowling, mini-golf and table tennis. There are also various restaurants and shops, plus a variety of holiday homes.

⑭
Fejø and Femø

Ⓐ E7 ⓘ Herredsvej 278 A, Fejø; www.fejoemoelle.dk

Danes love the islands of Fejø and Femø, on the Smålands-havet archipelago, thanks to their wealth of lovely beaches, orchards and cottages. Fejø lies in the Smålands Sea around 15 minutes from the North Lolland coast and is accessible by a ferry that heads out from Kragenæs early in the morning through to late evening. The island has two villages, Østerby and Vesterby, both of which are characterized by charming thatched houses, while its orchards produce most of the fruit in Denmark. The sight

⑫
Nakskov

Ⓐ E7 Ⓐ Lolland ⓘ Axeltorv 3; 54 92 21 72

Nakskov's origins date back to the 13th century. A reminder of its medieval past is the tower of Sankt Nikolai Kirke (Church), which rises up above the old quarter. One of Nakskov's oldest houses is Dronningens Pakhus, a quayside warehouse from 1590. Also on the quay is the Skibs- og Søfartsmuseet (Maritime and Ship Museum).

The majority of Denmark's sugar beet is grown on Lolland. Housed in a former factory, **Denmark's Sugar Museum** tells the story of the crop and of the Polish immigrants who came to work in the fields.

There are 20 small islands in Nakskov Fjord, some of them inhabited. Deliveries are still made using the **Postbåden**, a small boat that also welcomes tourists on board in summer. The route varies, but it always stops for a 1-hour lunch break

at Albuen (The Elbow), an area with numerous natural attractions. It is well worth paying a little extra and bringing a bike; after cycling around the islands, you can catch another boat back to Nakskov. As well as the morning excursions, there are also trips just before sundown.

Denmark's Sugar Museum

⊛ Ⓐ Løjtoftevej 22 Ⓞ Jun-Sep: 1-4pm Tue-Sun; Oct-May: 1-4pm Sat Ⓦ sukkermuseet.dk

Postbåden

⊛ Ⓐ Havnegade 27 Ⓒ 54 93 12 36 Ⓞ Jun-Aug: from 9am daily

⑬ ⊛ 🍽 💻 🛍
Lalandia

Ⓐ E7 Ⓐ Lolland 🚌 ⓘ Rødby, Lalandia Centret 1; www.lalandia.dk

Lalandia in Rødby is ideal for family holidays. The tropical holiday centre is sat on the southern coast of Lolland and has plenty to offer. The huge Lalandia Aquadome is filled with different types of pools, jacuzzis and rides, including Scandinavia's largest covered

12,000

The amount of sugar beet (in tons) processed in Nakskov every day.

→ The spire of Nysted's church rising above the harbour

of trees blossoming in May is breathtaking. Other highlights include Kernegaarden Farm, which provides accommodation with sea views, and the 13th-century Fejø Kirke on the beachfront – one of the oldest island churches in Denmark. The Fejø Mølle information centre, a working windmill and café, is also located in the middle of the island.

Femø is Fejø's little sister, famed for its lovely beaches where it's easy to find a secluded spot to bathe. The island is also popular for mid-level hiking and cycling trails, which all seem to lead to the sea. The island welcomes a jazz festival every August.

15
Tågerup
🅰E7 🅰Lolland 🚌

The main attraction of this small village situated a short way south of Maribo is its Romanesque-Gothic church, which contains some fine 15th-century frescoes. At the entrance to the church is a runic stone. Visitors are often surprised to find a building displaying the Polish flag. This is **Polakkasernen**, or the Polish Barracks, which contains various items left by Polish immigrants. The Poles moved to Lolland in great numbers between 1870 and 1920 in a bid to escape a feudal system that gave them few legal rights. Once they arrived, most Poles found employment in the local sugar beet fields.

A short way from here is **Lungholm Gods**, an early 15th-century residence with English-style landscaped grounds. The house is now used as a conference centre and spa. The footpaths around it are ideal for a pleasant ramble.

Polakkasernen
⊘ 🏠Højbygårsvej 34
🕐Easter, Jul-Aug: 2–4pm Tue-Sun 🌐polakka sernen.dk

Lungholm Gods
🏠Rødbyvej 24
📞54 60 02 53

> **Femø is Fejø's little sister, famed for its lovely beaches where it's easy to find a secluded spot to bathe. The island is also popular for mid-level hiking and cycling trails.**

16
Nysted
🅰F7 🅰Lolland 🚌

This small harbour town on Rødsand Bay was founded in the 13th century. Nysted's main historic monuments are a large Gothic church dating from the early 14th century, and a 17th-century tower. There are also many half-timbered houses and a water tower, which now serves as a viewpoint.

Ålholm Slot (Castle) is on the outskirts of Nysted and dates from the 12th century. It was crown property for many years and the rooms still contain many royal furnishings. In 1332 Christian II was held prisoner in the dungeons here on the orders of his half-brother. The castle is now in private hands and is not open to the public.

About 3 km (2 miles) north of Nysted is Kettinge, a small village with an old Dutch windmill and a church containing frescoes from around 1500.

⑰ Fanefjord Kirke

🅰F7 🏠Fanefjord Kirkevej 49, Askeby ⏰8am–6pm daily 🌐fanefjordkirke.dk

The small church of Fanefjord stands on top of an isolated hillock surrounded by green fields. From here it is possible to look out over the Baltic and Falster. Folklore tells that the Gothic church derives its name from Fanefjord Bay, whose waters come close to the building. The fjord was itself named after Queen Fane, wife of King Grøn Jæger, local rulers in the late Stone Age.

Built about 1250, the church served worshippers from ships anchoring in the busy harbour. According to records it was here that Bishop Absalon gathered his fleet before embarking on raids against the Wends on the south coast of the Baltic. Fanefjord Kirke is famous for

its frescoes, the oldest of which date from around 1350. The later paintings date from the mid-15th century and include frescoes painted in warm, rich colours by the Elmelunde Master, an artist about whom virtually nothing is known. A collection of votive ships hangs in the church. The oldest is a barquentine hanging above the entrance which commemorates a tragic shipwreck off the north coast of Møn.

---

⑱ Nykøbing F

🅰F7 🏠Falster 🚉🚌 🛈Færgestræde 1A; www.visitlolland-falster.com

Falster's capital city was a busy commercial centre in medieval times and was granted municipal status in the early 13th century by Valdemar II. In order to distinguish it from two other Danish towns of the same name, this Nykøbing is followed by the letter F (standing for Falster).

Detailed frescoes housed inside the unblemished Fanefjord Kirke *(inset)* ↓

Nykøbing F's main historic sight is a 15th-century church once formed part of a Franciscan monastery. Its richly decorated interior includes an eye-catching series of portraits of Queen Sophie (the wife of Frederick II). Another notable sight is the half-timbered Czarens Hus (Tsar's House), one of the oldest buildings in town. In 1716 the Russian Tsar, Peter the Great, stopped here overnight on his way to Copenhagen. Today, it houses the **Falsters Minder** museum. Among the exhibits are the reconstructed interiors of an 18th-century cottage and a 19th-century burgher's house.

A wonderful panorama can be seen from the town's water tower. The **Guldborgsund Zoo** is a little way east of the train station and has a variety of animals, including monkeys, donkeys and goats.

Falsters Minder

♿ 🏠Færgestræde 1A 📞54 85 13 03 ⏰10am–4pm Tue–Fri (Jul–Sep: also Mon), 10am–2pm Sat

Guldborgsund Zoo

♿ 🏠Østre Alle 97 ⏰May– mid-Oct: 9am–5pm daily; mid-Oct–Apr: 10am–4pm daily 🌐guldborgsundzoo.dk

⑲ Eskilstrup

Ⓐ F7 **Ⓞ Falster** 🍴🚌

This small town is a short trip from the E47 motorway and has two unusual museums. The **Traktormuseum** contains over 200 tractors and engines dating from 1880 to 1960. Alongside a wide selection of vintage Fiats, Fords and Volvos are rare Czechoslovakian and Romanian tractors. The oldest tractor is American and was built in 1917. There is also a steam traction engine built in England in 1889. Until 1925 it was still serving as a threshing machine. A number of small pedal tractors are provided for children.

About 3 km (2 miles) from the town centre is **Krokodille Zoo**. This is the largest collection of crocodiles in Europe and includes virtually every species of these sharp-toothed reptiles that exists worldwide. The smallest among them is the dwarf cayman, which grows up to 159 cm (62 in) in length. At the other end of the scale, the zoo's giant Nile crocodile Sobek is currently the largest crocodile in Europe.

As well as its resident crocodiles, the zoo also features a wide variety of other animals, including a green anaconda (the world's largest snake), turtles, tortoises and a number of rare clouded leopards. The zoo donates a percentage of the admission price to an international programme of scientific research and protection of crocodiles in the wild.

Traktormuseum

♿ Ⓐ Nørregade 17B ⏰ May-Jun & Sep: 10am–4pm Sat-Mon; Jul & Aug: 10am–4pm daily ☒ traktormuseum.dk

Krokodille Zoo

♿ Ⓐ Ovstrupvej 9 ⏰ Feb-mid-Jun & Sep-Nov: noon–4pm Tue-Sun; mid-Jun-Aug: 10am–5pm daily ☒ krokodillezoo.dk

↑ Admiring the view from the golden sands of gorgeous Marielyst beach

⑳ 🍴🛍 Marielyst

Ⓐ F7 **Ⓞ Falster** 🚌 **ⓘ** Marielyst Strandvej 54; www.visitlolland-falster.com

Thrice voted the best beach in Denmark, the town's 20-km (12-mile) stretch of white sand on the Baltic Sea has been among the foremost holiday havens in Denmark for a good century. Beach-goers enjoy the clean, shallow waters and dunes that run parallel to the coastline, which are in turn fringed by an ancient beech forest. Situated on the eastern end of the island, along with campsites, guesthouses and hotels, the town of Marielyst has about 6,000 summer cottages plus plenty of shops, restaurants and bars. The Surfcenter Falster has a wind- and kite-surfing school for all ages and in multiple languages.

Just south of Marielyst is the Bøtø Nor bird sanctuary, where cranes, ospreys and plovers can be spotted. An important place for spotting migratory birds in the autumn, the observation tower here offers spectacular views. Also not far is the small town of Væggerløse, which has an 18th-century windmill, now a glassblowing work-shop, and a late Romanesque church with late-medieval ceiling paintings.

TOP 5 SOUTHERN ZEALAND BEACHES

Marielyst
Ⓐ F7
Beautiful sandy beach.

Enø Strand
Ⓐ E6
Blue Flag beach in Karrebæksminde Bay.

Feddet Strand
Ⓐ F6
Golden sand strip near Præstø Fjord.

Ulvshale Strand
Ⓐ F6
Picnic-friendly spot on Møn with a backdrop of idyllic green forest.

Rødvig Strand
Ⓐ F6
Family-friendly beach near Stevns Klint.

---

21 ✏️

Fuglsang Kunstmuseum

🅰F7 ▯Nystedvej 71, Toreby, Lolland ⏰Apr–Jun & Sep–Oct: 11am–5pm Tue–Sun; Jul & Aug: 11am–5pm daily; Nov–Mar: 11am–4pm Wed–Sun 🌐aabne-samlinger.dk

Located in the vast grounds of Fuglsang Manor, between Nysted and Nykøbing F, this art museum was designed by British architect Tony Fretton. The modern white building provides a stark contrast to the green rural landscape. Inside is a collection of Danish art from the 18th century onwards, with a focus on the period from 1850 until 1950. Golden Age painters such as P C Skovgaard and Kristian Zahrtmann are represented, as are the Funen artists, Skagen School alumni and the CoBrA group.

---

22 ✏️ 🖼️

Liselund Slot

🅰F6 ▯Langebjergvej 4, Møn ⏰May–Sep: daily 🌐natmus.dk/liselund

Liselund is a colourful park with a tiny palace on the island of Møn. The gardens exude the classical Danish idyll combined

> ### NEW NORDIC TIPPLE
>
> When it comes to brewing, South Zealand excels. Gavnø Kloster has Denmark's only castle brewery *(www.gavnoe.dk)*. Isle of Møn Spirits creates small-batch gin with locally foraged botanicals *(www.isleofmoen.com)*. Noteworthy winemakers are Werning Wine *(www.werning wine.com)* and Wineyard Vesterhavegården *(www.vesterhave gaarden.dk)*.

↑ Delightful Liselund Slot, bounded by lush gardens

with the natural landscaping of Enlightenment philosophy and the ordered wildness of Romanticism. Here, thoughts are easily swept away in the atmosphere of a fairy tale from Hans Christian Andersen.

At one end is the diminutive Liselund Slot, named after the owner's beloved wife. The fairy-tale atmosphere chimes with the immaculate thatch on the building's roof (locals joke that this is the only thatched-roof palace in the world) and the reflection of its white walls in the lake. You can visit the park on your own or, during the summer months, join a tour through the palace (10:30am, 11am, 1pm & 3pm Wed–Sun).

23

Elmelunde

🅰F6 ▯Møn 🚌

Along with its famous cliffs, Møn has a number of churches with highly original frescoes. Built around 1075, the stone **Elmelunde Kirke** is one of the oldest in Denmark. The frescoes date from the 14th and 15th centuries and were restored in 1970 under the guidance of Copenhagen's National Museum.

The frescoes include images of Christ and the saints as well

as lively portrayals of demons and the flames of hell. Most are attributed to one prolific artist, known simply as the Elmelunde Master. The paintings served to explain biblical stories to illiterate peasants and are characterized by their quirky static figures with blank faces devoid of any emotion. More frescoes can be seen in Keldby Kirke, a little to the west, which also has a sumptuously carved 16th-century pulpit.

Elmelunde Kirke

▯Leonora Christines Vej 1 ⏰8am–3:45 daily (Apr–Sep: to 4:45pm) 🌐keldbyel melundekirke.dk

---

24

Kong Asgers Høj

🅰F7 ▯Møn

King Asgers mounds, located in a farmer's field near the village of Røddinge, are all that remain of Denmark's largest passage grave. The Stone Age corridor consists of a long underground passage that leads to a large chamber. It is advisable to take a torch.

→

Walking alongside the chalk-white cliffs of Møns Klint

A short way south stands yet another burial mound: the Klekkendehøj, which has two entrances placed side by side. The mound has been restored and is now illuminated.

At the south end of Møn is Grønjægers Høj, estimated to be about 4,000 years old. The burial site is one of the largest in Denmark and consists of 134 weighty stones arranged in an oval shape. According to local legend, the site is the final resting place of Queen Fane and her husband, Grøn Jæger.

25

Møns Klint

ⓐG6 ⓜMøn

Soaring above the aquamarine Baltic Sea, the lofty white cliffs of Møns Klint stand out in Denmark's gently rolling, flat landscape. The highest cliffs in the country attract hikers, cyclists, paragliders, kayakers and more. The cliffs are about 70 million years old and are formed of calcareous shells.

Geocenter Møns Klint is a high-tech, interactive science museum with

GREAT VIEW
Coastal Splendour

Møns Klint soar 120 m (394 ft) above sea level, creating a unique vista of the sea and the landscape. Møns also has Dark Sky ranking, meaning it's one of the best places in Europe to gaze at the stars.

climbing and excavation activities alongside exhibitions on dinosaurs and geology. After a clifftop hike many people head inland to explore Klinteskoven (Klint Forest), where Denmark's last known population of Large Blue butterflies flutter around rare orchids in the summer.

South of the cliffs, small boats leave for 2-hour cruises from Klintholm Havn, a good way to take in the coastal scenery. You'll find long sandy beaches beside the harbour.

Geocenter Møns Klint
⊛ ⓐStengårdsvej 8, Borre
ⓞTimes vary, check website
ⓦmoensklint.dk

---

26 ⊛ ⓨ ⓓ ⓗ

Middelaldercentret

ⓐF7 ⓜLolland ⓘVed Hamborgskoven 2 ⓞTimes vary, check website
ⓦmiddelaldercentret.dk

Lolland's Middle Ages Centre is a recreated medieval settlement that provides an interesting insight into what life was like in the 14th century. Staff in period costumes demonstrate crafts and games from medieval times, while the local inn serves a range of medieval-inspired food. A replica sailing ship lies in the harbour and a huge wooden catapult is ready for firing. Jousting tournaments are a regular feature during the summer, and visitors can also try their hand at archery. A walking trail in the nearby forest explains medieval customs. Along the way, visitors are warned about woodland spirits and invited to throw "ghost-repelling sticks" – just in case.

The centre can easily be reached from Nykøbing F by crossing the bridge that connects Lolland and Falster.

27 🏞️

Knuthenborg Safari Park

📍E7 📍Knuthenborg Alle, Maribo 🕐Times vary, check website 🌐knuthenborg.dk

Knuthenborg Safari Park provides the chance to see such exotic creatures as zebras, camels, antelopes and giraffes. The parkland itself has been in the hands of the same family since the 17th century. It was landscaped in the English style in the 19th century and the first animals were transported by ship from Kenya in 1969. The park's botanical garden has many rare trees and shrubs, and there is an attractive lake area that is ideal for picnics.

28

Stege

📍F7 📍Møn 🚌 ℹ️Storegade 75; www.visitsouth zealand-mon.com

Møn's commercial centre, Stege grew up around a castle built in the 12th century and reached the height of its power in the

→
Grand gatehouse guarding the snowy town of Stege

Middle Ages, when it prospered thanks to a lucrative herring industry. A reminder of those days is Mølleporten (Mill Gate), which once served as Stege's principal entrance. The town's museum, **Empiregården**, is a short way from here. The 13-century Romanesque Stege Kirke in the town centre had its frescoes painted over during the Reformation and exposed again in the 19th century.

Empiregården

🏛️ 📍Storegade 75 🕐Times vary, check website 🌐moensmuseum.dk

29 🏞️

Vallø Slot

📍F6 📞56 26 05 00 🕐Courtyard: 10am-6pm daily; garden: 8am-sunset daily

The secluded castle of Vallø is one of the most impressive Renaissance buildings in

Denmark. As early as the 15th century the islet was circled by a moat and featured a complex of defensive buildings. The castle owes its present shape to the influence of two enterprising sisters, Mette and Birgitte Rosenkrantz, who in the 16th century divided the estate between themselves into east and west. In 1737 the castle became a home for unmarried women of noble birth in their later years.

The castle is closed to the public. You are, however, free to stroll through the gardens and the former stable block, now a museum containing a mix of agricultural implements and equestrian accessories.

30

Fakse

📍F6 🚉🚌 🌐visitsouth zealand-mon.com

References to Fakse (or Faxe) can be found in records from the late 13th century, when it was an important area for limestone mining. Today the town is best known for its local brewery, Faxe Bryggeri.

The town's most historic building is a 15th-century Gothic church with wall paintings dating from around 1500. **Geomuseum Faxe** has over 500 types of fossils, including

↑ Zebras and antelopes grazing in Knuthenborg Safari Park

the 63-million-year-old remains of plants and animals.

Geomuseum Faxe

🏛 Kulturhuset Kanten, Østervej 2 🕐 Apr–Jun: 10am–5pm Fri–Sun; Jul–Aug: 10am–5pm daily; Sep–Mar: 10am–5pm Sat & Sun 🕐 Jul: Mon 🌐 kalklandet.dk/geo museum-faxe

---

31

Nyord

🅰 F6 🚌

Until the late 1980s, the only way to reach this small island was by boat. A bridge, built in 1986, now links the island with Møn, making it more accessible and so increasingly popular. Nevertheless, both the island and the pretty hamlet of the same name have changed little since the

> With cobbled streets and half-timbered houses, there is much to appreciate in Køge, one of Denmark's prettiest and most well-preserved medieval towns.

19th century. Nyord is a haven for bird-watchers; its salt marshes attract massive flocks of birds in spring and autumn, when the island is used as a stopping-off place for winged migrants.

32

Køge

🅰 F6 🚌 🚌 ℹ Vestergade 1; www.visitkoege.com

With cobbled streets and half-timbered houses, there is much to appreciate in Køge, one of Denmark's prettiest and most well-preserved medieval towns. Founded in 1288, Køge grew quickly thanks to its natural harbour. The heart of the town is its market square, where you will find a monument to Frederick VII and the town hall, the longest-serving public building of its kind in Denmark. The square still hosts weekly markets, and the streets leading from the square are lined with the half-timbered houses for which Køge is famous. The tower of Sankt Nicolai Kirke,

built in 1324, served for many years as a lighthouse and is now used as a viewpoint. The **Køge Museum** is located along Nørregade and occupies two early 17th-century buildings. Its exhibits include historic furniture, costumes and the local executioner's sword. Nearby is Borgring, a 10th-century viking fortress extraordinary for its size and shape. You can visit the excavation site and even take a guided tour.

Køge Museum

♿ 🏛 Nørregade 4 📞 70 70 12 36 🕐 Jul–Aug: 10am–5pm daily; Sep–Jun: 11am–4pm Tue–Sun

→ Statue of Frederick VII in Køge's main square

PICTURE PERFECT
Historic Houses

Køge has the largest concentration of half-timbered houses in Denmark. The best shot is looking north from Torvet at Kirkestræde, where you will find some of Denmark's oldest, built in 1527.

Harbour lined with sailing boats in Svendborg

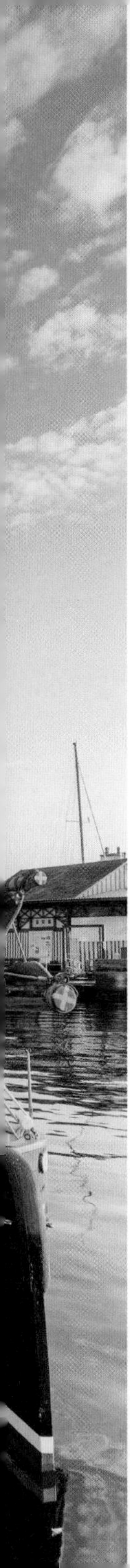

FUNEN

Funen (Fyn in Danish) is Denmark's second largest island and has some of Denmark's best scenery, from wide, sandy beaches and steep cliffs to lush pastures and blossoming orchards. Funen is separated from Zealand by the Store Bælt (Great Belt) and from Jutland by the Lillebælt (Little Belt). Nearly half of Funen's inhabitants live in Odense, the island's capital and birthplace of Hans Christian Andersen. Odense aside, there are no large towns on Funen and the island is sometimes described as the "garden of Denmark" thanks to the abundance of produce that grows in its fertile soil. The island escaped most of Denmark's wars with other nations and, as a result, has an exceptionally high number of well-preserved historic buildings and palaces. The best-known of these is Egeskov Slot, a Renaissance castle encircled by a moat.

The relatively small distances, gently rolling landscape and countless sights of interest make Funen an ideal area for cyclists. The south- western part of the island has a range of wooded hills, while Central Funen is mostly flat and only becomes slightly undulated in the northeastern region. The south, meanwhile, has most of the island's harbours and towns, while the northern and western parts are sparsely populated. An archipelago of southern islets includes Langeland, Ærø and Tåsinge as well as a number of tiny islands inhabited only by birds. This area is particularly popular with yachtsmen.

FUNEN

Must See
❶ Odense

Experience more
❷ Egeskov Slot
❸ Assens
❹ Nyborg
❺ Kerteminde
❻ Hindsholm
❼ Faaborg
❽ Svendborg
❾ Tåsinge
❿ Langeland
⓫ Marstal
⓬ Ærøskøbing

SOUTHERN AND
CENTRAL JUTLAND
p204

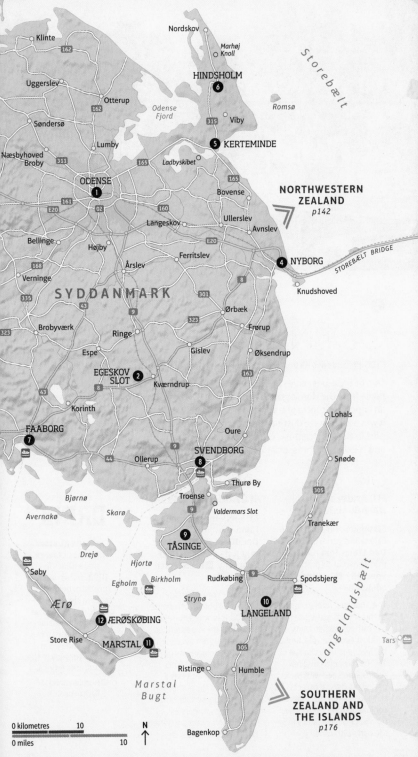

Æbelø

Klinte

162

Uggerslev

Otterup

162

Odense Fjord

Nordskov

Marhøj Knoll

HINDSHOLM 6

Storebælt

Romsø

Søndersø

Næsbyhoved Broby

311

Lumby

315

Viby

KERTEMINDE 5

165

ODENSE 1

165

Bovense

Ladbyskibet

NORTHWESTERN ZEALAND p142

161

E20

02

160

Langeskov

Ullerslev

Avnslev

E20

NYBORG 4

STOREBÆLT BRIDGE

Bellinge

Højby

Årslev

Ferritslev

Knudshoved

168

Verninge

SYDDANMARK

8

301

335

43

9

323

Ørbæk

Brobyværk

Ringe

Espe

Gislev

Frørup

Øksendrup

323

43

EGESKOV SLOT 2

Kværndrup

8

163

Korinth

Oure

FAABORG 7

44

Ollerup

SVENDBORG 8

Lohals

Snøde

305

9

Thurø By

Bjørnø

Troense

Avernakø

Skarø

9

Valdemars Slot

Tranekær

Drejø

Hjortø

TÅSINGE 9

Langelandsbælt

Søby

Egholm

Birkholm

Rudkøbing

9

Spodsbjerg

Ærø

ÆRØSKØBING 12

Strynø

LANGELAND 10

Store Rise

MARSTAL 11

Tars

Ristinge

305

Humble

Marstal Bugt

SOUTHERN ZEALAND AND THE ISLANDS p176

Bagenkop

0 kilometres   10

0 miles   10

N

↑ Enjoying a relaxed summer's day beside Odense River

❶ ODENSE

🅐D6 🚌🚉Odense ℹ️Vestergade 2; www.visitodense.com

One of the oldest cities in Denmark, Odense derives its name from the Nordic god Odin. In medieval times it was an important centre of trade and from the 12th century it was a pilgrimage destination before it became a major port in the 19th century. Odense has a rich cultural life and is loved for its associations with H C Andersen.

① 🔗
H C Andersens Barndomshjem

🅐Munkemøllestræde 3-5 🕐Jan-mid-Jun & mid-Sep-Dec: 11am-4pm Tue-Sun; mid-Jun-mid-Sep: 10am-5pm daily 🌐hcandersens odense.dk

The Andersen family moved to this small house close to the cathedral when Hans was just two years old, and he lived here until the age of 14. The museum has a few rooms, furnished with basic period household objects, but successfully manages to conjure up what life was like for a poor Danish family in the early 19th century.

② 🔗
H C Andersens Hus

🅐Hans Jensens Stræde 45 🕐Jan-mid-Jun & mid-Sep-Dec: 10am-4pm Tue-Sun; mid-Jun-mid-Sep: 10am-5pm daily 🌐hcandersen odense.dk

Denmark's most famous writer was born in this house in 1805. It is now a museum, and it was greatly extended and modernized to celebrate the 200th anniversary of Andersen's birth, in 2005. The exhibition includes a recreation of the author's study and numerous items belonging to Andersen, including his notes and letters. There is also an old rope; apparently Andersen was terrified by the thought of a fire and carried this with him wherever he went in readiness for an emergency evacuation. Hanging on one of the walls is a world map indicating all the countries in which Andersen's tales have been published in translation. A special collection includes copies of his works in 120 languages.

DRINK

Carlsens Kvarter
This historic tavern opened back in 1898, and serves a long list of beers and artisan ales from all over the world. Those in need of more solid fare can choose from a range of cheeses and sausages to enjoy in the cosy surroundings.

🅐Hunderupvej 19 🌐carlsens.dk

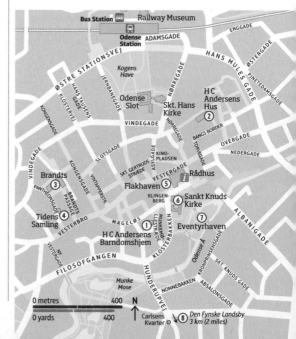

Close to the museum is Fyrtøjet (the Tinderbox), a children's cultural centre based on Andersen's stories.

③ Brandts

🏠 **Brandts Torv 1**
🕐 **10am–5pm Tue, Sat & Sun, 10am–9pm Wed–Fri**
🌐 **brandts.dk**

For more than 50 years Brandts's textile factory was the biggest company in Odense. It stood empty after its closure in 1977 and was reimagined as the cultural centre seen today. It houses museums, a cinema, galleries, shops, restaurants and cafés.

The Mediemuseet has displays on the history of print production and the latest electronic media. The collection offers a journey through 250 years of Danish art history.

④ Tidens Samling

🏠 **Farvergården 7**
🕐 **10am–4pm Mon–Sat**
🌐 **tidenssamling.dk**

Journey through Danish homes of the 20th century at this immersive museum of everyday life. Browse bookshelves, open drawers and try on clothes as you time travel through the decades. There's a great café where all generations can swap their own memories and experiences.

⑤ Flakhaven

For centuries this square was used for a local market and attracted merchants and farmers from all over Funen. The Rådhus (city hall), which dates from the 19th century, can be found in the square. Guided tours are available on Tuesdays and Thursdays during the summer months.

⑥ Sankt Knuds Kirke

🏠 **Klosterbakken 2** 🕐 **Apr–Oct: 10am–4pm Tue–Sat, noon–4pm Mon & Sun; Nov–Mar: noon–5pm Mon, 10am–5pm Tue–Sat, noon–4pm Sun** 🌐 **odense-domkirke.dk**

The cathedral is named after Canute (Knud) II, who ruled Denmark from 1080–86. The king's skeleton is on public display in a glass case in the basement. The present structure is one of Denmark's most beautiful examples of Gothic architecture and stands on the site of a Romanesque building.

⑦ Eventyrhaven

🏠 **H C Andersen Haven**
🌐 **hcandersenparaden.dk**

This lovely green space, overlooked by the cathedral, is a popular picnic spot. In summer, a castle is built on an island on the lake and becomes a stage where actors bring moments from Andersen's tales to life.

↑ Market stalls lining the pedestrianized Vestergade, Odense

⑧ Den Fynske Landsby

🏠 **Sejerskovvej 20**
🕐 **Times vary, check website**
🌐 **museum.odense.dk**

The "Funen Village" is an open-air museum south of the city centre. Here, you can imagine what life would have been like during H C Andersen's childhood. In summer, there are open-air theatre events.

EXPERIENCE MORE

❷
Egeskov Slot

🅰 D6 🏠 Egeskov Gade 18, Kværndrup 🕐 From 10am daily (closing times vary, check website) 🌐 egeskov.dk

This magnificent castle was built in the mid-16th century. Egeskov means "oak forest", and the castle was built over a pond on a foundation of oak trees. The interior has some grand rooms and a hall full of hunting trophies. The grounds were laid out in the 18th century and feature fountains and a herb garden.

---

❸
Assens

🅰 C6 🚌 🛈 Tobaksgaarden 7; www.visitassens.dk

Situated on the shores of the Lillebælt (Little Belt), Assens was once a busy harbour for ferries sailing between Funen and Jutland until a bridge was built across the strait. It has many historic buildings, including 18th- and 19th-century merchant houses and the 15th-century Vor Frue Kirke.

The most famous citizen was Peter Willemoes (1783–1808), a serviceman who distinguished himself in the Napoleonic Wars. His birthplace, **Willemoesgården**, is now a cultural history museum. The museum complex also includes a silver and glass collection, Ernsts Samlinger (guided tours only) and the Toldbodhus, which hosts changing exhibits in the town's old customs building.

Willemoesgården
🕸 🏠 Østergade 36 🕐 Times vary, check website 🌐 museumvestfyn.dk

---

❹
Nyborg

🅰 D6 🚂🚌 🛈 Torvet 2B; www.visitnyborg.dk

The castle of **Nyborg Slot** was built around 1170 by Valdemar the Great's nephew as part of the fortifications that guarded the Store Bælt. For nearly 200 years the castle was the scene of the Danehof assemblies (an early form of Danish parliament). As a result, the city was Denmark's capital from 1183 to 1413. The castle was also

Did You Know?

Tottenham Hotspur footballer Christian Eriksen was born on Funen in 1992.

the venue of the 1282 signing of a coronation charter that laid down the duties of the king. Over the centuries it gradually fell into ruin and was only restored after World War I. Some rooms are open to the public, including the royal chambers, while the ramparts and moat are now a park.

Nyborg Destilleri, Denmark's largest distillery, produces delicious gin and whisky. There's also a great restaurant on site here.

Nyborg Slot
🕸 🏠 Slotsgade 34 🚫 For renovation until 2021 🌐 nyborgslot.dk

Nyborg Destilleri
🕸 🏠 Holmens Boulevard 11 🕐 11am–10pm Wed–Sat, 11am–4pm Sun 🌐 nyborg destilleri.com

↑ Colourful houses along a cobbled street in Faaborg

❺ Kerteminde

D6 🚌 ℹ Strandvejen 6; www.visitkerteminde.dk

Much of this pretty seaside town is clustered around the 15th-century Sankt Laurentius Kirke (Church). One of the main attractions is **Fjord&Bælt**, a sea-life centre built in 1997. A 50-m- (164-ft-) long tunnel with large windows allows visitors to walk beneath the fjord and enjoy the underwater view. The **Johannes Larsen Museum** contains many paintings by the famous Danish painter (1867–1961), who once lived in Kerteminde.

Four kilometres (2 miles) southwest of Kerteminde is the Ladbyskibet, a 22-m- (72-ft-) long Viking ship that dates from the 10th century and was used as the tomb of a Viking chieftain.

Fjord&Bælt

⊛ 🏠 Margrethes Plads 1 ⏰ Feb-Jun & Sep-Nov: 10am-4pm Tue-Sun; Jul-Aug: 10am-5pm daily 🌐 fjord-baelt.dk

Johannes Larsen Museum

⊛ 🏠 Møllebakken 14 ⏰ Jun-Aug: 10am-5pm daily; Sep-May: 10am-4pm Tue-Sun 🌐 johanneslarsenmuseet.dk

← A boathouse sitting alongside idyllic waterfront homes in Nyborg

❻ Hindsholm

D5 🚌

The cliffs rising at the far end of the Hindsholm peninsula provide a splendid view over the coast and the island of Samsø. A little way inland is Marhøj Jættestue, an underground burial chamber from the 2nd century BC.

The small town of Viby, north of Assens, has a 19th-century windmill and an early Gothic church. According to legend, Marsk Stig, a hero of Danish folklore, was buried here in 1293. Before setting off for war, he left his wife in the care of the king, Erik Klipping. The king took the notion of "care" somewhat too far and when the knight returned he killed the king and was made an outlaw. Even his funeral had to be held in secret.

❼ Faaborg

D6 🚌 ℹ Torvet 19; www.visitfaaborg.com

Faaborg is a picturesque place with cobbled streets and half-timbered houses. Its famous monument, *Ymerbrønden*, sits in the market square and shows the figure of Ymer, a giant killed by Odin in Nordic mythology. The view from the town's Klokketårnet (Belfry) embraces the bay. The tower is all that remains of a medieval church.

Den Gamle Gaard is the house of a wealthy merchant from 1725. **Faaborg Museum** has a number of works by the "De Fynske Malere" group of Danish artists, which included Peter Hansen, Johannes Larsen and Fritz Syberg.

Den Gamle Gaard

⊛ 🏠 Holkegade 1 ⏰ Times vary, check website 🌐 ohavsmuseet.dk

Faaborg Museum

⊛ 🏠 Grønnegade 75 ⏰ Jul & Aug: 10am-5pm Tue-Sun; Sep-Jun: 11am-4pm Tue-Sun 🌐 faaborgmuseum.dk

---

EAT

Lieffroy

One of the best dining experiences on the island, Lieffroy serves French cuisine with local produce. The waterfront manor is stunning.

D6 🏠 Skræddergyden 34, Nyborg 🌐 lieffroy.dk

Ⓚ Ⓚ Ⓚ

Berthed boats lining
a jetty in Svendborg's
busy marina

> The island of Langeland has a number
> of good beaches and cycling paths.
> Windmills are dotted here and there,
> along with quaint hamlets and farms.

8
Svendborg

D6 🚊🚌 ℹ️ **Havnepladsen
2; www.visitsvendborg.dk**

Funen's second-largest town,
Svendborg is a busy port and
has strong links with shipbuilding. In the 19th century
its boatyards produced half
of all Danish vessels.

Most of the sights are within
reach of Torvet, the market
square. Closest is the 13th-
century Vor Frue Kirke, which
has a carillon consisting of 27
bells. Just west of Vor Frue Kirke
is Anne Hvides Gård, a half-
timbered building dating from
1560. **SAK Kunstbygningen**
(SAK Art Exhibitions) displays
works by the Danish sculptor
Kai Nielsen (1882–1924), who
was born in Svendborg. Other
museums include Naturama, a
natural history museum, and
Forsorgsmuseet, built in 1872
as a "poor farm". In 1906 there
were 450 such institutions in
Denmark; this, the only extant
one, houses a museum telling
the story of the country's poor.

SAK Kunstbygningen
⊛ 🅰️ Vestergade 27 📞 62 22
44 70 🕐 11am–4pm Tue–Sun

Forsorgsmuseet
⊛⊛⊛⊛🕐 🅰️ Viebæltegård
Grubbemøllevej 13 🕐 Mid-
Feb–late Dec: 10am–4pm
Tue–Sun 🆆 svendborg-
museum.dk

9
Tåsinge

D7 🚌

The major local attraction on
the island of Tåsinge, linked by
bridge to Funen and Langeland,
is **Valdemars Slot**, built in 1644
by Christian IV for his favourite
son Valdemar.

In the 1670s the king gave
the castle to Admiral Niels Juel
in recognition of his success
in the Battle of Køge Bay. The
castle has remained in the
hands of the Juel family ever
since. The royal apartments,
reception rooms and kitchens
are open to the public. In the
attic there is a collection of
trophies from African safaris,
and the quarters around the
lake house a small museum.

Near the castle, heading for
Svendborg, is the fishing port
of Troense. Its most attractive
street, Grønnegade, is lined
with half-timbered houses.

In Bregninge, the Tåsinge
Museum illustrates life at sea;
it also tells of the ill-fated love
affair between circus performer
Elvira Madigan and Swedish
lieutenant Sixten Sparre.

Valdemars Slot
⊛ 🅰️ Slotsalleén 100, Troense
🕐 May–Aug: 10am–5pm Tue–
Sun 🆆 valdemarsslot.dk

10
Langeland

E7 🚌🚌 ℹ️ **Rudkøbing
Torvet 5; www.langeland.
dk**

The island of Langeland has
a number of good beaches
and cycling paths. Windmills
are dotted here and there,
along with quaint hamlets
and farms. Off the southeast
coast of Funen, it can be
reached by bridge or from
Lolland by ferry.

The capital, Rudkøbing, is
the island's only sizeable
town. Its most famous citizen
was Hans Christian Ørsted
(1777–1851), a physicist who
made major advances in
electromagnetism. The house
in which he was born, **Det
Gamle Apotek** (The Old

→

Attractive huts
fringing a quiet
beach in Marstal

Pharmacy), has been arranged to re-create an 18th-century pharmacist's shop and herb garden. From here it is only a short distance to the market square, with its 19th-century town hall and a church founded in 1105.

Some 10 km (6 miles) north of Rudkøbing is Tranekær, whose main attraction is Tranekær Slot, a pink-coloured castle that dates from around 1200. About 30 km (18 miles) further south is the **Koldkrigsmuseum** (Cold War Museum), where you can explore a submarine and a bunker.

Det Gamle Apotek
⊛ ⊛ 🄰 Brogade 15, Rudkøbing 🅲 63 51 63 00 🄲 For guided tours (Jul)

Koldkrigsmuseum
🄰 Vognsbjergvej 4B, Bagenkop 🄲 Apr & Oct: 10am–4pm daily; May–Sep: 10am–5pm 🅆 langelandsfortet.dk

---

⑪
Marstal
🄰 D7 🄰 Ærø 🚢🚌 🄵 62 52 13 00

Marstal is the largest town on the island of Ærø. Its history has long been associated with the sea, and in the 18th century it was a busy port with about 300 ships arriving every year.

🔍 HIDDEN GEM
Dukkehuset

Ærøskøbing is known for its narrow, cobbled streets and picturesque architecture. The town's most eccentric dwelling is a tiny, crooked, half-timbered cottage known as Dukkehuset (Dolls' House) at Smedegade 37. The owner, who lives next door, rents it out.

The **Søfartmuseum** (Maritime Museum) occupies four buildings near the harbour and has a splendid collection of items, including model schooners and seafaring paintings.

The dependence of the locals on the sea is also apparent in the church on Kirkestræde, built in 1738. The altarpiece depicts Christ calming the rough waves, and there are votive sailing ships hanging up around the building. Gravestones of local sailors can be seen outside. The church clock was created by Jens Olsen, who built the World Clock in the Rådhus in Copenhagen (p102).

Søfartmuseum
⊛ 🄰 Prinsensgade 1 🄲 Times vary, check website 🅆 marmus.dk

---

⑫
Ærøskøbing
🄰 D7 🄰 Ærø 🚢🚌 🄵 Ærøskøbing Havn 4; 62 52 13 00

Many of the 17th-century houses lining the cobbled streets of Ærøskøbing are a reminder of times gone by when it was a prosperous merchant town. The oldest house is from 1645 and can be found at Søndergade 36. Also in Smedegade is **Flaske-Peters Samling**, a museum devoted to Peter Jacobsen, who first went to sea at the age of 16. Known as "Bottle Peter", he created about 1,700 ships in bottles before he died in 1960. Also in the museum is the cross he made for his own grave. The **Ærø Museum** has displays on the history of the island and its people, including a collection of paintings from the 19th century.

Flaske-Peters Samling
⊛ 🄰 Smedegade 22 🄲 81 55 59 72 🄲 May, Jun & Sep: 11am–3pm; Jul & Aug: 10am–4pm daily

Ærø Museum
⊛ 🄰 Søndergade 16 🄲 62 52 29 50 🄲 Times vary, call ahead

SOUTHERN AND CENTRAL JUTLAND

Jutland derives its name from the Jutes, a Germanic tribe that once inhabited this peninsula. When the Vikings, who occupied the islands to the east, began to encroach on this territory, the mixing of the two tribes gave rise to the Danes as a distinct people. After Denmark's defeat during the Schleswig Wars in 1864, Jutland was occupied by Prussia, and subsequently, as part of Schleswig, remained under German control. It was not until a plebiscite in 1920 that it once more became part of the kingdom of Denmark. After the final resolution of this Danish-German border dispute, many families decided to remain on the "other" side. The expatriate minorities are still active on both sides of the border.

As well as the scenic lowlands and undulating hills and meadows found on the eastern side of central Jutland, this region has beautifully preserved medieval towns, traditional hamlets, parks, castles and ancient Viking burial grounds.

On the islands of Fanø and Rømø the influence of the nearby Netherlands can be seen in the tiles decorating some of the houses. The Wadden Sea around these islands makes for excellent exploration, either on a seal or oyster safari. The milder east coast features wealthy borough towns with fine museums.

SOUTHERN AND CENTRAL JUTLAND

Must Sees

1 Aarhus
2 Ribe
3 LEGOLAND®

Experience More

4 Ebeltoft
5 Moesgård Museum
6 Horsens
7 Silkeborg Lake District
8 Silkeborg
9 Givskud Zoo
10 Herning
11 Ringkøbing Fjord
12 Jelling
13 Vejle
14 Rømø
15 Fanø
16 Esbjerg
17 Kolding
18 Tønder
19 Sønderborg
20 Haderslev
21 Fredericia

FUNEN
p194

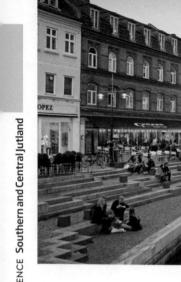

↑ Relaxing and enjoying the social scene along Aarhus river at dusk

❶

AARHUS

🅐D4 🚉Aarhus H 🚌 🛈Banegårdspladsen 20; www.visitaarhus.com

Denmark's second-largest city dates back to Viking times and was called Aros, meaning "at the river's mouth". Today Aarhus boasts a vibrant cultural life, with innovative museums and venues, as well as lively cafés and bars. The city is also a major centre for wind energy.

① 🏍

Rådhus

🅐Rådhuspladsen
Ⓦaarhus.dk/Aarhus-Raadhus

The city hall, a prime example of Danish Modernism, was designed by Arne Jacobsen and Erik Møller. Completed in

PICTURE PERFECT
Møllestien

In summer, head to Møllestien. Roses grow around the doorways of the 18th-century cottages, painted pink, blue and orange, that line this picturesque cobbled lane. Perfect Instagram fodder.

1941, the building is clad with dark Norwegian marble and topped with a rectangular clock tower, which affords a good view of the city. The interior has a lighter feel and the large council chamber and Civic Room are both worth seeking out.

② 🏛 🍽 🖥

Musikhuset

🅐Thomas Jensens Allé 2
Ⓒ11am-6pm daily
Ⓦmusikhusetaarhus.dk

The city's concert hall is one of Denmark's foremost cultural centres. The glass-fronted building opened in 1982 and is home to the prestigious Jutland Opera Company and Aarhus Symphony Orchestra,

which holds concerts most Thursday evenings. The building is worth visiting if only to see its vast glazed hall, planted with luxuriant palm trees. The centre features its own café, which often has concerts, and a restaurant, the Richter, named after Johan Richter, the main architect of the building.

③ 🏛

Vikingemuseet

🅐Sankt Clemens Torv
Ⓒ10:15am-4pm Mon-Fri,
10:15am-5pm Sat & Sun
Ⓦvikingemuseet.dk

In a building across from the cathedral, next to the Nordea Bank, is this museum devoted to the Viking era. The prime exhibit is a section of archaeological excavation that was carried out in Sankt Clemens Torv, a square named after the city's patron saint. Fragments of the original Viking ramparts, discovered in 1964, are on display along with items dating from AD 900 to 1400 including a skeleton, a reconstructed house, pottery and runic stones. Similar discoveries at nearby Store Torv have confirmed the importance of Aarhus as a major centre of Viking culture.

④
Vor Frue Kirke

📍 Frue Kirkeplads 🕐 May-Sep: 10am-4pm Mon-Fri; Oct-Apr: 10am-2pm Mon-Fri, 10am-noon Sat
🌐 aarhusvorfrue.dk

Vor Frue Kirke is a complex of three churches in a former Dominican monastery. The oldest section of this complex is the 11th-century Roman-esque stone crypt. The highlight here is a replica of an early crucifix featuring a Christ with Viking plaits. The star adornment inside the church is a 16th-century wooden altarpiece carved by Claus Berg.

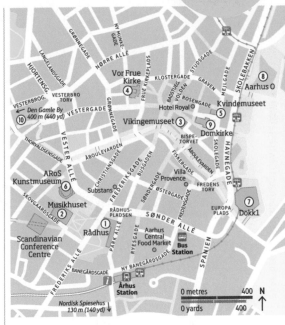

⑤ 🔖📺🖥️
Kvindemuseet

📍 Domkirkeplads 5 🕐 10am-5pm Mon-Sat (to 8pm Wed), 10am-4pm Sun 🌐 kvindemuseet.dk

The Women's Museum is at the forefront of worldwide debate, discussion, research and education surrounding sex, gender and women's issues. It has established a reputation for its imaginative exhibitions, events and campaigns relating to women's issues. Denmark is famed for its approach to equality but this has not always been the case, and this museum offers a brilliant exploration of the country's suffrage history. Since 1984 the museum has gathered a collection of objects, photographs and documents that illustrate the many challenges facing women, past and present, in Denmark and all across the world. The museum is based in the former City Hall. There is also a hands-on exhibition aimed at and about children, and a charming, vintage-style café.

↑ Exhibits housed under historic beams at Kvindemuset

→
Olafur Eliasson's colourful walkway circling the ARoS Kunstmuseum

⑥ 🛝 🍽
ARoS Kunstmuseum

📍 Aros Allé 2 🕐 10am–5pm Tue–Sun (to 10pm Wed)
🌐 aros.dk

This stunning gallery occupies ten storeys and is crowned with a circular rainbow-coloured walkway. Designed by Olafur Eliasson, *Your rainbow panorama* offers unique and breathtaking views of Aarhus. The collection inside spans the Golden Age to the present day, with modern art pieces stealing the show.

⑦ 🛝 🖥
Dokk1

📍 Hack Kampmanns Plads 2
🕐 8am–10pm Mon–Fri, 10am–6pm Sat & Sun
🌐 dokk1.dk

This seven-sided glass-and-concrete building, completed in 2015, contrasts dramatically with the red brick and green copper of Aarhus's older buildings. Looming majestically over the old harbour, it's the anchor of Aarhus's ambitious, rejuvenated waterfront, and is a triumph of Modernist

2017

The year that Aarhus held the title of European Capital of Culture.

Scandinavian design, worth visiting for its architecture alone. The building is surrounded by a changing array of art installations, and there are open-air play areas for families on its terraces. Dokk1 also houses the city's public library and the council's citizens' services department.

⑧ 🛝
Aarhus Ø

This exciting project on the city's waterfront is a work in progress. Dubbed Aarhus Ø, the area has numerous archi-tectural highlights, including the aptly named Iceberg, an apartment block that looks like the set for a sci-fi movie. There's also the star-shaped Navitas science and inno-vation campus. Visitors can

↑ The stunningly modern Dokk1 building, illuminated at night

EAT

Substans

There are two imaginative menus to choose from here, both featuring beautifully presented dishes. Dishes include scallops with tomatoes and cod with carrot, hazelnut and lovage.

🏠 Frederiksgade 74
🕐 Lunch, Sun-Tue
🌐 restaurant substans.dk

Ⓚ Ⓚ Ⓚ

Aarhus Central Food Market

This food market is a hive of activity. Food stalls are based in and outside and offer an exciting choice of both Danish and international snacks, drinks and street food. Live music frequently acts as an accompaniment.

🏠 Skt Knuds Torv 7-9
🌐 aarhuscentral foodmarket.dk

Ⓚ Ⓚ Ⓚ

Nordisk Spisehus

Collaborating with Michelin-starred chefs from across the globe, Nordisk Spisehus promises innovative New Nordic cuisine. Menus change monthly, but diners can expect fine seafood and ingredients such as caviar and wild-foraged fungi all year round.

🏠 M P Bruuns Gade 31
🕐 Sun 🌐 nordisk spisehus.dk

Ⓚ Ⓚ Ⓚ

ascend the observation tower at Bassin 7 – a striking metal structure cantilevered out over the water – for a view of the waterfront. In July and August the Harbour Bath's 50-m (164-ft) open-air pool is popular with swimmers.

---

⑨

Domkirke

🏠 Store Torv 🕐 May-Sep: 9:30am-4pm Mon-Fri; Oct-Dec: 10am-3pm Mon & Wed-Sat, 10:30am-2pm Tue 🌐 aarhus-domkirke.dk

Aarhus's main house of worship is at the heart of the city's oldest district. The original cathedral was built in 1201 but was destroyed by fire in the 14th century. It was rebuilt in the late 15th century in a Gothic style, and is easily Denmark's longest cathedral, with a nave that spans nearly 100 m (328 ft). Until the end of the 16th century most of the cathedral walls were covered with frescoes. Sadly, these were largely whitewashed over during the Reformation, but fortunately many have since been restored.

The five-panel altarpiece dates from 1479 and is the work of Bernt Notke of Lübeck. The Baroque pipe organ dates from 1730.

---

⑩

Den Gamle By

🏠 Viborgvej 2 🕐 Times vary, check website 🌐 dengamleby.dk

This open-air museum has 75 half-timbered houses from the 17th, 18th and 19th centuries, plus neighbourhoods from 1927 and 1974. One exhibit that shouldn't be missed is a Danish town that looks as it would have done in the 19th century at the time of Hans Christian Andersen.

Aside from exploring the scenery, there are opportunities to enjoy a ride on a horse-drawn wagon, visit workshops and try your hand at various crafts, and learn more in a number of small museums. The atmosphere at Den Gamle By is especially vibrant during the Living History season (Easter–Dec), when actors play key characters in the town, such as the vicar and the town crier.

②

RIBE

AB6 **A**Esbjerg Municipality **A** **i**Torvet 3; www.
visitribe.com

This is Scandinavia's oldest town and makes for a
lovely visit. Ribe was once a thriving river port and its
population takes pride in the town's Viking, mercantile
and early Christian heritage. Crooked, half-timbered
houses fronted with painted doors line the labyrinth
of cobbled streets and hint at the town's historic past.

①

Ribe Domkirke

ATorvet **O**Apr & Oct:
11am–4pm daily; May–mid-
Sep: 10am–5pm daily; Nov–
mid-Mar: 11am–3pm daily
Wribe-domkirke.dk

Bells chime at midday and
at 3pm from Ribe's medieval
cathedral in memory of Queen
Dagmar, wife of Valdemar II
(1170–1241). She died in child-
birth here in Ribe, in 1212, and
her image stands within, next
to that of her husband. Other
relics here include the oldest
royal tombstone in Scandinavia, that of Christoffer I.
    Visitors can climb to the top
of the 14th-century bell tower
for stunning views of the
Wadden Sea. The cathedral's

foundations were laid around
1150 on the site of a wooden
church built in AD 856 by
St Ansgar, one of the earliest
Christian missionaries to
Scandinavia. It was completed
around 1250.

②

Det Gamle Rådhus

AVon Stockens Plads
OTimes vary, check
website **W**detgamle
raadhusiribe.dk

The Old Town Hall is a gracious
red-brick building standing
opposite the cathedral. Built
in the late 15th century, it
stands as a reminder of Ribe's
past prosperity, with polished
wooden beams supporting its

coffered ceiling. A collection of
headsmen's swords and instruments of torture awaits inside.

③

Ribe Kunstmuseum

ASct Nicolajgade 10
OSep–Jun: 11am–4pm
Tue–Sun; Jul–Aug 11am–
5pm daily **W**ribe
kunstmuseum.dk

The town's stunning art
gallery houses a collection of
Danish art dating from 1750
to 1950, and houses examples
of work by painters from the
Skagen School and the
Golden Age. Highlights of
the collection include work

↑ Light and airy
interior of the Ribe
Kunstmuseum

Did You Know?

Night watchmen have patrolled the streets of Ribe since the 14th century. You can join them in summer.

by Michael Anker (1849-1927), renowned for his portrayals of fishing folk. Be sure to enjoy the gallery garden.

---

④ 🎨 Ⓜ

Ribes Vikinger

🏛 Odin Plads 1 🕐 Jun-Aug: 10am-5pm daily; Sep-May: 10am-4pm Tue-Sun 🌐 ribesvikinger.dk

This engaging museum re-creates the hustle and bustle of Ribe's oldest market square, a central part of life in the Viking trading port from AD 700 to 1700. There are guided tours and appealing hands-on activities for younger visitors.

---

⑤ 🎨 Ⓜ

Ribe Vikingecenter

🏛 Lustrupvej 4 🕐 Times vary, check website 🌐 ribevikingecenter.dk

The world of Ribe's Viking explorers, traders and

← An attractive waterfront scene in Ribe, with its half-timbered houses

warriors comes to life at this open-air museum, around 2 km (1.2 miles) from the town centre. Visitors can try their hand at age-old skills such as archery, wood-whittling and metalwork and watch Viking warriors in mock combat.

---

⑥ 🎨 Ⓜ

Vadehavscentret

🏛 Okholmvej 5, Vester Vedsted 🕐 10am-4pm daily 🌐 vadehavscentret.dk

This is the jumping-off point for adventures in the unique marine environment of the Wadden Sea, a region of sandbanks, islands and tidal lagoons, where seals bask at low tide and huge flocks of wading water birds patrol the shoreline. Tours from the Wadden Sea Centre introduce visitors to wildlife and local seafood, such as oysters. The centre's exhibition explains everything related with the sea, from wildlife to the weather.

Must See

EAT

Kolvig

Inside this historic merchant's factory on the riverfront, Kolvig's chefs specialize in traditional Danish cuisine using ingredients from the Wadden Sea. The terrace is a particularly lovely spot.

🏛 Mellemdammen 13 🕐 Sun 🌐 kolvig.dk

Ⓚ Ⓚ Ⓚ

Porsborgs

Tucked in the heart of the old town, opposite the Domkirke, this cozy vaulted cellar café is popular with both locals and visitors alike. Seasonal, locally-sourced dishes are best washed down with a Danish craft brew.

🏛 Torvet 3 🌐 pbvinbar.dk

Ⓚ Ⓚ Ⓚ

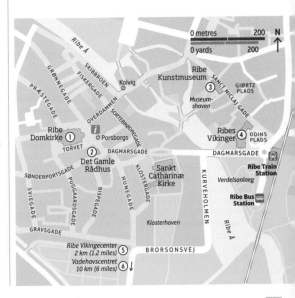

TOP 5 UNMISSABLE ATTRACTIONS

Miniland
Experience the world in miniature; visit Copenhagen's Nyhavn, New York's Statue of Liberty and London's Tower Bridge.

LEGO® Train
Jump aboard the LEGO® train to see all the park's sights – great if you're pressed for time.

Pirate Splash Battle
Take a boat trip past the dastardly LEGO® pirates. Beware of the water cannons; if you don't fire first, you'll be shot at!

King's Castle Show
This action-filled medieval spectacular stars stuntmen.

Polar X-plorer
This dizzying roller coaster swoops over Polar Land's amazing animal residents.

LEGOLAND®

C5 ⬥ Nordmarksvej 9, 7190 Billund ⬥ Billund ⬥ Times vary, check website ⬥ legoland.dk

Billund's LEGOLAND® is a mini-brick mecca, loved by little and big kids alike. Take a spin on one of the park's rides, visit iconic landmarks built entirely of LEGO® bricks or build your own masterpiece. All sorts of family magic awaits at one of Denmark's most popular attractions.

LEGO® bricks were invented in the 1930s by Danish toymaker Ole Kirk Christiansen. The company's name derives from the Danish phrase "leg godt", which means "play well", and is today one of the world's most famous brands. Denmark's Billund amusement park opened in 1968 and was followed by a spate of similar parks across the world. The various areas of the park are themed, from the medieval castle of Knights' Kingdom and the colourful Duplo Land playground, to the aquarium at Atlantis and the reconstructed cities and landmarks of Miniland. There are a variety of eateries offering sustenance after all that adventure, all with their own LEGO® theme. Note that some rides close at dusk before the rest of the park.

INSIDER TIP
Every Little Helps

Advance online tickets are always cheaper than those bought on the door on the day. Family passes are also available online and are cheaper than individual tickets.

Did You Know?

20 million LEGO® bricks
are snapped together
in Miniland.

↑ Enjoying the magical
surroundings of
LEGOLAND®Billund

1 Miniland recreates many
famous destinations, like
Copenhagen's Nyhavn.

2 The Haunted House
includes lots of interactive
fun, all made of mini-bricks.

3 Kids can wreak havoc at
the Pirate Splash Battle.

STAY

Hotel LEGOLAND®
Playfully decorated
rooms promise a unique
night's sleep at Hotel
LEGOLAND®. Themes
include knights, pirates
and princesses,
promising something
for everyone. There are
also "business" rooms
for those preferring a
more sedate stay.

⌂LEGOLAND®,
Nordmarksvej, 7190
Billund ⊡LEGOLAND.dk

Ⓚ Ⓚ Ⓚ

EXPERIENCE MORE

❹ Ebeltoft

🗺D4 🚌 🛈S A Jensens Vej 3; 86 34 14 00

Ebeltoft, which forms part of the Mols Bjerge national park, is over 700 years old. Many of the town's cobbled streets are lined with 17th-century half-timbered houses and Ebeltoft houses Denmark's smallest *rådhus* (town hall).

In the harbour you'll find **Fregatten Jylland**, a restored wooden ship that took part in the Battle of Helgoland in 1864. Groups can arrange overnight stays on board and get a sense of a sailor's life. A large museum annex focuses on maritime history. The nearby **Glasmuseet** specializes in contemporary glass artworks, including several pieces by Dale Chihuly and Harvey Littleton.

Fregatten Jylland

⊗ 🏠S A Jensen Vej 2-4 🕒Mid-Feb-Nov: 10am-4pm daily (late Jun-Aug: to 6pm); Dec: 10am-4pm Sat & Sun 🌐fregatten-jylland.dk

Glasmuseet

⊗ 🏠Strandvejen 8 🕒Apr-Oct: 10am-5pm daily (Jul-Aug: to 6pm); Nov-Mar: 10am-4pm Wed-Sun 🌐glasmuseet.dk

❺
Moesgård Museum

🗺D4 🏠7 km (4 miles) south of Aarhus 🌐moesmus.dk

This large prehistoric museum is situated on a hill known as Hill of the Elves, a short drive south of Aarhus. There are many highlights, ranging from its collection of runic stones, the largest in Scandinavia, to a hoard of swords, axes, shields and other items found at Illerup Ådal, near Skanderborg, from about 200 AD. Its star exhibit is Grauballe Man, a mummified body from around 80 BC discovered in a bog.

In late July, Moesgård is the venue for a lively and entertaining Viking festival, Vikingtræf, which features battles, a Viking marketplace and performing horses.

❻ Horsens

🗺C5 🏠38 km (24 miles) south of Aarhus 🚍🚌 🛈Fussingsvej 8; www.visithorsens.dk

This is the birthplace of Vitus Bering (1681–1741), the Danish explorer who discovered Alaska and the straits that separate it from Siberia (these were subsequently named after him). The guns from Bering's ship stand in the town's park and mementos from his travels are on display in **Horsens Museum**.

Pretty cobbled streets and half-timbered houses of Ebeltoft ↑

← Wild swimmers taking a dip in the waters of Silkeborg Lake District

Did You Know?

The average Dane lights 3.5 kg (8 lb) of candles per year, more than any other nationality.

Horsens Museum

◈ 🏠 Sundvej 1A 🕐 Jul–Aug: 10am–4pm daily; Sep–Jun: 11am–4pm Tue–Sun 🌐 horsensmuseum.dk

7

Silkeborg Lake District

🅰 C4

The stretch between Silkeborg and Skanderborg and the area to the north is a land of lakes and hills known as Søhøjlandet. Here, you will find Jutland's largest lake, the Mossø, as well as Denmark's longest river, the Gudenå (176 km/109 miles). The Lake District also has some of the country's highest peaks. In summer it is a favourite destination for canoeists and cyclists, as well as hikers, all of whom make the most of the lakeland scenery.

Gjern is known for its vintage car museum (with about 70 models, the oldest dating from the early 20th century), while Tange Sø boasts Elmuseet, an electricity museum situated next to the country's largest power station.

Other places worth visiting in the Lake District include the church in Veng, which was built around 1100 and is thought to be the oldest monastery in Denmark, and, on the shores of the Mossø, the ruins of Øm Kloster, the most well-preserved Cistercian monastery in Denmark.

8

Silkeborg

🅰 C4 🏠🚆 ℹ️ Østergade 13; www.silkeborg.com

Silkeborg owes much of its past prosperity to the paper factory, built in 1846, which was at one time powered by the local river. **Museum Silkeborg** occupies a former manor built in 1767. Most visitors head straight for the Tollund Man, one of the best-preserved prehistoric bodies in the world.

The city is also famous for its art galleries, including **Museum Jorn**, with works by the Danish artist Asger Jorn and other members of the CoBrA movement.

In summer a 19th-century paddle steamer sails through the lakes to Himmelbjerget, where a 25-m- (82-ft-) high tower offers great views.

Museum Silkeborg

◈ 🏠 Hovedgårdsvej 7 🕐 10am–5pm daily 🌐 museumsilkeborg.dk

Museum Jorn

◈⏰ 🏠 Gudenåvej 7–9 🕐 11am–5pm Tue–Fri, 10am–5pm Sat & Sun 🌐 museumjorn.dk

---

CYCLING IN THE SILKEBORG LAKE DISTRICT

It's a known fact that many Danes love to cycle, and a popular year-round destination for cycling is the splendid Lake District around Ry, Silkeborg and Skanderborg. Here 250 km (155 miles) of trails loop through lush forests, across verdant meadows and around luminous lakes. A 41-km (25-mile) day trip around Lake Julsø is a great way to soak up the scenery. An alternative is a 23-km (14-mile) tour around Lake Salten Langsø, where hilly woodland alternates with flat moorland. Silkenborg.com and visitskanderborg.com are good resources for route maps.

EAT

Brdr. Price
Beloved celebrity chefs Adam and James Price run this stylish bistro in the town square. In addition to fresh oysters and an excellent wine list, the kitchen turns out time-honoured Danish dishes.

🅐B4 🅠Torvet 3, Herning 🅦brdr-price.dk

Ⓚ Ⓚ Ⓚ

Bryggeriet
Home-brewed, freshly tapped beer is the focus in this gastro pub on the town square. But don't miss the food: you'll relish hearty dishes designed for brew pairings.

🅐B4 🅠Torvet 3C, Herning 🅒Sun 🅦bryggeriet.dk

Ⓚ Ⓚ Ⓚ

Givskud Zoo

🅐C5 🅠Løveparken 🅒Apr–mid-Oct: from 10am daily (closing times vary, check website) 🅦givskudzoo.dk

A short way north of Jelling is Givskud Zoo (or Zootopia), home to the largest pride of lions in Scandinavia as well as some 700 other animals representing 70 species. Givskud is part-zoo, part-safari park, and many animals wander freely. Fenced-off areas provide children with the opportunity to stroke some of the park's more domesticated animals or have fun feeding the camels.

Givskud Zoo is also a major scientific establishment with around 50 endangered species. One of its programmes resulted in deer and antelope reared at the park being reintroduced into the wilds of Pakistan in the late 1980s.

10 Herning

🅐B4 🅐🚌 🅘Østergade 21; www.visitherning.dk

The town of Herning was established in the late 19th century following the arrival of the railway. Herning has twice been named Denmark's "city of the year" and is home to Messecenter Herning, the largest entertainment complex and exhibition centre in Scandinavia. **Frilandsmuseet** tells the story of the town as well as allowing you to explore the history and archaeology of the region. Housed in a building designed by American architect Steven Holl, the **HEART Herning Museum of Contemporary Art** is known for exhibiting and preserving art from the mid-20th century onwards, including works by artists like Carl-Henning Pedersen, a representative of the CoBrA movement.

> Herning has twice been named Denmark's "city of the year" and is home to Messecenter Herning, the largest entertainment complex and exhibition centre in Scandinavia.

← Works on display at the HEART Herning Museum of Contemporary Art

Frilandsmuseet
⊕ ⌂ Museumgade 32
🕐 10am–4:30pm Tue–Fri, 11am–4:30pm Sat & Sun (Jul: also Mon) 🖿 museummidtjylland.dk

HEART Herning Museum of Contemporary Art
⊕ ⌂ Birk Centerpark 8
🕐 10am–5pm Tue–Sun
🖿 heartmus.dk

11
Ringkøbing Fjord
🅰 A4 🛈 Ringkøbing, Torvet 22; Hvide Sande, Nørregade 2B; www.visitvest.dk

A thin strip of land separates Ringkøbing Fjord from the North Sea. This sandy spit is about 1 km (half a mile) wide and has many summer cottages tucked into the dunes. The only water access between the sea and the fjord is through a channel in the town of Hvide Sande. Ringkøbing Fjord is popular with windsurfers and the calm waters of the bay are suitable for novices; the North Sea is more challenging.

On the bay's northern shore is Ringkøbing, a former port, now an inland harbour. Standing in Torvet, the main square, are some of the town's most historic buildings, including Hotel Ringkøbing (1600). The **Ringkøbing-Skjern Museum** is a collective of 14 different museums and historical sites around Ringkøbing Fjord that promote local cultural history.

Fiskeriets Hus (House of Fisheries) at Hvide Sande has a display of specimens from the North Sea and fjord waters. A paved footpath, suitable for wheelchairs, leads from here to Troldbjerg, the town's main viewpoint. Another good view is from the lighthouse on the Nørre Lyngvig dune, 5 km (3 miles) north of Hvide Sande.

The southern marshes of the fjord form the Tipperne Nature Reserve. Access is restricted to a few hours on Friday or Sunday mornings so as not to disturb the birds.

Ringkøbing-Skjern Museum
⊕ ⌂ Herningvej 4
🕐 Times vary, check website
🖿 levendehistorie.dk

Fiskeriets Hus
⊕ ⌂ Nørregade 2B, Hvide Sande 🕐 10am–5pm daily (Nov–Easter: to 4pm)
🖿 fiskerietshus.dk

→ An engraved depiction of Christ on a replica 10th-century Jelling stone

---

12
Jelling
🅰 C5 🚌 🛈 Gormsgade 23; www.visitvejle.com

For Danes Jelling is a special place: this unassuming village served as the royal seat of Gorm the Old, a 10th-century Viking who conquered Jutland, Funen and Zealand to create a new dynasty that has ruled Denmark to this day.

Jelling Kirke and the two burial mounds beyond it have revealed much of Denmark's ancient history. In the late 1970s, archaeologists found what are thought to be Gorm's remains on the site. These were reburied under the floor of Jelling Kirke and marked with a silver sign. Close to the church are two runic stones. The larger one, known as the "Danes' Baptism Certificate", was erected in AD 965 by Gorm's son, Harald Bluetooth. Visible on the stone is a depiction of Christ – probably the oldest in Scandinavia – and an inscription considered to be the first written record of the word "Denmark". The complex was declared a UNESCO World Heritage Site in 1994.

Kongernes Jelling, an exhibition centre opposite the church, is devoted to the history of the Vikings and the Danish monarchy.

The atmosphere of Jelling is best enjoyed during the annual Viking Fair, a weekend-long event in July. A further reminder of Denmark's past is at Fårup lake, where a full-scale replica of a Viking ship takes visitors on cruises of the lake.

Jelling Kirke
⌂ Thyrasvej 1 🕐 8am–5pm Mon–Sat (May–Aug: to 8pm), noon–5pm Sun
🖿 jellingkirke.dk

Kongernes Jelling
⊕ ⌂ Gormsgade 23 🕐 Times vary, check website
🖿 natmus.dk

Sun setting over Hvide Sande, near Ringkøbing Fjord

⑬
Vejle

▲C5 🚗🚌 ℹ️Banegårds-
pladsen 6; www.visitvejle.
com

Vejle is loved for its beech
trees (the national tree and
the first to burst into leaf in
springtime). The town also
makes a good base for visiting
LEGOLAND® (p214) and Jelling
(p219). Its main point of
interest is Sankt Nicolai Kirke,
a 13th-century Gothic church,
which surprisingly displays the
human remains of a woman,
known as Haraldskær Woman.
The body was found in 1835 in
a peat bog; forensic tests have
revealed that the woman lived
around 450 BC.

Rådhustorvet, Vejle's main
square, contains the town hall,
which stands on the site of a
Dominican monastery. The
Vejle Museum is spread over
a number of locations in town.
The exhibition in Den Smidtske
Gard, an early 19th-century
burgher's residence, covers 800
years of Vejle's history. On the
edge of town, Vejle Vindmølle,
built in 1890, is also part of
the museum.

The Ecolarium aims to raise
awareness of environmental
issues and alternative energy.

Ravninge Broen is a Viking-era
bridge in the Ravninge Enge
(Meadows) exhibition centre.

Vejle Museum

🕐Times vary, check website
🌐vejlemuseerne.dk

⑭
Rømø

▲B6 🚌 ℹ️Nørre Frankel 1;
www.romo.dk

The largest Danish island in
the North Sea, Rømø was a
prosperous whaling base in
the 18th century. Its western
shores are fringed with wide
stretches of beach. The island
is connected to Jutland by a
causeway that passes through
marshland rich in birdlife.

In the village of Toftum is the
Kommandørgården (Captain's
House), which dates from 1748
and has retained some of its
original interior decor, including
wall coverings consisting of
4,000 Dutch tiles. A short way
north, in the hamlet of Juvre,
is a whale jawbone fence from
1772. In Kirkeby, next to the
walls that surround the late-
Gothic church, are whalers'
gravestones from Greenland.
The histories of captains have
been carved by local artists.

The main point of interest at
the south end of the island is
Havneby, which has a labyrinth
park. A ferry goes from here
to the tranquil island of Sylt, in
Germany, just to the southwest.

⑮
Fanø

▲B6 🚌 ℹ️Skolevej 5-7,
Nordby; www.visitfanoe.dk

The island of Fanø may just be
even more beautiful than its
big sister Rømø, further south,
and boat-only access means
there are fewer tourists. The
traditional seafaring town of
Nordby is full of idyllic thatched
houses, blooming gardens, and
cobblestone streets lined with
boutiques and cafés. It is also
home to Fanø Krogaard, built
in 1664, one of the oldest inns
in Denmark. The other island
village, Sønderho, with its 18th–
19th-century architecture, has
been awarded Denmark's most
beautiful village and is worth a
wander. Fanø has some of the
longest beaches in Denmark;
the stretch from Fanø Bad to
Rindby Strand offers the best
swimming. Fanø is also famous
for the Fanø International Kite
Fliers Meeting, which takes
place in June.

↑ A boat in Esbjerg, with stylish, modern homes sitting on the water

16

Esbjerg

🅰B6 🚌🚆⛴ 🛈 Skolegade 33; www.visitesbjerg.dk

In 1868, the former fishing village of Esbjerg began to develop into a harbour from which Jutland's farmers and producers could export goods. Today it is one of Denmark's largest commercial ports.

Despite lacking a medieval district, Esbjerg has several places worth visiting. For years the town's main symbol was its **Vandtårnet** (Water Tower), which was erected in 1897.

Today, it serves as an observation platform, from which you can take in a panoramic view of Esbjerg. Close to the tower is the Musikhuset (Concert Hall), built in 1997.

The **Esbjerg Art Museum** contains one of Denmark's finest collections of Danish contemporary art. The **Fiskeri-og Søfartsmuseet** (Fisheries and Maritime Museum), 4 km (2 miles) northwest of the town centre, has a large aquarium and various marine-related displays. Most of the sealife in the aquarium comes from the North Sea. Its most popular inhabitants are the seals, most of which have been rescued. This vast museum complex also features a collection of navigation instruments and model vessels, a number of fishing boats placed outside the building and a reconstructed coastal lifeboat station. Outside the museum grounds, on the seashore, are four 9-m- (30-ft-) tall snow-white stylized figures of seated men, entitled *Man Meets the Sea*, created by Svend Wiig Hansen to mark the town's centennial in 1995. The maritime theme continues in the harbour, where the **Horns Rev Lightship** is moored.

←

Beautiful ink-hued skies over a dune beach in Fanø

Vandtårnet
♿ 🏠Havnegade 22 📞76 16 39 39 🕐Jun-mid-Sep: 10am-4pm Tue-Sun

Esbjerg Art Museum
♿ 🏠Havnegade 20 📞75 13 02 11 🕐10am-4pm Tue-Sun

Fiskeri-og Søfartsmuseet
♿ 🏠Saltvandsakvariet Tarphagevej 2-6 📞76 12 20 00 🕐10am-5pm daily (Jul-Aug: to 6pm)

Horns Rev Lightship
♿ 📞21 62 11 04 🕐Apr, Sep & Oct: 10am-noon Mon; May-Aug: 11am-4pm Mon-Fri

⑰ Kolding

🅰C5 🚌🚆 ℹAkseltorv 8; www.visitkolding.dk

Families often use Kolding as a base camp for LEGOLAND®, but it's worth visiting the town in its own right. The seaport's most famous landmark is the hilltop castle of Koldinghus, which was built as a fortification in the 1200s. More about the castle and the urban history of Kolding is told at the municipal museum, **Museet på Koldinghus**, housing a number of artifacts of local interest. Art lovers will appreciate the **Kunstmuseet Trapholt** on the outskirts of town, which is dedicated to visual arts, crafts and design. Perched above Kolding Fjord, there are spectacular views to enjoy.

Museet på Koldinghus

⊛ 🅰Markdanersgade 11 🕙10am–5pm daily 🌐koldinghus.dk

Kunstmuseet Trapholt

⊛ 🅰Æblehaven 23 🕙10am–5pm daily (to 8pm Wed) 🌐trapholt.dk

↑ Narrow alley between traditional, half-timber houses in Kolding

GREAT VIEW
Old Lille Bælt Bridge

Built in 1935, the Old Lillebælt Bridge offers one of the best photo ops over the Lille Bælt Strait, the narrow channel that snakes between the islands of Funen and Jutland.

⑱ Tønder

🅰B7 🚌🚆 ℹStoregade 2–4; www.romo.dk

Situated just 4 km (2.5 miles) from the border, Tønder has strong links to German culture. Founded as a fishing port in the Middle Ages, the town has survived floods, annexations, and economic crashes only to reinvent itself as the centre of lacemaking. Its most famous resident is the renowned furniture designer Hans J Wegner. Fine lace, tools, and many of Wegner's chairs are displayed in the art museum **Kunstmuseet i Tønder**. The town centre is a good place to begin exploring, with narrow streets and traditional houses. The best-known is Det Gamle Apotek (The Old Pharmacy) at Østergade 1, which has a Baroque doorway from 1671. The market square contains a 16th-century rådhus (town hall) and 16th-century Kristkirken.

Kunstmuseet i Tønder

⊛⊛⊛🅰Wegners Plads 1 🕙Jun–Aug: 10am–5pm daily; Sep–May: 10am–5pm Tue–Sun 🌐msj.dk

⑲ Sønderborg

🅰C7 🅰Als 🚌🚆 ℹPerlegade 50; www.visit sonderborg.com

Sønderborg (South Castle) owes its name to a **castle** built by Valdemar I in 1170.

→ Sun setting over the pretty waterfront town of Sønderborg

Today the town is popular with holiday-makers as it straddles the Als Sound. The Gendarmstien (Gendarme trail) along the coast towards Germany attracts many hikers.

The town's history is brought to life at the **Historiecenter Dybbøl Banke**. In the spring of 1864 the area was the scene of a fierce battle between Danish and Prussian forces. Dybbøl Mølle, a windmill that was damaged in the fighting, is now regarded as a national symbol. Sønderborg itself was nearly destroyed and southern Jutland annexed by Prussia and later Germany before being returned in 1920.

Sønderborg Castle

⊛ 🅰Sønderbro 1 🕙Times vary, check website 🌐msj.dk

Historiecenter Dybbøl Banke

⊛ 🅰Dybbøl Banke 16 🕙Early Apr–mid-Oct: 10am–5pm daily 🌐1864.dk

⑳ Haderslev

🅰C6 🚌 ℹBispebroen 3; www.visithaderslev.dk

The present-day capital of southern Jutland is situated between a narrow fjord and a lake. It was a market town

in the 13th century and has many period buildings.

During the Reformation in the 16th century, Haderslev was a major centre of Protestantism and in 1526 it became the site of the first Protestant theological college. The 13th-century Haderslev Domkirke boasts a splendid altarpiece featuring a 14th-century crucifix and statues of the apostles.

The most enchanting of the town's buildings are found on Torvet, a square flanked by half-timbered houses. Nearby, the simply titled **Archaeology** museum has exhibits on the history of the area and its own miniature open-air museum. Haderslev is also famous throughout Denmark for the harbourfront StreetDome skate park.

Archaeology
⊗ ⬛ Dalgade 7 ⬛ Jun-Aug: 10am-4pm Tue-Sun; Sep-May: 1-4pm Tue-Sun
ⓦ msj.dk

21

Fredericia

🅰 C5 🚉 🚌
ℹ Prinsessegade 27; www.visit fredericia.dk

Situated on the shimmering Lillebælt between Jutland and Funen, Fredericia is a busy port with a view of two coastlines. Frederick III built Fredericia on this strategic section of the Lillebælt in 1650. Its ramparts are some of the best preserved in northern Europe. In 1849 the northwest section was the scene of a battle between the Danes and the Prussian army, commemorated here by the *Landsoldaten* monument by the Prinsens Port (Prince's Gate). The nearby water tower provides the best views of the area. The **Fredericia Museum** has displays on the town's military and civilian history. Fredericia is also one of the top spots for wildlife; the Lille Bælt has one of the highest concentrations of porpoises in the world.

Fredericia Museum
⊗ ⬛ Jernbanegade 10
⬛ Noon-4pm Tue-Sun (mid-Jun-mid-Aug: daily) ⬛ Jan
ⓦ fredericiahistorie.dk

→

The bronze *Landsoldaten* statue commemorating the 1849 Battle of Fredericia

A wind turbine in Hvide Sande, near Ringkøbing Fjord

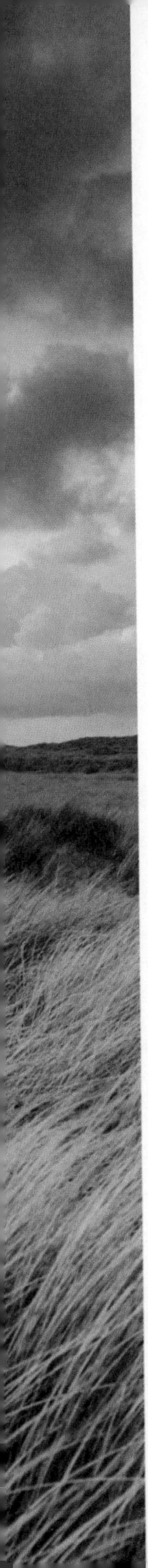

NORTHERN JUTLAND

The least populated and the wildest part of this region is its northern end, which is shaped by its proximity to the sea. On the northwestern side, facing Skagerrak, the scenery is dominated by dunes that display the clear effects of frequent sea breezes that shift the sand by up to 10 m (33 ft) each year. Many visitors embark on trips to Grenen, Denmark's northernmost point, which is washed over by the waters of the Baltic and the North Sea. This area is sometimes referred to as the "Land of Light" and enjoys more hours of sunshine than anywhere else in Denmark. The extraordinary light has long been appreciated by artists, who came here in search of inspiration in the 19th century and famously settled around Skagen. Another distinct feature of northern Jutland's landscape are its heathlands. They covered one third of this region until the mid-19th century; now they can be seen only here and there.

The university town of Aalborg is the area's only large city but, in the summer months, the seaside resorts of Skagen and Løkken-Blokhus do get busy. The most important of the area's historic sights are the Lindholm Høje prehistoric burial ground and the 1,000-year-old Viking fortress at Fyrkat, which includes a replica Viking farmstead.

NORTHERN JUTLAND

Must Sees
1. Limfjorden
2. Aalborg
3. Skagen

Experience More
4. Hirtshals
5. Råbjerg Mile
6. Den Tilsandede Kirke
7. Frederikshavn
8. Sæby
9. Fårup Sommerland
10. Lindholm Høje
11. Holstebro
12. Hjerl Hede Frilandsmuseum
13. Kongenshus Mindepark
14. Voergård Slot
15. Fyrkat
16. Viborg
17. Mønsted
18. Rebild Bakker
19. Mariager
20. Randers
21. Gammel Estrup

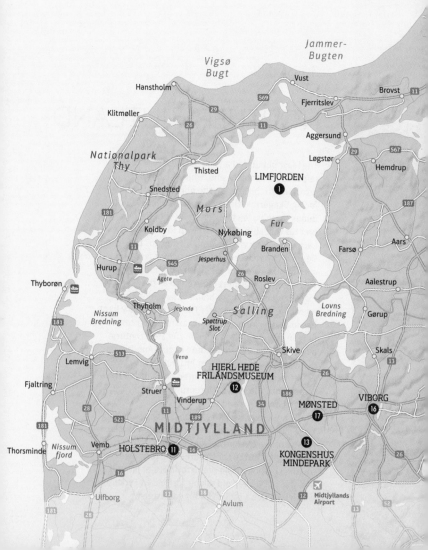

↑ Kristiansand,
Brevik, Larvik

Oslo ↑

Grenen

SKAGEN **3**

DEN TILSANDEDE KIRKE **6**

RÅBJERG MILE **5**

*Ålbæk
Bugt*

HIRTSHALS **4**

Ålbæk

40

597

55

Sindal

35

Hjørring

FREDERIKSHAVN **7**

→ Göteborg

585

E39

Tårs

553

Vrå

Løkken

Ør Vrå

585

SÆBY **8**

FÅRUP
SOMMERLAND **9**

543

Brønderslev

180

541

VOERGÅRD
SLOT **14**

Pandrup

Hjallerup

E45

Aabybro

55

Vodskov

Asaa

Aalborg Airport ✈

LINDHOLM HØJE **10**

AALBORG **2**

Nibe

Svenstrup

Limfjord

Hals

583

N O R D J Y L L A N D

Egense

595

E45

Støvring

507

Dokkedal

*Aalborg
Bugt*

Skørping

541

13

Øster Hurup

18
REBILD
BAKKER

180

Als

Hadsund

29

541

Ajstrup Bugt

Hobro

MARIAGER **19**

15
FYRKAT

Hald

Randers Fjord

E45

507

16

503

Fornæs

547

RANDERS **20**

GAMMEL
ESTRUP **21**

Langå

46

Auning

16

Grenå

525

21

Gudenå

Djursland

Bjerringbro

E45

Hornslet

Aarhus
Airport ✈

Trustrup

**SOUTHERN AND
CENTRAL JUTLAND**
p204

Lystrup

L æ s ø

Vesterø
Havn

Byrum

Hornfiskrøn

**NORTHERN
JUTLAND**

0 kilometres   15

0 miles   15

N
↑

❶ LIMFJORDEN

🅰B2–C2 🚉Thisted 🚌Thisted, Nykøbing Mors 🚢Nykøbing Mors
ℹ️Store Torv 6, Thisted, 97 92 56 04; Havnen 4, 97 72 04 88
🌐danishfjordholiday.com

Neighbouring Norway isn't the only Scandi country with dazzling fjords. Limfjorden is Denmark's largest body of inland water and its various islets and waterways are home to sea birds, ancient fossils, bike trails, charming villages and so much more.

Although narrow inlets connect it to both the Kattegat strait and the North Sea, Limfjorden resembles a lake. The significance of this area can be deduced from the many Bronze Age burial mounds, churches and castles that pepper the landscape. According to legend, when God created Jutland he first built a model. It was so good that he placed it at the centre of Limfjorden; this is Mors Island, found at the heart of the area. The Hanklit Cliffs on the northern tip of Mors have particularly stunning views. In summer, ferries offer trips to the smaller islands and other areas, including the colourfully planted Jesperhus Park on Mors, the stunning coves of Lovns Bredning and the port city of Aalborg (p232).

> **The Hanklit Cliffs on the northern tip of Mors have particularly stunning views.**

1 A Danish sailing ship, *Loa*, is moored at Limfjorden's capital, Aalborg.

2 Protected by a moat and ramparts, the medieval castle of Spøttrup Borg has changed very little since 1500.

3 The modern Musikkens Hus in Aalborg overlooks the Limfjorden.

Did You Know?

Fur, one of Limfjorden's islands, is home to fossils that are 55 million years old.

TOP 5 HIGHLIGHTS OF LIMFJORDEN

Jesperhus Park
This attractive park is planted with half a million flowers.

Fjerritslev
Between the fjord and North Sea, this lovely town brewery now houses a museum.

Lovns Bredning
Enchanting coves and diverse birdlife can be found here.

Spøttrup Borg
A medieval castle protected by a moat.

Nibe
This idyllic fjord town used to be famous for its herring markets, which supplied the royal table.

←

Waves lapping along the coast of Lemving in Limfjorden

↑ Cycling past Aalborg's half-timbered houses in summertime

2

AALBORG

C2 Aalborg Nordkraft, Kjellerups Torv 5; www.visitaalborg.com

North Jutland's capital is situated on the south bank of the Limfjorden (p230). It was founded by the Vikings and rapidly acquired a strategic significance as a hub of trade and transport. Aalborg prospered in the 17th century thanks to a thriving herring industry and many of its buildings date from this time. It remains a commercial hub and is the seat of the regional government.

1

Historiske Museum

 Algade 48 10am–5pm Mon–Sat nordjyllands historiskemuseum.dk

Just west of the cathedral is the local history museum. Its varied collection includes archaeological finds from Lindholm Høje (p238) and rare glassware and ancient coins. The museum's star exhibits include a reconstructed drawing room from an early 17th-century merchant's house. Most interesting of all, perhaps, is the skeleton of a 40-year-old female who died around AD 400. Her body was discovered in a peat bog.

2

Jens Bangs Stenhus

 Østerågade 9 To the public

A Dutch Renaissance-style house, this five-storey edifice, decorated with gargoyles and floral ornaments, was built in 1624 for Jens Bang, a wealthy merchant. Its façade facing the Rådhus (city hall) includes a stone figure of a satyr sticking its tongue out – this was intended to symbolize the owner's attitude towards the city's councillors, who refused to admit him into their ranks. The cellars house a wine bar that also serves traditional Danish food.

3

Utzon Center

 Slotspladsen 4 11am–5pm Tue–Fri (to 9pm Thu); 10am–5pm Sat & Sun utzoncenter.dk

The Utzon Center, a power-house of architectural and design exhibitions, is the last building created by the late Jørn Utzon, in collaboration with his son Kim. Utzon, the man responsible for the Sydney Opera House, grew up in Aalborg. The centre also

↑ Admiring artworks in the innovative Utzon Center

EAT

Mortens Kro
Signature dishes on the menu include lobster salad and braised veal shanks. Set tasting menus combine modern Danish cuisine with global influences.

🏠**Mollea 4**
🌐**mortenskro.dk**

Ⓚ Ⓚ Ⓚ

---

features a restaurant, library and an auditorium. It is located by the waterfront, next to the harbour pool, where you can go for a swim.

---

④
Aalborghus Slot

🏠**Slotspladsen 1**
🕐**8am–9pm daily**
🌐**kongeligeslotte.dk**

This modest half-timbered castle was built on the orders of Christian III and completed in 1555. The dank dungeons and underground passages make for an eerie walk.

---

⑤ ⊘ ⊘
Helligåndsklostret

🏠**Klosterjordet 1, C W Obels Plads** 🕐**Late Jun–mid-Aug: 2pm Mon–Fri (for tours only)** 🌐**aalborgkloster.dk**

This convent was founded in 1431 and is considered one of the best-preserved buildings of its type in Scandinavia. The only original part of the convent is the west wing; the north and the east wings are 16th century. Guided tours allow visitors to look at the frescoes in the hospital chapel, step into the

refectory with its starry vault and listen to the story of a nun who was buried alive as punishment for having a relationship with a monk.

---

⑥
Rådhus

🏠**Gammel Torv 2** 🕐**To the public**

The yellow-painted Baroque city hall was completed in 1762 and stands on the site of a demolished Gothic town hall. The motto written above the main door translates as "Wisdom and Determination" and was used by Frederick V, who was on the throne when the city hall was built.

---

⑦
Vor Frue Kirke

🏠**Niels Ebbesens Gade** 🕐**9am–2pm Mon–Fri, 9am–noon Sat** 🌐**vorfrue.dk**

The Church of Our Lady dates back to the 12th century. In the 16th and 17th centuries it was the main place of Christian worship in Aalborg. The surrounding area

makes for a lovely stretch of the legs, especially the cobbled street of Hjelmerstald.

---

⑧ ⊘ ⊡
Kunsten Museum of Modern Art Aalborg

🏠**Kong Christians Allé 50** 🕐**10am–5pm Tue–Sun (to 9pm Wed)** 🌐**kunsten.dk**

Designed by Finnish architect Alvar Aalto in conjunction with Danish architect Jean-Jacques Baruël, this striking marble museum has a wonderful collection of Danish and European modern art. Light, airy interiors make for a great space, and there's also a good café and attractive grounds to explore.

Did You Know?

Aalborg is the country's leading producer of Danish schnapps, *akvavit*.

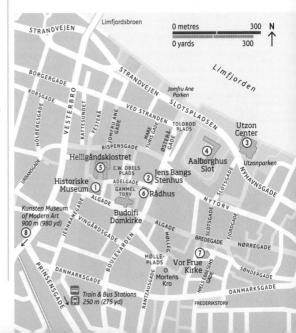

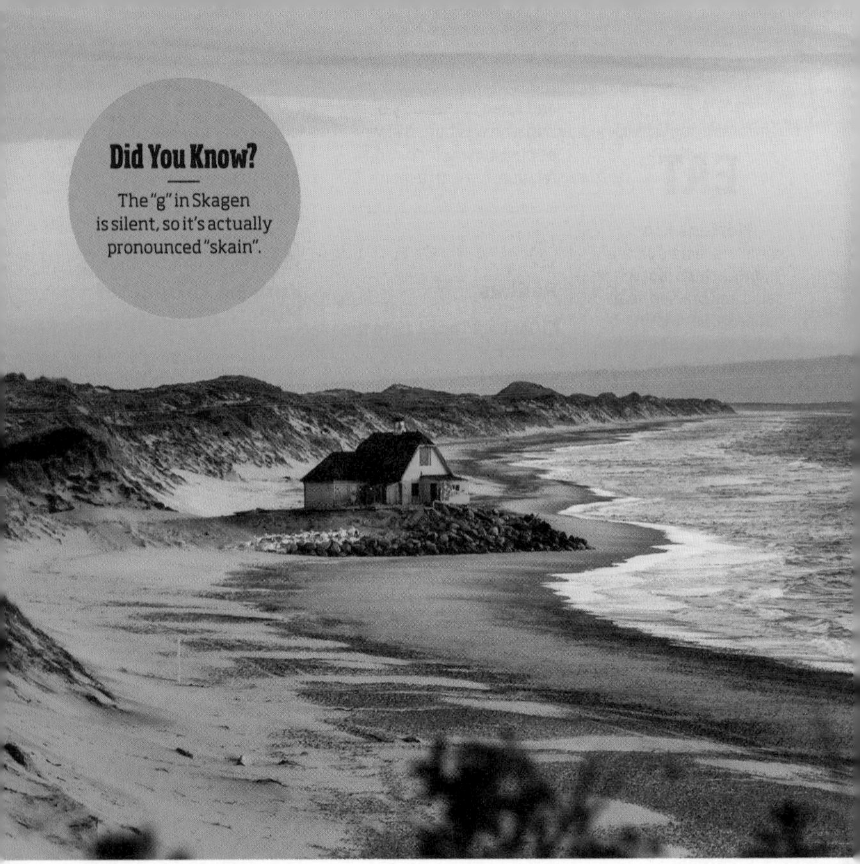

Did You Know?

The "g" in Skagen is silent, so it's actually pronounced "skain".

3

SKAGEN

D1 Vestre Strandvej 10, Skagen; www.toppenafdanmark.com

Denmark's northernmost point is both rugged and radiant. Sometimes referred to as "The Land of Light", Skagen's beautiful skies and white sand beaches have long drawn visitors to the area, most famously the 19th-century Skagen School of painters, who immortalized the ethereal landscape on canvas. See the scenery for yourself with a bohemian holiday by the sea.

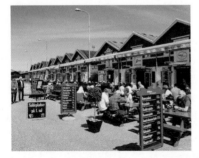

The fishing town of Skagen has a reputation for beauty, particularly Gammel Skagen (Old Skagen), which is characterized by white picket fences and quaint yellow houses. The harbour-front is dotted with working fishing boats and authentic red fisherman cabins, much like it was 200 years ago. Today these sit alongside seafood restaurants and ice creameries. Those

←

Visitors enjoying one of the tempting seafood restaurants in Skagen

SKAGEN SCHOOL

Nineteenth-century Danish artists flocked to Skagen, charmed by the lustrous light and rugged coastline that leant itself perfectly to the style of art popular at the time. Leading members of the Skagen School were Peder S Krøyer, Anna and Michael Ancher, Carl Locher, Christian Krogh and Oscar Björk. Skagen Museum displays a collection of their art-works, while charmingly quaint Brøndums Hotel is where these bohemians once socialized; the painting above is *Artists' Luncheon at Brøndum's Hotel*, by Peder S Krøyer.

↑ Pretty beaches around Gammel Skagen, home to dwellings and seals *(inset)*

interested in the area's art history should head to Drachmanns Hus where Holger Drachmann lived, and Anchers Hus, the former home of Anna and Michael Ancher.

Life's a Beach

Beyond Skagen are a plethora of beaches. Along the east coast, beaches such as Skagen Sønderstrand, Damstederne and Hulsig are family-friendly, with wide swathes of sand and gentle currents. On the west coast are Højen and Kandestederne, both perfect for barefoot walks along the sand, plus the spectacular Råbjerg Mile, famous for its 40-m (131-ft) high sand dunes. Note that the area's northernmost beach at Grenen is not safe for swimmers as the sea can be particularly boisterous. The second tallest lighthouse in Denmark, the Skagen Grå Fyr, offers splendid sea views.

↑ The historic Skagen Grå Fyr looming over sand dunes

EXPERIENCE MORE

4

Hirtshals

🅰C1 🚢🚍 ℹ Dalsagervej 1;
www.visithirtshals.dk

Towards the end of the 19th century Hirtshals was no more than a small fishing hamlet; now it is one of Jutland's major ports. Regular ferry links with Kristiansand, Oslo and Moss in Norway make this small town an important stepping stone to Denmark's Scandinavian neighbours. The town has a thriving fishing harbour; every day, at 7am, it is the venue for auctioning the night's catch.

The greatest attraction is the **Nordsøen Oceanarium**, a sea-life centre that is situated about 1 km (half a mile) east of the town centre. Its vast aquarium contains 4.5 million litres (990,000 gallons) of sea water, making it one of the biggest in Europe, and is home to herring, mackerel and sharks. A diver feeds the fish every day at 1pm. The oceanarium also has numerous displays on issues surrounding fishing in North Sea waters and the ecology of the region. Outside is a seal pool, which has regular feeding times at 11am and 3pm.

Hirtshals also has an extensive network of walking and cycling trails, one of which leads west to a lighthouse, whose tower you can climb to enjoy views over the landscape. A little way north, Husmoderstranden beach has many safe places to play and swim.

Hirtshals Museum has an exhibition of everyday objects illustrating the significance of the sea to the local population in the early 20th century.

Nordsøen Oceanarium

⊘ 🏠 Willemoesvej 🕐 Jan-Mar & Nov: 9am-4pm (to 5pm Sat, Sun & hols); Apr-Jun, Sep & Oct: 10am-5pm; Jul & Aug: 9am-6pm daily 🔽 nordsoen oceanarium.dk

---

5

Råbjerg Mile

🅰D1 🚌 🔽 visitaalborg.com

North Jutland has its own desert, the Råbjerg Mile, the largest drifting dune in Europe. It covers an area of 1,000 sq m (3,200 sq ft) on the west coast and moves about 15 m (50 ft) northeast towards Skagen and the Kattegat every year. The undulating natural phenomenon makes for excellent photo opportunities at the top of the dune, 40 m (130 ft) above sea level. The dune was formed on the west coast (Råbjerg Stene) in the 16th century during the great sand migration and is expected to reach the main road to Skagen within a century. Råbjerg Mile is 16 km (10 miles) southwest of Skagen, off route 40 towards Kandestederne. It can also be reached by bike from Vestkyststien. Råbjerg Stene can be reached by footpath from Råbjerg Kirke.

↑ Sun rising over a stunning and isolated lighthouse on the coast of Hirtshals

⑥
Den Tilsandede Kirke

🅐D1 🚌 ℹ️ Skagen Klitplantage, Skagen; www.visitdenmark.com

The Sand-Buried Church, once the largest in the Skagen area, is the stuff of legend. Today only its white tower is visible, poking out of the golden sand. The church, which bears the name of Saint Laurence, the patron saint of seafarers, was built in the 14th century; it lies 4 km (2 miles) south of Skagen within the Skagen Klitplantage nature reserve and is clearly signposted from route 40. Sand migration began in the 16th century, reaching the church at the end of the 18th century. The congregation eventually had to dig their way into the church to attend services. The struggle continued until it was closed by royal decree in 1795.

---

⑦
Frederikshavn

🅐D1 🚌🚆⛴️ ℹ️ Skandiatorv 1; www.visitfrederikshavn.dk

Jutland's main international ferry port has a number of important historical sights. The Krudttårnet (Gunpowder Tower) is all that remains of a 17th-century citadel that once guarded the port. Today the tower houses a small military museum. The 19th-century Frederikshavn Kirke houses a painting by Michael Ancher, one of the best-known of the Skagen School. The **Kystmuseet Bangsbo** lies about 3 km (2 miles) south of the centre. This 18th-century manor house has an eclectic collection that includes objects relating to the town's history

↑ Riding the hair-raising Orkanen roller coaster in Fårup Sommerland

and the Danish Resistance during World War II. Perhaps the best exhibit is a reconstructed 12th-century Viking merchant ship.

Kystmuseet Bangsbo

♿ 🅐 Dronning Margrethes Vej 6 🕐 Times vary, check website 🌐 kystmuseet.dk

---

⑧
Sæby

🅐D2 🚌🚆 ℹ️ Algade 14; www.saeby-museumm.dk

Saeby's skyline is dominated by Vor Frue Kirke (Church of Our Lady), once a 15th-century monastery and richly decorated with frescoes and a beautiful altarpiece from around 1520. Next to the church is the grave of Peter Jakob Larssøn, a 19th-century buccaneer who went on to become mayor. Sæby has a compact centre with half-

timbered houses and an attractive harbour. A 1920s schoolroom and a violinmaker's workshop can be seen in the **Sæby Museum**.

A short distance north of town is Sæbygård, a well-preserved 16th-century manor set in a small beech forest.

Sæby Museum

♿ 🅐 Algade 1–3 🕐 Times vary, check website 🌐 kystmuseet.dk

---

⑨
Fårup Sommerland

🅐C2 🅐 Pirupvejen 147 🕐 Times vary, check website 🚫 Mid-Sep–Apr 🌐 faarupsommerland.dk

This amusement park is set in a forest close to the beach, between Saltum and Blokhus. Among the thrills and spills are wild roller coasters and Denmark's largest, wettest water park. There are also gentler attractions for younger visitors. Once the splashing is over, visitors can cook in the grill area, jump on trampolines or take in a film at the 4D cinema.

> **The Sand-Buried Church, once the largest in the Skagen area, is the stuff of legend. Today only its white tower is visible, poking out of the golden sand.**

⑩ ✦ 🍴

Lindholm Høje

🅰C2 🄰Vendilavej 11
🕒Until dusk; museum:
10am-5pm Tue-Sun (Nov-
Mar: to 4pm) 🆆nordmus.
dk/lindholm-hoje-museet

Denmark's largest Iron Age and Viking burial ground has survived so well due to a sand deposit that kept it hidden until 1952, when archaeologists unearthed nearly 700 graves. The Viking-era graves have been made to resemble ships. Other finds discovered in the vicinity indicate that between the 7th and 11th centuries this was an important Viking trading centre. Lindholm Høje comes to life each year during the Viking festival held in the last week of June. The rest of the year you can visit the museum and even try Viking-era food served in its restaurant.

⑪

Holstebro

🅰B4 ⬛🚍 🛈Kirkestraede
13; www.visitholstebro.dk

Records of Holstebro date back to the 13th century, but the town was often plagued by fire and has few historic sights. Continuing a centuries-old tradition, the town bells chime every day at 10pm, reminding citizens to put out their fires.

In front of the 19th-century town hall is a sculpture by the renowned Swiss artist Alberto Giacometti. The nearby Neo-Gothic church is 20th century and houses the remains of a 16th-century altar.

Holstebro Kunstmuseum has a sizeable collection of paintings (including works by Picasso and Matisse), as well as

$\longrightarrow$

Stones marking the Viking burial grounds of Lindholm Høje

150

The number of Viking stone ships unearthed at Lindolm Høje.

sculptures and ceramic work by contemporary Danish and international artists. It also has an interesting programme of temporary exhibitions.

The **Strandingsmuseet St George**, 45 km (28 miles) to the west of Holstebro, tells the story of the shipwrecks that took place off the coast of Jutland in 1811.

Holstebro Kunstmuseum
✦ 🄰Museumsvej 2A
🕒Sep-Jun: noon-4pm Tue-
Fri, 11am-5pm Sat & Sun;
Jul-Aug: 11am-5pm Tue-Sun
🆆holstebrokunstmuseum.dk

Strandingsmuseet St George
✦ 🄰Vesterhausgade 1E,
Thorsminde 🕒Early Feb-
late Nov: 10am-5pm daily
🆆strandingsmuseet.dk

⑫ ✦ 🍴

Hjerl Hede Frilandsmuseum

🅰B3 🄰Hjerl Hedevej 14
🕒Times vary, check
website 🆆hjerlhede.dk

Just northeast of Holstebro is an open-air museum that re-creates the development of a Danish village from 1500 to 1900. The collection of buildings includes an inn, a school, a smithy and a dairy. In the summer guides wear period clothes and demonstrate traditional skills such as weaving and bread-making.

⑬ ✦ 🖥

Kongenshus Mindepark

🅰C4 🄰Vestre Skivevej
142, Daugbjerg, Viborg
🕒All year round
🆆kongenshus.dk

A small section of Denmark's uncultivated heathland can be explored at Kongenshus Mindepark. For many years early pioneers attempted to cultivate this windswept and inhospitable area. In the 18th century an army officer

from Mecklenburg, Germany, leased the land from Frederick V. With the king's help, he built a house and named it Kongenshus (King's House). However, after 12 years the officer abandoned the land and returned home. The observation tower next to the café is a good place to take in the scenery.

↑ Sumptuous interiors of Voergård Slot, an attractive castle *(inset)*

14

Voergård Slot

🅰 D2 🏛 Voergård 6, Dronningelund 🕒 Easter-Oct: 11am–4pm on certain days, check website; tours compulsory 🌐 voergaard slot.dk

This Renaissance castle is one of Denmark's most stylish buildings. Its splendid portal was intended originally for the royal castle of Fredensborg *(p165)*. Initially the estate was part of a religious complex but passed into private hands after the Reformation. Its large collection of art includes works by Raphael, Goya, Rubens and Fragonard. Also on display are many pieces of furniture and porcelain (including a dinner set made for Napoleon I).

15

Fyrkat

🅰 C3 🏛 Fyrkatvej 37B, Hobro 🕒 Jun–Aug: 10am–5pm daily; Sep: 10am–3pm daily 🌐 nordmus.dk/vikingecenter-fyrkat

In 1950 the remains of a Viking settlement dating from around AD 980 were discovered in the fields 3 km (2 miles) from the town of Hobro. The entire settlement was surrounded by ramparts 120 m (394 ft) in diameter and the entry gates to the fortress, aligned strictly with the points of the compass, were linked with each other by two intersecting streets. An ancient burial site containing 30 graves was discovered just outside the main camp. Today, a Viking-style farmstead north of the settlement re-creates many aspects of Viking life. Visitors can try on a Viking tunic and bake bread over an open fire.

STAY

Hotel Krogen
This 150-year-old guesthouse was once a palatial villa. Aside from the romantically furnished rooms, the hotel's unique feature is the miniature railway encircling the garden. Aalborg's bustling centre is conveniently within walking distance, in spite of the hotel's sense of rural isolation.

🅰 C2 🏛 Skibstedsvej 4, Aalborg 🌐 krogen.dk
Ⓚ Ⓚ Ⓚ

←
Colourful frescoes above the gilded altar in Viborg's Domkirke

train, which travels into the pit, past limestone columns and underground lakes.

18
Rebild Bakker

🅐 C3 🛈 Rebildvej 25A, Rebild; www.rebildporten.dk

Rebild Bakker is part of Rold Skov, Denmark's largest forest. In 1912, after fundraising among Danish expatriates in the USA, a section was turned into this park. An array of wildlife lives in the park, including foxes, deer, squirrels, martens, badgers and numerous birds. Every Sunday afternoon at the nearby **Fiddlers Museum**, visitors can take part in a lively square dance. The museum explores the way in which the surrounding forest has shaped the economy of the area and the lives of the local people by looking at forest trades, including hunting and poaching.

Fiddlers Museum
🅐 🛈 Cimbrervej 2 ⏰ Times vary, check website 🅦 spillemandsmuseet.dk

16
Viborg

🅐 C3 🚌 🛈 Tingvej 2A; www.visitviborg.dk

Viborg, whose history dates back to the 8th century, grew up around two scenic lakes. After the original 12th-century cathedral was torn down in the 19th century, the twin-towered **Domkirke** was completed in 1876. This huge granite building houses some valuable relics as well as a crypt dating from 1130 – all that remains of the original cathedral. Other features include a gilded altarpiece and a vast 15th-century candelabra. The cathedral's frescoes form an illustrated Bible and are a tribute to the original medieval decoration. The **Viborg Museum** contains a variety of exhibits relating to the town's history, including some items that date from the Viking era.

Domkirke
🅐 Sankt Mogensgade 4 ⏰ Times vary, check website 🅦 viborgdomkirke.dk

Viborg Museum
🅐 Hjultorvet 4 🛈 87 87 38 38 ⏰ Jul-mid-Aug: 11am-5pm Tue-Sun; mid-Aug-Jun: 1-4pm Tue-Fri, 11am-5pm Sat & Sun

17
Mønsted

🅐 C3 🛈 Mønsted Kalkgruber: Kalkværksvej 8 ⏰ Apr-Oct: 10am-5pm daily 🅦 monsted-kalkgruber.dk

The world's largest chalk mine was in operation from the 10th to the 20th centuries. Today, however, the bizarre and vast underground space is used as many things, including a venue for classical concerts and a space for ripening cheese.

A walk through this underground maze is an unforgettable experience as some of the chambers are as large as cathedrals. Visitors can wander at their own pace through the galleries, but they must wear safety helmets. For those who prefer more comfort, there is a mine

19 Mariager

A D3 🚌 **i** Torvet 1B; www. visitmariagerfjord.dk

In the Middle Ages Mariager was a major centre of pilgrimages, owing to the nunnery built here in 1410. Today, it is a quiet fjord town, with cobbled streets and picturesque houses engulfed in roses. The main reminder of the convent is the church standing on a wooded hill. Though it is much smaller than the original 14th-century building it is possible to imagine what the convent would have been like from a scale model in **Mariager Museum**, which is in an 18th-century merchant's house.

At **Mariager Saltcenter** visitors can learn about salt production, make their own crystals and take a bath in Denmark's own Dead Sea.

Mariager Museum
🔖 **A** Kirkegade 4A **O** Mid-May-mid-Sep: noon-4pm daily **W** nordmus.dk/ mariager-museum

Mariager Saltcenter
🔖 **A** Ny Havnevej 6 **O** 10am-4pm daily (to 5pm Sat, Sun & hols) **W** salt center.dk

20 Randers

A D3 🚃🚌 **i** Rådhustorvet 4; www.visitranders.com

Randers was already a major market town by the Middle Ages. Its most important historic sight is the 15th-century Sankt Morten's Kirke. Hanging inside is a model ship dating from 1632. The three-storey Paaskesønnernes Gård nearby is late 15th century and one of the city's oldest houses. The most popular attraction is **Randers Regnskov**, a tropical zoo that houses 200 animal species and 450 species of plants in a tropical rainforest environment. Here, regardless of the time of year, the temperature remains at a constant 25° C (77° F), with very high humidity. Among the many animals kept at the zoo are crocodiles, gibbons, butterflies, tapirs and snakes. There is also an area focusing on Danish farm animals.

Randers Regnskov
🔖 **A** Tørvebryggen 11 **O** 10am-4pm Mon-Fri, 10am-5pm Sat & Sun **W** regnskoven.dk

18,000

The number of bats living in the limestone caves of Mønsted during the winter.

21

Gammel Estrup

A D3 **A** Randersvej 2-4 **O** Times vary, check website **W** gammelestrup.dk

This estate near the village of Auning on the Djursland peninsula is one of the region's major attractions. The 15th-century manor house is surrounded by a moat and now houses a museum. Its interiors, replete with period furniture, paintings and tapestries, include reception rooms, a chapel and an alchemist's cellar. The Dansk Landbrugsmuseum focuses on Denmark's agricultural past.

Rosenholm Slot, a short drive from Gammel Estrup, is a 16th-century castle built on a small island in a lake. It was here that Count Rosenkrantz, immortalized in Shakespeare's *Hamlet*, lived.

↑ Crossing over the moat that surrounds the grand Gammel Estrup manor house

Chimneys of a traditional smokehouse in Hasle

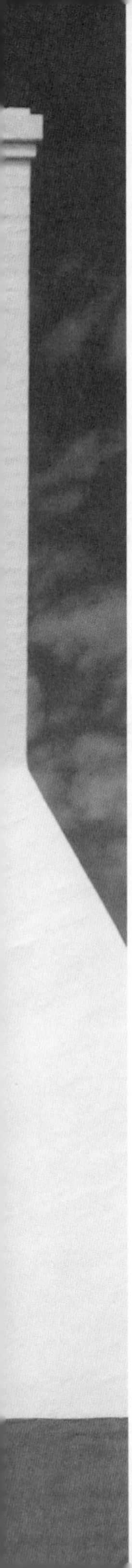

BORNHOLM

Far out in the Baltic, the idyllic island of Bornholm has an atmosphere all of its own. Bornholmers are fiercely proud of their ancestry. Among the older generation is a distinctive dialect that is as unique to the island as the *rundkirke* (round churches) that are found here. The discovery of ancient burial mounds and engravings suggest that Bornholm was inhabited by 3000 BC. At one time the island was an important centre for trade, and coins have been unearthed from as far afield as Rome and the Near East. The name "Bornholm" appeared for the first time in AD 890 at a time when the island was inhabited by the Vikings. From the mid-12th century much of Bornholm became the property of the Archbishop of the city of Lund, which at that time belonged to Denmark. For a period in the 17th century it was controlled by Sweden but the islanders' strong allegiance to Denmark resulted in a rapid withdrawal of Swedish forces. Following the surrender of Germany in May 1945 Bornholm was occupied by the Soviets until the Danish army established a permanent garrison.

Bornholm has developed a reputation for its fantastic regional cuisine, and boasts local delicacies and a thriving fishing industry; don't leave without sampling its smoked herring, known as *røget bornholmer*.

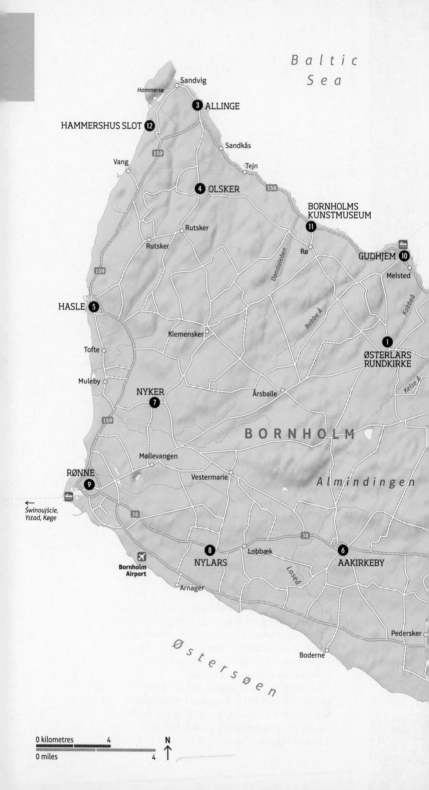

Baltic Sea

Sandvig

Hammersø

3 ALLINGE

HAMMERSHUS SLOT 12

Sandkås

Vang

159

Tejn

158

4 OLSKER

BORNHOLMS KUNSTMUSEUM

11

Rutsker

Rutsker

Dandaleleten

Rø

GUDHJEM 10

Melsted

159

HASLE 5

Tofte

Klemensker

Baabe Å

Kobbeå

Muleby

NYKER 7

Årsballe

1

ØSTERLARS RUNDKIRKE

Kelse Å

BORNHOLM

159

Møllevangen

Vestermarie

Almindingen

RØNNE 9

← *Świnoujście, Ystad, Køge*

38

Bornholm Airport

8 NYLARS

Løbbæk

Loseå

38

6 AAKIRKEBY

Arnager

Pedersker

Østersøen

Boderne

0 kilometres   4
0 miles   4

N ↑

Christiansø

BORNHOLM

Must See
1 Østerlars rundkirke

Experience more
2 Svaneke
3 Allinge
4 Olsker
5 Hasle
6 Aakirkeby
7 Nyker
8 Nylars
9 Rønne
10 Gudhjem
11 Bornholms Kunstmuseum
12 Hammershus Slot
13 Joboland

158
Bølshavn   Listed
Østermarie
13 JOBOLAND   2 SVANEKE
Ibsker   Årsdale
Ølene
158
Øle Å   Neksø
38   Bodilsker
Balka
Povlsker   Snogebæk
Dueodde

*Baltic
Sea*

BORNHOLM

Kołobrzeg ↓

1
ØSTERLARS RUNDKIRKE

🗺 F3 📍 Vietsvej 25, Østerlars 🚌 1 or 9 (from Gudhjem) 🕐 Apr-Oct: 10am-5pm Mon-Sat; Nov-Mar: 10am-2:45pm Tue-Sat 🌐 oesterlarskirke.dk

Round churches are unique to the island of Bornholm and Østerlars is by far the most impressive. Constructed way back in the 12th century, the church's masonry includes 2-m- (7-ft-) thick granite walls.

The church is Bornholm's oldest, dating from 1150, and is dedicated to St Laurentius, or "Lars" in Danish. The roof was originally constructed with a flat top to serve as a battle platform for hurling projectiles at attackers before the conical roof was added in 1744. The church consists of a circular nave with wide walls and seven buttresses that were added later in the 17th and 18th centuries.

Inside, a baptismal font stands inside a massive central column. This is decorated with 14th-century frescoes that depict scenes from the life of Christ. Above the religious space are two additional floors. The church is still used for Sunday services today.

Round the Garden

The church grounds also contain three runic stones, which are believed to date from the 11th century. Look out for the stone at the entrance that reads "Edmund and his brother erected this stone to the memory of their father Sigmund. May Christ, St Michael and St Mary help his soul."

↑ A fresco adorning the whitewashed walls of the church

WHY ROUND?

The logic behind the island's round churches isn't clear but it is most likely that they were built as protective sanctuaries; Bornholm's location in the Baltic meant it was vulnerable to attack. The distinctive thick walls and round shape of the churches helped withstand battering rams, while valuables could be stored on the upper levels. Here archers would also have a good vantage point.

→ Bornholm's oldest and largest round church, Østerlars Rundkirke

> **INSIDER TIP**
> **Gudhjem**
>
> A 20-minute bike ride away is Gudhjem *(p252)*, which has breathtaking scenery along the Helligdomsklipperne (Sanctuary Cliffs). After, enjoy a hard-earned meal at Gudhjem Røgeri *(www.smokedfish.dk)*.

↑ The round church of Østerlars sitting in pretty gardens

EXPERIENCE MORE

② Svaneke

 F3 🚌 *ℹ* Grønningen 30; 56 95 95 00

In the 1970s this appealing town won the European Gold Medal preservation award and Svaneke continues to maintain its unspoilt historic character. A short distance south of the town centre is Svaneke Kirke. A majestic swan adorns the spire of this 14th-century church, and the image of a swan is also included in the town emblem: Svaneke translates as "Swan Corner".

As well as being one of the most photogenic towns on the island, Svaneke is also famous for its windmills. These can be seen standing by each of the town's exit roads. The best preserved is the Årsdale Mølle (1877) on the road to Nexø. Svaneke is also home to an unusually square lighthouse, southeast of the harbour near to Hullehavn, a small inlet that's ideal for swimming. In the local glass factory, Pernille Bülow, you can watch workers skilfully produce designer glassware.

③ Allinge

F3 🚌 *ℹ* Sverigesvej 11; 56 95 95 00

Allinge and nearby Sandvig, 2 km (1 mile) to the northwest, are treated as one town though the two have slightly different characters. Allinge has most of the commercial facilities, while Sandvig is quieter, with walking trails and neatly tended gardens. Allinge's church is mostly from the 19th century, although it grew out of a chapel erected five centuries earlier. Inside hangs a painting that once adorned the chapel in Hammershus Slot (*p253*).

On the outskirts of Allinge is a cemetery for Russian soldiers, with a granite obelisk proudly displaying the Soviet star at the top – a reminder of the Red Army, who occupied

🔍 HIDDEN GEM
Gården Madkulturhuset

This place celebrates Bornholm's food culture through interactive food events (*www.gaarden.nu*). The space is a unique venue for the island's producers and guests to create and taste Bornholm's stellar cuisine.

Bornholm from the end of World War II until March 1946.

On the outskirts of Allinge is Madsebakke Helleristninger – the biggest and the most precious set of rock carvings in Denmark. These enigmatic Bronze Age drawings of ships, boats and feet are thought to be 4,000 years old. Another curiosity is Moseløkken quarry, where visitors can learn all about the excavation of granite on Bornholm and even have a go at splitting a piece themselves (May to September).

↑ A fishing boat moored alongside storage warehouses, Bornholm

STAY

Stammershalle Badehotel

This waterfront hotel offers understated seaside luxury in what feels like a stylish and welcoming home. The on-site restaurant is a foodie haven.

🅰F3 🅐Søndre Strandvej 128, Gudhjem 🅦stammershalle-badehotel.dk

Green Solution House

Sustainability should not mean compromising on comfort. Spacious and streamlined rooms feature modern Danish design. In-demand eatery GSH is a classic with a modern twist.

🅰F3 🅐Strandvejen 79, Rønne 🅦greensolution house.dk

Ⓚ Ⓚ Ⓚ

④ Olsker

🅰F3 🚌

The village of Olsker, *south of* Allinge, has one of the best-known of Bornholm's distinctive *rundkirke* (round churches). For many years historians believed these unique structures were of pagan origin, but more recent theory is that they were in fact intended for defensive purposes; piracy was rife in the region in the 12th century. They also served as supply warehouses. This granite building is the most slender of Bornholm's four round churches and has nine windows. It was erected in the mid-12th century in honour of St Olaf, a Norwegian king who died in 1031 and who is revered in Denmark. The hill on which the church stands affords an excellent view of the surroundings, which would have made it ideal for keeping watch.

← The attractive Svaneke lighthouse perched on Bornholm's rocky coastline

⑤ Hasle

🅰F3 🚌 🅘Søndre Bæk 20; www.hasleroegeri.dk

One of Bornholm's oldest towns, Hasle is mentioned in records as early as 1149. The herring industry has long been the town's main revenue source, although locals were once also employed in mining brown coal until 1946. The town is popular with fans of smoked herring. Hasle Smokehouse is the last place in Bornholm to use traditional methods. There are smoking sessions every day from May to October and it is possible to follow the smoking process from early morning to late evening, when the herring and other fish products are finished and ready to be eaten.

In the centre of town stands a 15th-century church with a stunning altarpiece made in Lübeck in 1520. According to one local story the altar was a gift from a sailor who miraculously escaped a sinking ship.

A monument in the town square commemorates Peder Olsen, Jens Kofoed and Poul Anker, who became the local heroes of an uprising against the Swedes in 1658.

On the outskirts of town, on the road towards Rønne, is a huge runic stone – the largest one on the island.

6

Aakirkeby

🅰F3 🚍 **𝒊** Torvet 30; 56 95 95 00

During the Middle Ages this was the most important town on the island and the seat of Bornholm's church and the lay authorities. As a result, the 12th-century Aa Kirke is the island's largest church. The Romanesque building contains a number of treasures including a 13th-century baptismal font and an early 17th-century pulpit. Climbing to the top of the church's bell tower affords great views of the town.

A more modern attraction is **NaturBornholm**, a state-of-the-art natural history museum situated on the southern outskirts of town. The museum takes visitors back 2,000 years and provides an entertaining way to learn about the flora and fauna of the island. Behind this centre is a gigantic natural fault in the bedrock created around 400 million years ago, which marks the boundary between the continental plates of Europe and Scandinavia.

NaturBornholm

⊛ 🏠 Grønningen 30 ⏱ Apr–Oct: 10am–5pm daily 🌐 natur bornholm.dk

7

Nyker

🅰F3 🚍

The smallest of Bornholm's four historic *rundkirke* (round churches) is in the small town of Nyker. The church is just two storeys high and lacks external buttresses, giving it a simple, clean exterior. In keeping with its name (**Nykirke** or New Church), it is the most recently built of the churches. A Latin inscription found on the late-Gothic chalice kept within proclaims that the church is dedicated to All Saints.

Other items to look out for in Nykirke include the splendid frescoes that decorate the main pillar of the church, which depict the Stations of the Cross, and a stone laid in the portico with a Resurrection scene dating from 1648. Another highly interesting object is an 18th-century tablet carved with the names of the local inhabitants who died as a result of two plagues that sadly devastated the area in 1618 and 1654.

Nykirke

⊛ 🏠 Ellebyvej 1A ⏱ Easter–mid-Oct: 8am–4pm Mon–Fri 🌐 ny-kirke.dk

HIDDEN GEM
🔍 Høstet Sea Buckthorn Farm

On the southeast side of the island, rows of buckthorn bushes laden with orange berries slope down to the sea. A good spot to sample these fruits during the summer months is the Høstet plantation. Taste berries, buckthorn juices and marmalades (www.høstet.dk).

8

Nylars

🅰F3

Some 7 km (4 miles) southeast of Rønne, the tiny village of Nylars developed in the early 1900s after the railway line between Rønne and Nexø was opened. The village doesn't have as much to offer as other towns and villages on the island, but is home to the most well-preserved of Bornholm's four round churches, **Nylars Kirke**. This *rundkirke* was built in 1150 and is dedicated to St Nicholas, the patron saint of sailors. The porch houses two ancient rune stones, the oldest of which is from around 1050. To climb the stairs to the upper levels it is necessary to squeeze through very narrow passages. For invaders trying to reach the upper floor this presented quite an obstacle. The frescoes adorning the distinctive pillar that rises through all three levels of the building depict biblical scenes from Genesis, including the creation of Adam and Eve and their expulsion from the Garden of Eden.

Nylars Kirke

⊛ 🏠 Kirkevej 10 ⏱ Sunrise–sunset 🌐 nylarskirke.dk

←

Dandelions blossoming outside Nyker's historic round church

Boat masts piercing the sky above Rønne's pretty harbour ↑

9

Rønne

F3 ✈️🚌 ℹ️ **Nordre Kystvej 3; www.bornholm.info**

One-third of Bornholm's entire population lives in Rønne. The town has grown up around a natural harbour, and two of the first buildings that you see when approaching from the Baltic are the 19th-century lighthouse and Sankt Nicolai Kirke, built in 1918. Rønne's two main squares are Store Torv and Lille Torv (Big Market and Little Market). Store Torv was originally used for military parades but is now the venue for a market held twice weekly.

The Tinghus at Store Torv 1 dates from 1834 and was once used as the town hall, courthouse and jail. A number of picturesque cobbled streets lead off from Rønne's Store Torv, and many of the early 19th-century houses are still standing, in spite of a series of bombing raids carried out by the Soviets in May 1945. One of the more unusual buildings is found in Vimmelskaftet; its width allows for only one window. Standing at the corner of Østergade and Theaterstræde is the beautifully restored Rønne Theatre, one of the oldest theatres in Denmark, dating from 1823. **Bornholms Museum** has a good local history section that includes archaeological finds, a small collection of paintings and a selection of 6th-century tablets known as *goldgubber*. Over 2,000 of these tablets engraved with small figures have been found on the island. **Bornholms Forsvarsmuseum** (Military Museum) is housed in a citadel built south of the town centre around 1650. The defensive tower houses a large collection of weapons, ammunition, uniforms and one of the oldest cannons in Denmark.

Bornholms Museum
🔊 🏛️ Sankt Mortensgade 29
🕐 Times vary, check website
🌐 bornholmsmuseum.dk

Bornholms Forsvarsmuseum
🔊 🏛️ Arsenalvej 8 🕐 May-Oct: 10am-4pm Mon-Fri
🌐 bornholmsforsvars museum.dk

> A number of picturesque cobbled streets lead off from Rønne's Store Torv, and many of the early 19th-century houses are still standing, in spite of a series of bombing raids.

EAT

Kadeau
Located in a renovated beach pavilion in the south of the island, this Michelin-starred restaurant is surrounded by sea, beach and forest. Its sparse decor enhances the tasting experience: a flurry of 9 to 12 dishes, which are exclusively regional, exciting and innovative. Reservations essential.

F3 🏛️ Baunevej 18, Aakirkeby 🌐 kadeau.dk

Ⓚ Ⓚ Ⓚ

————————

Christianshøjkroen
In the large forest of Almindingen, the historic, half-timbered Christianshøjkroen draws a lunch crowd with new spins on classic *smørrebrød*. Reservations recommended.

F3 🏛️ Segenvej 48, Aakirkeby
🌐 christianshojkroen.dk

Ⓚ Ⓚ Ⓚ

⑩

Gudhjem

Ⓐ F3 ***i*** **Ejnar Mikkelsens Vej 17; 56 95 95 00**

Gudhjem – or "God's Home" – is built on a steep hill overlooking the Baltic Sea. The picturesque harbour, cobbled streets and brightly painted half-timbered houses with their red-tiled roofs make it a popular and picturesque spot with visitors in summer. The village has long been associated with the fishing industry and, in 1893, Gudhjem acquired Bornholm's first proper smokehouse. The famous "Sun over Gudhjem", a herring smoked in its skin and served with egg yolk, is a must for lovers of Danish cuisine. A late 19th-century church sits in the centre of the village. Close by are the remains of

---

📷 PICTURE PERFECT
Sanctuary Cliffs

Stretching between Tejn and Gudhjem, the sharp Sanctuary Cliffs - or Helligdomsklipperne - offer amazing photo ops. Travel by boat from Gudhjem and the approach reveals 60-m- (195-ft-) high cliff caves. A cliffside staircase also leads to the coastal path.

---

a much older chapel, dating to the 13th century.

The **Oluf Høst Museet** has a large selection of paintings by the beloved Bornholm artist Oluf Høst, who died in 1966. The collection is housed in the artist's attractive home, which he built in 1929. An old railway station houses the **Gudhjem Museum**, dedicated to local history.

Oluf Høst Museet

⊛ Ⓐ Løkkegade 35 Ⓒ Apr-May, Sep-Oct: 11am–5pm Wed-Sun; Jun-Aug: 11am–5pm daily Ⓦ ohmus.dk

Gudhjem Museum

Ⓐ Stationsvej 1 Ⓒ 61 22 33 65 Ⓒ Apr-Sep: 10am–5pm Mon-Sat, 2–5pm Sun

---

⑪

Bornholms Kunstmuseum

Ⓐ F3 **Ⓓ Otto Bruun Plads 1, Gudhjem** 🚌 **2 (Rønne); 4, 8 (Gudhjem)🚌** **Ⓦ bornholms-kunstmuseum.dk**

Akin to Danish art icons such as Copenhagen's ARKEN *(p130)* and the Louisiana Museum *(p146)* in Humlebæk, Bornholm's Kunstmuseum is a mecca for art lovers. Situated on the Helligdomsklipperne (Sanctuary Cliffs), about 9 km (6 miles) north of Gudhjem,

the art museum occupies a strikingly contemporary building that overlooks the sea, offering a stellar backdrop to its treasure trove of artworks. The spacious, three-storey gallery has an impressive permanent collection by artists from the early 20th-century group of painters known as the Bornholm School, including Karl Isakson, Olaf Rude, Oluf Høst and Edvard Weie. The Bornholm School had a distinctive style of classic Modernism, using subdued colours inspired by the natural beauty of the island's famously unique landscapes and light.

A stroll through the museum grounds is worthwhile, if not for the colourful contemporary sculptures arranged around the gardens then for the views. Here you can admire the rocky shoreline and the distant islet of Christiansø, where the Bornholm School painters often decamped to find seclusion and inspiration. A 6-km- (4-mile-) path runs parallel to the top of the cliffs into Gudhjem. In good weather, a boat service runs between Gudhjem and the museum. From April to November longhorned, long-haired highland cattle graze in the field next to the museum. The cows are allowed to wander freely and graze as they help to keep bushes and scrub down.

←

Red-tiled rooftops of Gudhjem, with the Baltic Sea beyond

12 🎨 Ⓜ️ 💻 🏛️

Hammershus Slot

🅰️ F3 🕐 All year round

The atmospheric ruins of Hammershus Slot are the largest in northern Europe and stand on a 70-m- (230-ft-) high cliff. The medieval fortification was built in the 13th century on the orders of the Archbishop of Lund. Legend has it that Hammershus was originally intended to be built at a different site, but the walls erected during the day would mysteriously vanish overnight. Having decided that a change of location was necessary, horses were let loose; the spot where they finally came to a stop was chosen as the new site. The entrance to the castle leads over a stone bridge that was once a drawbridge. The ruins also include what remains of a brewery, a granary and a bakery. The impressive square tower, Manteltårnet, was used in the Middle Ages for storing the country's tax records and later served as the quarters of the castle's commander and as a prison. In 1660 Leonora Christina, daughter of Christian IV, and her husband were imprisoned in the tower, accused of collaboration with the Swedes. Technological improvements in artillery eventually diminished the castle's defensive capabilities as its brick walls became vulnerable to attack from powerful cannons. It was abandoned in 1743 and much of the castle was used as building material for local homes. An exhibition in **Hammershus Visitor Centre** includes a model of the castle as it was at its peak.

Hammershus Visitor Centre

🅰️ Slotslyngvej 9, Allinge 🕐 10am-4pm daily (Jun-Aug: to 5pm)

13 🎨

Joboland

🅰️ F3 🚗 3 km (2 miles) from Svaneke, Højevejen 4 🕐 Times vary, check website 🌐 joboland.dk

This amusement park's greatest attraction is its aquapark, where the water is kept at a constant 25° C (77° F). It contains five water slides and a 125-m- (410-ft-) long Wild River, which adventurous visitors can ride on a rubber tyre. It is also possible to sail a boat, whizz down a "death slide" and walk across a rope bridge. During the high season the park lays on additional shows and games for children, such as treasure hunts. Joboland also has its own small zoo with a variety of animals, including peacocks, monkeys and exotic birds.

> ## Did You Know?
>
> Bornholm is also known as Rock Island (*klippeøen*) and Sunshine Island (*solskinsøen*).

↑ Exploring the ruins of Bornholm's medieval Hammershus Slot

A CYCLING TOUR OF
BORNHOLM

Length 51 km (32 miles) **Difficulty** There are a number of hills on Bornholm so a reasonable level of fitness is needed **Nearest town** A few minutes outside of Allinge

The best way to explore beautiful Bornholm is by bike, and you'll find cycle groups are a common sight here. The island has 235 km (146 miles) of well- signposted cycling routes, many of which connect to the main towns and take in gorgeous views along the coastline. The routes provide an ideal way to enjoy Bornholm's lush meadows, rolling fields and verdant forests, particularly as most are far away from busy roads. Rønne, Allinge, and Gudhjem are good places to start. English language brochures are available at tourist information centres.

Hasle (p249) *is a pleasant town with a number of traditional smokehouses.*

Rønne (p251) *is Bornholm's capital and has a distinctive 19th century lighthouse.*

0 kilometres   4
0 miles   4

N ↑

Bornholm Airport receives domestic flights only.

← Church spire piercing the sky in the leafy town of Rønne

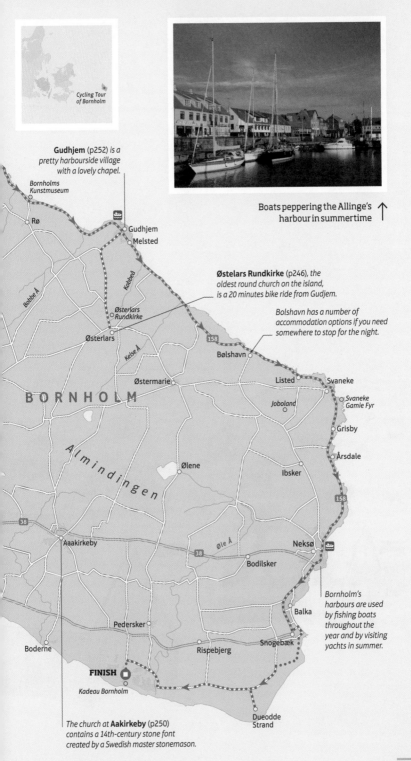

Gudhjem (p252) *is a pretty harbourside village with a lovely chapel.*

Bornholms Kunstmuseum

Rø

Gudhjem

Melsted

Kobbed

Østelars Rundkirke (p246), *the oldest round church on the island, is a 20 minutes bike ride from Gudjem.*

Bolshavn has a number of accommodation options if you need somewhere to stop for the night.

Bobbe Å

Østerlars Rundkirke

Østerlars

Kelse Å

158

Bølshavn

Østermarie

Listed

Svaneke

BORNHOLM

Joboland

Svaneke Gamle Fyr

Grisby

Almindingen

Ølene

Ibsker

Årsdale

158

38

Aaakirkeby

38

Øle Å

Neksø

Bodilsker

Bornholm's harbours are used by fishing boats throughout the year and by visiting yachts in summer.

Balka

Pedersker

Snogebæk

Boderne

Rispebjerg

FINISH

Kadeau Bornholm

Dueodde Strand

The church at **Aakirkeby** (p250) *contains a 14th-century stone font created by a Swedish master stonemason.*

Boats peppering the Allinge's harbour in summertime ↑

Snow-topped houses in the town of Tasiilaq, Greenland

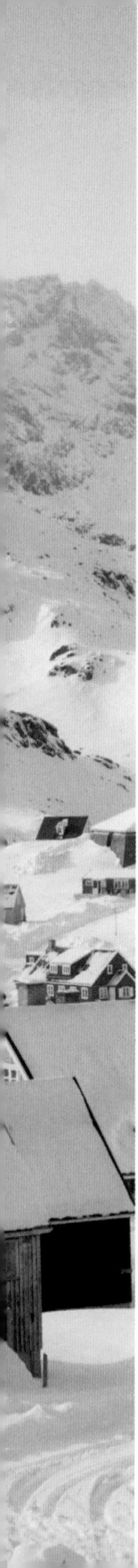

GREENLAND AND THE FAROE ISLANDS

These two far-flung territories of Denmark offer spectacular adventure and some of the world's most stunning scenery. Intrepid visitors are attracted by the solitude and natural beauty, including Greenland's vast frozen glaciers and wondrous Northern Lights, and the remote settlements and varied birdlife of the Faroe Islands.

Greenland was granted home rule in 1979; the Faroe Islands in 1948. Both have their own government but, due to the fact that Denmark retains responsibility for matters such as defence, both are represented in the Danish parliament. Native Greenlanders share a common heritage with the Inuit of Alaska and northern Canada. Denmark's links with the island began in the 10th century when Viking settlers arrived here and began trading with the Greenlanders. The island was named by Erik the Red, a Viking chief who reached the southern end of Greenland around AD 985.

Early settlers on the Faroe Islands were from Norway, but the Scandinavian neighbour fell under Danish rule in the 14th century and the islands came with it. Denmark ceded Norway to Sweden in 1814 under the Treaty of Kiel but the Faroes continued under the Danish crown until demands for independence led to eventual home rule.

GREENLAND

Lincoln Sea

Kap Morris Jesup

Peary Land

○ Nord

CANADA

Knud Rasmussen Land

Greenland Sea

Kong Frederik VIII Land

Danmarks
○ Havn

6 QAANAAQ
(THULE)

○ Savissivik

Qimusseriarsuaq

○ Daneborg

Baffin Bay

GREENLAND

Kong Christian X Land

Ymers Øer

Traill Øer

○ Upernavik

Scoresby Land

○ Ittoqqortoormiit
(Scoresbysund)

1 UUMMANNAQ
(UMANAK)

Disko Øer

Qeqertarsuaq ○
(Godhavn)

Aasiaat ○
(Egedesminde)

2 ILULISSAT
KANGERLUA

Kong Christian IX Land

KANGERLUSSUAQ
(SØNDRE STRØMFJORD)

○ Aputiteeq

Sisimiut ○
(Holsteinsborg)

4 ✈ Kangerlussuaq
Airport

Arctic Circle

ICELAND

Reykjavík

○ Maniitsoq

5

TASIILAQ
(AMMASSALIK)

3 NUUK
(GODTHÅB)

Paamiut ○
(Frederikshåb)

Atlantic

Ivittuut ○

Ocean

Narsarsuaq
Airport

Narsarsuaq ○ ✈

THE
SOUTHERN
FJORDS

Qaqortoq ○
(Julianehåb)

7

○ Nanortalik

Kap Farvel

Labrador Sea

| 0 km | 200 |
| 0 miles | 200 |

N ↑

GREENLAND

Experience

1 Uummannaq (Umanak)

2 Ilulissat Kangerlua

3 Nuuk (Godthåb)

4 Kangerlussuaq
(Søndre Strømfjord)

5 Tasiilaq (Ammassalik)

6 Qaanaaq (Thule)

7 The Southern Fjords

FAROE ISLANDS

FAROE ISLANDS

Fugloy
Kirkja
Svinoy
Svinoy
Viðareiði
Múli
Viðoy
Hvannasund
Kunoy
KALSOY
Kunoy
Borðoy
Klaksvík
Mikladalur
Gjógv
Eiði
Oynadarfjørður
Leirvik
Tjørnuvík
Fuglafjørður
Saksun
EYSTUROY
STREYMOY
Vestmanna
Kollafjørður
Saltangará
MYKINES
VÁGAR
Kvívík
Toftir
Mykines
Bøur
Sørvágur
Sandavágur
Syðradulur
TÓRSHAVN
Vága Airport
Miðvágur
Nólsoy
FAROE
Koltur
Nólsoy
ISLANDS
Hestur
Kirkjubøur
Hestur

Norwegian
Sea

Skopun
Sandoy
Sandur
Skálavík
Skúvoy
Dalur
Skúvoy

Stóra Dímun

Sandvik
Litla Dímun
Hvalba
Atlantic
Tvøroyri
Ocean
Famjin
SuÐuroy
Hov
Vágur
Sumba

FAROE ISLANDS

Experience

8 Tórshavn
9 Streymoy
10 Mykines
11 Vágar
12 Eysturoy
13 Kalsoy

0 km   8
0 miles   8

N

EXPERIENCE

Uummannaq
Umanak

F1 **i** Hotel Uummannaq, PO Box 202; (+299) 95 15 18

Despite its location 400 km (250 miles) north of the Arctic Circle, Uummannaq enjoys more days of sunshine than anywhere else in Greenland. The charm of this town, situated on a small island, is due in part to its colourful houses set on a rocky shore against the backdrop of the Hjertetjeldet ("Heart Shaped") mountain. A nearby museum, housed in a late 19th-century hospital, contains hunting implements, kayaks and a display devoted to German scientist Alfred Wegener's 1930 expedition across the inland ice on propeller-driven sledges.

Nearby is the Inuit village of Qilakitsoq, where mummified bodies were discovered in a cave in 1972, now housed in Nuuk's National Museum.

In winter you can take an exhilarating trip on a dogsled across the frozen fjord. Rumour has it that Santa Claus lives in Uummannaq. Hikes to his hideaway be arranged for fortunate visitors.

Ilulissat Kangerlua

F1 **i** Fredericap Aqq 7A; www.northgreenland.com

The town of Ilulissat looks out over Disko Bay, known for the collection of icebergs that occupy its waters. Almost 10 per cent of the icebergs in Greenland's waters come from the nearby Ilulissat Kangerlua (Icefjord), a UNESCO World Heritage Site, where the glacier can reach over a kilometre (half a mile) thick and the icebergs can be as big as the town itself. The sight and sound of the ice cracking apart is an unforgettable experience. The glacier can be reached by boat from Ilulissat.

Ilulissat's most famous inhabitant was the explorer Knud Rasmussen (p166). His former house now contains various objects associated with everyday life in Greenland.

Nuuk
Godthåb

E1 **i** Hans Egedesvej 29; www.visitgreenland.com

Often overlooked by travellers eager to explore nature's wild beauty, Greenland's capital

> **GREAT VIEW**
> ### Myggedalen
> The most iconic view of Nuuk is at the end of Isaajap Aqqutaa road, a short walk from the Old Harbour. Here a postcard-perfect swatch of old wooden houses in Myggedalen (Mosquito Valley) brightens the horizon. In summer, it's the ideal place to watch the midnight sun set over the water.

←

Traditional wooden houses lining the icy coastline in Ilulissat, Greenland

has undergone a renaissance in the last five years. Modern architecture has altered the skyline, while independent boutiques and restaurants are reinvigorating local traditions.

Nuuk was founded in 1728 by Danish missionary Hans

Egede, who established a year-round trading post here. Nuuk, with its commanding position on a fjord with a mountain as backdrop, is the largest and oldest town on the island. It is also the seat of government. More information about the town's history can be found at the **National Museum**, whose permanent exhibits include a collection of Inuit costumes and three mummified bodies found near Uummannaq.

Katuaq Cultural Centre is an excellent example of Nuuk's modern architecture and the heart of the town's social life. Designed to resemble the Northern Lights, the exterior is an undulating expanse of wood and glass. Inside you will find a café, a library, a cinema and the Greenland Art School.

The best time to visit is in the summer, when beautiful humpback whales can be seen in the bay.

Did You Know?

Greenland is the world's largest non-continental island and has the world's sparsest population.

National Museum

⊘ ⬛ Hans Egedesvej 8
⬛ Jun-mid-Sep: 10am-4pm daily; mid-Sep-May: 1-4pm Tue-Sun ⬛ en.nka.gl

Katuaq Cultural Centre

⊘ ⓘ ⬚ ⬛ Imaneq 21
⬛ Times vary, check website
⬛ katuaq.gl

4

Kangerlussuaq
Søndre Strømfjord

⬛ E1 ⓘ Albatros Arctic Circle - Polar Lodge & Old Camp, Mitaarfit Aqq, PO Box 1009; www.wogac.com

Situated near the fjord of the same name, Kangerlussuaq was home to US base Blue West 8 until 1992. Remnants of the military presence can still be found all around the town, from the world's northernmost 18-hole golf course and the repurposed barracks to shards of aircraft embedded in nature.

If you like the great outdoors, Kangerlussuaq is a must. The area is today inhabited by reindeer, musk ox, arctic foxes and polar hares, and it's an excellent destination for hiking, biking, camping and fishing trips. A popular daytrip is to Russells Glacier, part of the Greenland ice sheet some 25 km (16 miles) away. About 10 km (6 miles) away is the vast Sugarloaf Mountain, which has a wonderful view of the Greenland ice sheet from its peak. Kangerlussuaq is also the only place in Greenland where you can drive to the Greenland ice sheet.

NORTHERN LIGHTS IN GREENLAND

A bucket list experience, the Northern Lights can often be seen in Greenland. Head out on a clear evening in deep winter for the highest probability of a full light show. They can also be seen in autumn. Kangerlussuaq is a good and popular viewing spot, while Disko Bay, East Greenland and Nuuk are also contenders. Visit Greenland provides information on tours *(www.visitgreenland.com)*.

EAT & DRINK

Godthaab Bryghus
Craft-beer lovers flock to the island's most venerable brewery.

🄰E1 🄰Imaneq 30, Nuuk 🄦heca.gl

Sarfalik
Housed in the Hotel Hans Egede, Sarfalik concocts top dishes using local ingredients.

🄰E1 🄰Aqqusinersuaq, Nuuk 🄦uk.hhe.gl

Ⓚ Ⓚ Ⓚ

Kritinemutt
Locals come to this rustic log cabin in droves for live music.

🄰E1 🄰Aqqusinersuaq 7, Nuuk Ⓒ(+299) 34 80 90 Ⓒ Sun

Cafétuaq
This bright, modern café excels at budget-friendly New Nordic.

🄰E1 🄰Imaneq 21, Nuuk 🄦katuaq.gl

Ⓚ Ⓚ Ⓚ

5
Tasiilaq
Ammassalik

🄰E1 🄘PO Box 506, Skæven Ujuaap Aqqulaa 48; www.eastgreenland.com

Situated on the shores of a fjord, surrounded by high mountains, Tasiilaq is one of eastern Greenland's larger towns. The first Europeans arrived here about 100 years ago, and tourism is becoming increasingly important. From here, you can go whale watching, visit the nearby "Valley of Flowers" (in summer this is a splendid opportunity to enjoy the Arctic flora, including the national flower of Greenland, the broad-leafed willow) or climb the cairn that towers over the town, from which there are some stunning views. The cairn was raised in 1944 to celebrate the 50th anniversary of Tasiilaq.

The town's other points of interest include a pentagonal church built in the mid-1980s and the town's first church, built in 1908 in the traditional style. The church has been beautifully restored and now houses the town's museum, with artwork and artifacts from around Greenland.

80

The percentage of Greenland's land mass covered by an ice cap and glaciers.

6
Qaanaaq
Thule

🄵F1 🄘PO Box 75; (+299) 97 14 73

Greenland's northernmost town was built in the 1950s. Its inhabitants follow a traditional way of life, hunting for seals, walruses and polar bears. Inhabitants speak Danish and Kalaallisut, and some speak the Inuktun language. The famous midnight sun lasts from mid-April to the end of August.

About 500 km (311 miles) east is the vast North and East Greenland National Park, covered by an inland ice cap and home to musk ox, polar bears and, in summer, walruses. Permission to enter must be obtained from the Expedition Office of the Government of Greenland (exp@nanoq.gl).

ACKNOWLEDGMENTS

The publisher would like to thank the following for their kind permission to reproduce their photographs:

Key: a-above; b-below/bottom; c-centre; f-far; l-left; r-right; t-top

123RF.com: Everst 235c; Anton Ivanov 28br; Audrius Merfeldas 122bc; Lillian Tveit 47cra.

4Corners: Susy Mezzanotte 12–3b; Maurizio Rellini 11t, 16c, 37crb, 58–9, 64cl.

Aamanns: 30bl; Columbus Leth 68–9t.

Aarhus Festival: Martin Dam Kristen 51cr.

Alamy Stock Photo: AF Archive 48br, 48–9t; Stig Alenäs 55bl, 95cra; Antiqua Print Gallery 53cla, 56bc; Art Collection 4 235tr; The Artchives 33cr; Aurora Photos / Thomas Bekker 266–7t; Photoshot License / Avalon 81cb; Frank Bach 12cl, 198t, 222–3b; Greg Balfour Evans 234bl; Wild Wonders of Europe / Bartocha 18, 176–7; Anna Berkut 113tr; Bernard Bialorucki 94b; DanitaDelimont.com / Walter Bibikow 49br; mauritius images GmbH / Walter Bibikow 22cl; Brian Bjeldbak 50bl; Stuart Black 24cr, 164tl; Chronicle 54bl, 54br; Bernhard Classen 250bl; Lordprice Collection 53cr; Craft Images 81t; Marco Cristofori 203b; Ian Dagnall 101tl, 156cl, 216–7t, 240tl; Danita Delimont / Tom Norring 110–1b; Didi 69crb; imageBROKER / Wolfgang Diederich 53tr; Elizabeth Whiting & Associates / Ewastock Diningrooms 81bc; dpa picture alliance 192bl, 216b; Michael Dwyer 166bc; Adam Eastland 81clb, 81br, 97clb; mauritius images GmbH / Thomas Ebelt 235br; Oliver Hoffmann / Your Rainbow Panorama by Olafur Eliasson 26–7c; Sina Ettmer 75t; eweliyi 138b; Folio Images / Gustaf Emanuelsson 252–3t; PE Forsberg 155bl; John Furnes 173t; Gaia Moments 129tl; Dylan Garcia 191b; Adam Gasson 80bl; Kevin George 31crb; Elly Godfrey 40–1b; Axel Göhns 220–1; StockimoNews / J. Gomes 50cr; Gonzales Photo / Jonas Kjaer 132b, / Kim M. Leland 47cl, 113b, 237tr, / Thomas Rasmussen 95cla, / Peter Troest 64br; Manfred Gottschalk 154t, / Han (2012) by Elmgreen & Dragset © DACS 2019 148t; AGE Fotostock / Christian Goupi 209bl; Tim Graham 53tl, 158–9b; Granger Historical Picture Archive 43cl,49cl, 163br; Jonathan Gröger 50cla; Guido Paradisi 186tl, 201tr; hemis.fr / Walter Bibikow 19cb, 22br, 34–5b, 188clb, 204–5, 218–9t, 238br; / Bertrand Gardel 13t, 79tr, 96–7t, 106–7t, / paintings © Walter Dahn 77, / Ludovic Maisant 80crb, 89tl, 108t, 112tl; Heritage Image Partnership Ltd 55tr; Oliver Hoffmann 210–11t; Peter Hollbaum-Hansen 35cl; Ralph Lee Hopkins 261clb; Stephen Hughes 166t; incamerastock / ICP 21, 256–7; imageBROKER 95cr; Novarc Images / Felis Images 129cra; Interfoto 53br, 54–5t; Janine Wiedel Photolibrary 146clb; John Peter Photography 231tl, 231cra; Jon Arnold Images Ltd 6–7, 63tr, 118–19; imageBROKER / Olaf Krüger 35tr; Aliaksei Kruhlenia 99cra; Joana Kruse 83br; Corbis / Tim De Waele / LC 50cra; Yadid Levy 133tr; Melvyn Longhurst 103br; LOOK Die Bildagentur der Fotografen GmbH / jan madsen 170tl, 174cra, / Roetting+Pollex 189tr, / Thomas Roetting 46b, 247; Lars Madsen 50cl; Mauritius Images Gmbh 230–31b, / ClickAlps 267cra, / Raimund Linke 175bl; Alexander Maximov 151cra; Neil McAllister 37tr; Antony McAulay 17, 142; Henk Meijer 36–7t, 37cl; Michal_Fludra_travel 253b; Tony Miller 139tl; robertharding / Roberto Moiola 28clb; Monradus 255tr; Miguel Angel Morales 134–5; Michael Morrison 254b; Christian Mueringer 248–9b; Eric Nathan 114bl; Niday Picture Library 55cra; Niels Poulsen mus 33bl, 136t, 173br; imageBROKER / NielsDK 100–101b, 149tr, 157t; AGB Photo Library / Alan Nielsen 54cr; North Wind Picture Archives 52br, 55br; OJPHOTOS 64cr, 171b, 182tl, 183b, 188b; Painters 32bl; Panther Media GmbH / Dagmara 186–7b; Kim Petersen 51cl, 63bl, 123bl, 124–5t,126–7, 167b; Photogenic 172b; Niels Poulsen DK 41tr, 51br, 95bc; PSL Images RF 57bl; Niels Quist 51tl, 163cra, 174t; Radius Images 200–201b; Dirk Renckhoff 85tr; Robertharding / Michael Runkel 84t, 224bl; Marcin Rogozinski 35br, 101cra,129cr; Jon Bower

Scandinavia 111tr; TravelCollection / Wolfgang Schardt 31cl; jean Schweitzer 240–41b; Guido Paradisi / artist Flemming Skude 185tl; Jeremy Sutton-Hibbert 146br; Morten Svenningsen 13cr; Mariusz Świtulski 22t; Jochen Tack 22t; traveler 78bl; travelimages 24t, / Chromosaturation light-installation (1965–2016) by Carlos Cruz-Dies 11cr, / Reclining Figure No. 5 (Seagram) by Henry Moore © The Henry Moore Foundation. All Rights Reserved, DACS 2019 www.henry-moore.org 2019 147br; Damian Tully 39cl; Lillian Tveit 162bl; United Archives GmbH 146bc; Taras Verkhovynets 105bc; VPC Coins Collection 57tr; F. Vrouenraths (Denmark) 162–3t; Wdnet Studio 85b; Westend61 GmbH 45tr; Jan Wlodarczyk 26tl; Xinhua 181br; Zoonar GmbH 128–9b.

ARKEN Museum of Modern Art: Tina Agnew 130bl; Anders Sune Berg / Love's Paradox (Surrender or Autonomy, Separateness as a Precondition for Connection.) (2007) and 2-Amino-5-Bromobenzotrifluoride (2011) by Damien Hirst © Damien Hirst and Science Ltd. All rights reserved, DACS 2019 131br; Hanne Fuglbjerg / Greenhouse (1995) by Thorbjørn Lausten 130–31t; Torben Petersen 130crb.

AWL Images: Walter Bibikow 4, 20t, 226–7; Marco Bottigelli 99t.

Bakken Kbh / Michael Lauritsen Dahl: 66tl.

Brus Bar: 38–9t.

The Coffee Collective A/S: 22c, 69cla.

Depositphotos Inc: cascoly 52t; eastfrisian 234t.

Dreamstime.com: Leonid Andronov 109br; Rui Baião 152–3, 159tr; Bernard Bialorucki 87br; Biathlonua 239cr; Bigandt 180–81t; Oliver Foerstner 164–5b; Luisa Vallon Fumi 122t; Galinasavina 82t; David Hyldkrog 160bl; Kkllggnn 193br; Valerii Kotenko 231tr; Radiokafka 38b, 39br; Rndmst 106br; Rphstock 2–3, 236b; Shure23 47br; Lillian Tveit 26tr.

Getty Images: 221A 88bl; 500px / Morten Christoffersen 224–5t, / Frank Jensen 46tl; alxpin 151t; Marco Bottigelli 44tl; Cultura / Richard Lewisohn 41br; danefromspain 212–213t; De Agostini / G. Dagli Orti 42tl, 184b, 239t; EyeEm / Thomas Dicker 140–41; Flottmynd 190tr; gaiamoments 129bc; Manfred Gottschalk 199tr; G. Jespersen 146cb; Keystone 56–7t; Martin Llado 28t; Lookphotos / Thomas Roetting 44–5b; Frank Lukasseck 19tl, 194–5; MB Photography 263t; Roberto Moiola 62bl, 90; Moment / Kevin Boutwell 10–11b, / Nick Brundle Photography 10c, / Hanneke Luijting 45br, / Posnov 8–9; Pixelicious Planet 268–9; Plougmann 169tr; Radiokukka 64t; Robertharding / Richard Ashworth 54tl; Roetting+Pollex 40tl; SeanPavonePhoto 115tl; SHSPhotography 57bc; Josef F. Stuefe 52bl; taranchic 232t; UIG / MyLoupe 101cr; UK Press / Mark Cuthbert 57cra; Ullstein Bild 56br; Thomas Winz 208t.

iStockphoto.com: AleksandarGeorgiev 117tl; Alexkotlov 264–5; alxpin 136–7b; Benedek 103tl; BirgerNiss 168crb, 168b; ClarkandCompany 24bl, 161t, 192–3t; cmfotoworks 249tl; danefromspain 42–3b; E+ / ClarkandCompany 31tr; LeoPatrizi 13br, / mura 62cl, 70; Esemelwe 20bl, 242–3; Explora_2005 260–61t; fotoVoyager 86–7t; Gestur Gislason 185bc; Alex_Ishchenko 223tl; kjekol 262–3b; mikeinlondon 76cl; miroslav_1 266bl; nemchinova 10clb; NMelander 210bl; SeanPavonePhoto 104–5t; shishic 50br; stigalenas 225br; TT 27tr; unikatdesign 251tl; Westersoe 202t; Zastavkin 124bl.

Koks: 28cl.

©2019 The LEGO Group: 215clb, 215cb, 215bc; Arne Müller 214–15t.

Louisiana Museum of Modern Art: 146–7; Kim Hansen 32–3t; Jeremy Jachym 146c.

National Museum Of Denmark Besøg Nationalmuseets hjemmeside: Sille Arendt 150bl; Roberto Fortuna 218bc.

Penguin Random House

Main Contributors Taraneh Ghajar Jerven, Robin Gauldie, Doug Sager, Monika Witkowska, Johanna Hald

Senior Editor Alison McGill

Senior Designer Laura O'Brien

Project Editor Lucy Richards

Project Art Editors Bess Daly, Ben Hinks, Bharti Karakoti, Mark Richards, Priyanka Thakur, Vinita Venugopal

Designer Van Anh Le

Factchecker Kathleen Sauret

Editors
Sophie Adam, Matthew Grundy Haigh, Penny Phenix, Zoë Rutland, Lucy Sara-Kelly

Proofreader Kathryn Glendenning

Indexer Helen Peters

Senior Picture Researcher Ellen Root

Picture Research Ashwin Adimari, Sumita Khatwani, Laskmi Rao, Surya S Sarangi, Mark Thomas

Illustrators Michał Burkiewicz, Dorota Jarymowicz, Paweł Marcza, Paweł Pasternak

Cartographic Editor James Macdonald

Cartography Subhashree Bharati, Simonetta Giori

Jacket Designers Bess Daly, Maxine Pedliham

Jacket Picture Research Susie Watters

Senior DTP Designer Jason Little

DTP Ashok Kumar, Mrinmoy Mazumadar

Senior Producer Stephanie McConnell

Managing Editor Rachel Fox

Art Director Maxine Pedliham

Publishing Director Georgina Dee

First edition 2005

Published in Great Britain by Dorling Kindersley Limited, 80 Strand, London, WC2R 0RL

Published in the United States by DK Publishing, 1450 Broadway, Suite 801, New York, NY 10018

A CIP catalog record for this book is available from the British Library.

A catalog record for this book is available from the Library of Congress.

ISSN: 1542 1554
ISBN: 978 0 2413 6538 0

Printed and bound in China.

www.dk.com

↑ An other-worldly ice formation in Greenland's Southern Fjords

❼
The Southern Fjords

🅰E1 ℹLundip Aqqutaa B 128, Nanortalik; www. visitgreenland.com

While crowds descend on the fjords of Norway, Greenland remains quieter and no less beautiful. The mighty Tasermiut Fjord in South Greenland has all the quintessential Greenlandic icons: steep granite cliffs, ice floes and cresting whales. Your visit will most likely start off from the southernmost town in Greenland, Nanortalik, a sleepy, picture-book village filled with colourful clapboard houses. The 70-m (43-mile) boat journey ends when you meet the massive ice sheet. Other options include trekking, kayaking or sailing on smaller craft. The granite cliffs dotted along the fjord are popular with adrenaline-seeking climbers. The nearby Torssuqatoq fjord is similarly gorgeous, and culminates at Aappilattoq, a photogenic village surrounded by steep mountain terrain.

TOP 5 EXPERIENCES IN GREENLAND

Wildlife Safari
Thrilling encounters with wildlife on land and sea include polar bears, whales, oxen, reindeer and eagles.

Dogsledding
Soak up arctic landscapes from a new perspective to the soundtrack of dogs' paws on snow.

Coastal Boat Cruise
Small vessels and the coastal ferry allow access to crowded ice floes and narrow fjords.

Skiing
From cross-country skiing expeditions to adrenaline-pumping heli-skiing, Greenland has many high-impact powder experiences.

Kayaking
The kayak links ancient culture, rugged modern expeditions and everyday life for inhabitants.

← Husky dogs pulling a sled through the wilderness near Tasiilaq

The staggeringly beautiful Mulafossur waterfall, Faroe Islands

8

Tórshavn

⌂F2 🚌🚌 🛈Niels Finsens gøta 17; www.visit torshavn.fo

The Faroe Islands' capital is a lively and picturesque place with a long, fascinating history. In the 11th century Tórshavn became a venue for Viking gatherings known as Althings, an early form of the Faroese parliament. The meetings were used to settle quarrels and to trade, and a permanent settlement developed around the annual event.

Some of the earliest inhabitants of the Faroes were Irish friars, and Tórshavn's oldest building is the 15th-century Munkastovan, or Monks' House, one of the few buildings to survive a fire in 1673.

The ruins of Skansin Fort, built in 1580 to defend the village from pirates, can still be seen. The fort acquired its present shape in 1780 and was used by British troops during World War II. Today, it provides a good viewpoint for surveying the town's busy harbour.

Søvn Landsins (Historical Museum) illustrates the Faroes' seafaring history, including boats and fishing equipment, as well as religious artifacts and items from the Viking era.

Søvn Landsins

⊛ ⌂Brekkutún 6, Hoyvík 🕐Mid-May–mid-Sep: 10am–5pm daily (from 2pm Sat & Sun); mid-Sep–mid-May: 2–5pm Thu & Sun 🖳savn.fo

9

Streymoy

⌂F2 🛈Niels Finsens gøta 17; (+298) 30 24 25

The largest of the Faroe Islands has a varied terrain and is criss-crossed by ancient paths once used to travel between settlements. Beyond the capital city Tórshavn, Saksun is a small village on the shores of an inlet that leads into Pollur lake – a fine spot to fish for trout and salmon. The **Dúvugarðar Museum**, located in an old turf-roofed farmhouse, has exhibits on island life from medieval times to the 1800s as well as a flock of around 300 sheep. Traces of a group of 8th-century Irish friars have

been found in the village of Kirkjubøur, at the south end of Streymoy. Written records show that Kirkjubøur was a busy place in medieval times. A reminder of those days is the 12th-century church of St Olaf, the archipelago's oldest historic site.

About half an hour's drive southwest from Tórshavn is **Vestmanna**, a coastal village famous for Vestmannabjørgini, (Bird Cliffs), where you'll find thousands of sea birds inhabiting the huge cliff face, such as fulmars, kittiwakes, guillemots, razorbills and puffins. Many visitors enjoy a boat tour to the cliffs. The two-hour tours embark from the village, and take in the narrow sounds and deep grottoes carved by the surf.

Vestmanna is also known for the Viking remains found here, which support the theory that it was one of the first places in the Faroes to be settled. Even its name suggests that "Men from the West" lived here.

Dúvugarðar Museum

⌂Saksunarvegur 31, Saksun 📞(+298) 59 44 55 🕐Mid-Jun–Aug: 2–5pm daily

Vestmanna

🖳puffin.fo 🖳visit-vestmanna.com

↑ Traditional turf-roof cabins in the village of Saksun, on Streymoy

---

⑩

Mykines

🅰F2 ✈ 🛈Flogvøllurin 2, Sørvágur; (+298) 33 34 55

The islanders here live in a tiny village of colourful turf-topped houses, and are vastly outnumbered by birds. This is one of the hardest islands to reach, but the trip is worth it. The islet of Mykineshólmur is a good spot to view gannets and large colonies of puffins. It is connected to the island by a footbridge built 24 m (79 ft) above the sea.

---

⑪

Vágar

🅰F2 ✖🖶 🛈Flogvøllurin 2, Sørvágur; www.visit vagar.fo

Vágar's modern airport was originally used as a landing strip by the Royal Air Force. This mountainous island has some of the region's most stunning sights, including the towering needle rock Trollukonufingur ("Troll Woman's Finger"). Lake Sorvagsvatn is a little way from Midvagur, Vágar's largest town, and due to an optical illusion appears to float high above the sea from a certain angle. Sandavagur, a nearby village,

↑ The populated waterfront of Tórshavn, the Faroe Islands

is the birthplace of Venceslaus Ulricus Hammershaimb, creator of the Faroese alphabet.

---

⑫

Eysturoy

🅰F2 🛈Í Støð 1, Fuglafjørður; www.visit runavik.fo

The second-largest island of the archipelago is connected to Streymoy by a road bridge, jokingly described as the only bridge across the Atlantic.

Eysturoy has a number of unique features. At 882 m (2,894 ft), Slættaratindur is the Faroes' highest point. The summit can easily be reached by climbing the mountain's eastern ridge; the views from the peak are breathtaking.

Close to Fuglafjørður is the Varmekelda, or Warm Spring, which has invigorating thermal waters of 16–18° C (60–64° F) and is believed to have healing properties. Further north is the village of Oynadarfjorður. Just beyond its shore are the Rinkusteinar (Rocking Stones), two huge blocks that move with the motion of the sea.

---

⑬

Kalsoy

🅰F2 ✈ 🛈Tingstøðin, Klaksvík; (+298) 45 69 39

Nicknamed the "Flute" because of its elongated shape, this rugged island is ideal for hikes. Many walkers head towards Kap Kallur, at the northern tip, where the lighthouse makes an excellent point from which to view the cliffs. Puffins can often be spotted. The sea stacks at Eysturoy's northern tip can be seen on a clear day.

↑ A couple of resting Atlantic puffins, a frequent sight on Kalsoy island

NEED TO KNOW

Icy waters of Uummannaq, Greenland

Before You Go...270

Getting Around...272

Practical Information...............................276

BEFORE
YOU GO

Forward planning is essential to any successful trip. Be prepared for all eventualities by considering the following points before you travel.

AT A GLANCE

CURRENCY
Danish Krone (DKK)

AVERAGE DAILY SPEND

SAVE
850Kr

SPEND
1350Kr

SPLURGE
1950Kr+

BOTTLED WATER
15Kr

COFFEE
35Kr

BEER
43Kr

DINNER FOR TWO
650Kr

ESSENTIAL PHRASES

Hello	Hej
Goodbye	Farvel
Please	Vær så venlig
Thank you	Tak
Do you speak English?	Taler du engelsk?
I don't understand	Jeg forstår det ikke

ELECTRICITY SUPPLY

Power sockets are types C or K, fitting two-pronged plugs and those with a grounding pin. Standard voltage is 230v.

Passports and Visas

Passports are required for everyone entering Denmark. Residents of 120 nations must apply for tourist visas prior to travel; British, EU, American, Australian and Canadian citizens do not need visas. Check with the **Danish Immigration Service** for more information. Increased borded controls put in place since 2016 means that those entering the country from the Schengen Area should be prepared to have their passport checked.

Danish Immigration Service
w nyidanmark.dk
Schengen visas
w schengenvisainfo.com

Travel Safety Advice

Visitors can get up-to-date travel safety information from the UK Foreign and Commonwealth Office, the US State Department and the Australian Department of Foreign Affairs and Trade.

Australia
w smartraveller.gov.au
UK
w gov.uk/foreign-travel-advice
US
w travel.state.gov

Customs Information

Visitors from outside the EU are permitted duty-free shopping and can claim a VAT refund on goods as they leave the country. An individual is permitted to carry the following for personal use:

Tabacco products 800 cigarettes, 400 cigarillos, 200 cigars, or 1 kg smoking tobacco.

Alcohol 10 litres of alcoholic beverages above 22 per cent strength, 90 litres of wine and 110 litres of beer.

Cash You cannot enter or leave the EU with €10,000 or more in cash (approximately 75,000Kr or the equivalent in other currencies) and you must declare it to the customs authorities.

If travelling outside the EU limits vary, so always check restrictions before departing.

Insurance

It is wise to take out an insurance policy covering theft, loss of belongings, medical problems, cancellation and delays.

The Danish National Health Service gives free healthcare to citizens but does not cover visitors to the country. Those travelling from EU countries should secure a European Health Insurance (**EHIC**) card, which covers visitors from the European Economic Area (EEA). Note that this is for non-emergency treatment only.

Travellers from outside the EU must arrange their own private medical insurance.

EHIC
🌐 gov.uk/european-health-insurance-card

Vaccinations

No inoculations are needed for travellers visiting Denmark.

Money

Credit, debit and prepaid currency cards are accepted almost everywhere. Contactless payments are also common. ATMs can be found in all tourist areas, though may not be available 24 hours a day. It is the custom to pay cash for transactions under 100Kr.

Booking Accommodation

Denmark offers a wide variety of accommodation options, from luxury five-star hotels, and family-run B&Bs, to budget hostels and stylish private apartments.

Hotels generally offer substantial discounts for online bookings, while local tourist offices offer inexpensive accommodation in family homes. Remote accommodation, including rural farmstays and B&Bs, should be booked well in advance.

Travellers with Specific Needs

Denmark is constantly improving its access to both buildings and rural outposts, but it does not yet offer full accessibility. A number of buses provide wheelchair access, and all taxis accept collapsible wheelchairs. Travellers can phone the national train company Danske Statsbaner (**DSB**) for accessibility at specific stations or to arrange for assistance. **Visit Denmark** lists accessible sites, including holiday lets and even fishing spots. **God Adgang** is also a great resource, listing and rating venues and service providers across Denmark.

DSB
📞 70 13 14 15
Visit Denmark
🌐 visitdenmark.com
God Agang
🌐 godadgang.dk

Language

Danish is the only official language of Denmark, and is an official language in Greenland and the Faroe Islands. An estimated 86 per cent of all Danes speak English as a second language.

Closures

Mondays Generally, if a museum or restaurant is open on a Sunday, it may well be closed on Monday.

Weekends Banks are closed all weekend. Many shops close at 4pm on Saturday and remain closed on Sunday, though larger stores usually remain open.

Public holidays All offices and banks are closed but many museums and attractions remain open. Transport services may be reduced.

PUBLIC HOLIDAYS

New Year's Day	1 Jan
Occupation Day	9 Apr
Easter Sunday	12 Apr (2020) 4 Apr (2021)
Workers' Day	1 May
Liberation Day	5 May
Ascension Day	21 May (2020) 13 May (2021)
Constitution Day	5 Jun
St John's Eve	23 Jun
Christmas Eve	24 Dec
Christmas Day	25 Dec
Third Day of Christmas	26 Dec

GETTING
AROUND

Whether you are visiting for a short city break or an extended rural retreat, discover how best to reach your destinations and travel like a pro.

AT A GLANCE

PUBLIC TRANSPORT COSTS

COPENHAGEN

24Kr

SINGLE JOURNEY
Bus, metro, train, water bus

AARHUS

20Kr

SINGLE JOURNEY
Bus & light rail

ODENSE

24Kr

SINGLE JOURNEY
Bus

TOP TIP
It's free to take a bike on Copenhagen's S-train; there is a charge for the Metro.

SPEED LIMIT

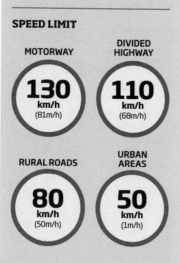

MOTORWAY

130 km/h
(81m/h)

DIVIDED HIGHWAY

110 km/h
(68m/h)

RURAL ROADS

80 km/h
(50m/h)

URBAN AREAS

50 km/h
(1m/h)

Arriving by Air

Most international flights arrive at Copenhagen's Kastrup Airport (CPH), the country's largest and Scandinavia's busiest airport. Kastrup is the main hub of Scandinavia Airlines (SAS). Billund (BLL), increasingly used by budget airlines, is closest to LEGOLAND®. Aalborg (AAL), Aarhus (AAR), Esbjerg (EBJ) and Sønderborg (SGD) also have international airports.

Train Travel

International Train Travel
It is possible to travel to Denmark by rail from any major city in Europe via the national DSB rail network. Students and budget travellers with **Eurail** or the European-only **InterRail** passes have access to the entire Denmark network. Note that all such passes must be purchased outside Denmark prior to arrival.
Eurail
W eurail.com
InterRail
W interrail.eu

Domestic Train Travel
All regions of Denmark are served by the national railway company **DSB**. Work is underway on high-speed tracks, starting with a 250 km/h (155m/h) link to Ringsted, just west of Copenhagen.

Standard tickets are valid for travel at any hour, on the day specified. They also include free travel for two children under 12 per adult ticket. Business class tickets include reserved seats and complimentary snacks. Considerable discounts can be had by purchasing "orange tickets", available online only and up to two months in advance. Orange tickets cannot be changed or refunded, and do not include seat reservation.

Journey Planner is a comprehensive timetable and route planner for all types of train travel. It also includes details on onward travel by bus and even by bike, to any destination in Denmark.
DSB
W dsb.dk
Journey Planner
W rejseplanen.dk

GETTING TO AND FROM THE AIRPORT

Airport	Distance to city	Taxi fare	Public Transport	Journey time
Aalborg	6 km (4 miles)	120Kr	bus	12 mins
Aalund	4 km (3 miles)	200Kr	bus/rail	10 mins
Aarhus	43 km (27 miles)	700Kr	bus	40 mins
Billund	4km (3 miles)	150Kr	bus	7 mins
Bornholm	5 km (3 miles)	100Kr	bus	7 mins
Copenhagen Kastrup	8 km (5 miles)	240Kr	bus/rail/metro	20 mins
Esbjerg	10 km (8 miles)	120Kr	bus	14 mins
Hans Christian Andersen (Odense)	8 km (5 miles)	126Kr	bus	24 mins
Sønderborg	7 km (4 miles)	150Kr	bus	15 mins

RAIL JOURNEY PLANNER

This map is a handy reference for travel on Denmark's main scenic and passenger lines. Journey times given are for the fastest available service on each route

Aarhus to Aalborg	1.5 hrs
Copenhagen to Aalborg	4.5 hrs
Copenhagen to Aarhus	3 hrs
Copenhagen to Esbjerg	3 hrs
Copenhagen to Horsens	2.5 hrs
Copenhagen to Odense	1 hr
Odense to Aalborg	3 hrs
Odense to Aarhus	1.5 hrs
Odense to Esbjerg	1.5 hrs
Odense to Horsens	1 hr
Horsens to Aarhus	0.5 hrs

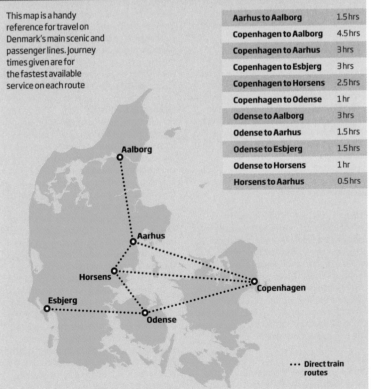

Aalborg

Aarhus

Horsens

Esbjerg

Odense

Copenhagen

••• Direct train routes

Public Transport

Denmark has one of the most advanced public transport systems in the world. Service perks include free minibuses in Odense and 24 hours daily metro in Copenhagen, not to mention free taxis if your bus is late in Odense or Aalborg.

Public Transport Operators

DOT (Copenhagen)
🅦 dinoffentligetransport.dk
Metroselskabet (Copenhagen)
🅦 intl.m.dk
Midttrafik (Aarhus)
🅦 midttrafik.dk
Fynbus (Odense)
🅦 fynbus.dk
Nordjyllands Trafikselskab (Aalborg)
🅦 nordjyllandstrafikselskab.dk

Buses

Denmark's buses are comfortable and modern. Copenhagen also has popular blue and yellow water buses. Tickets can be bought online, at vending machines or on board the bus provided you have exact change. They must always be validated before travel. There are severe fines for travelling without a ticket. In Copenhagen, get on the bus in the front and exit at the back or middle; in Aarhus, enter the bus by the back door.

Long Distance Bus Travel

Budget flights and train travel are the most popular means for getting between cities, but coaches do still operate. It is possible to travel to Denmark by coach from London, via Brussels, in under 24 hours with **Flixbus**. There are more frequent coach options from the main German cities with **Eurolines**. Both firms travel extensively within Denmark.
Flixbus
🅦 flixbus.co.uk
Eurolines
🅦 eurolines.de

Metro

Copenhagen and Frederiksberg share the only underground subway system in Denmark, with 22 stations on two lines and 34 modern, driverless trains. The network will more than double in size, with 24 new stations on the Cityringen, Nordhavn and Sydhavn extensions appearing between 2019 and 2024. Waiting time between trains, at peak hours, is as little as two minutes. Copenhagen is the only world capital with a 24-hour subway system.

Taxis

Official taxis are clearly identified and can be hailed when the yellow "taxa" light is illuminated. There are also stands and taxis can be booked by phone. Prices vary between companies, but all charge extra at night and on weekends, with extra fees for large items of baggage. Uber was popular in Copenhagen but left when new Danish laws required them to have meters.

Driving

Denmark is one of the most pleasant countries in Europe for driving. Distances are comfortable, traffic is relatively light, the roads are extremely well maintained and flat, and local drivers are not aggressive.

Driving to Denmark

For visitors making a driving tour of Europe, the fastest route to Denmark is the motorway north of Hamburg. It is route 7 in Germany and the E45 in Denmark, where it continues all the way to the north. From Calais in France, the Danish border is an eight-hour drive. Coming from Sweden, via Malmö, cars cross the Øresund Bridge. Dozens of car ferry routes offer even more alternatives.

Car Rental

Valid driving licences are all accepted, whatever the country of issue, but drivers must be at least 21 years of age and have held their licence for one year or more. Drivers under 25 incur daily surcharges of up to 125Kr. There is no upper age limit. Rental cars with automatic transmission are rare, and must be booked in advance. Returning a car to a different location from where it was picked up incurs a significant surcharge.

Driving in Denmark

Foreign drivers are required to carry their passport, driving licence, registration and insurance documents at all times. Police are quick to stop those speeding, and radar and camera controls are widespread. Tailgating or changing lanes without using indicators will attract police intervention.

Denmark's motorways are marked by green signs. There are no tolls on motorways, but payment is required on the Øresund Bridge crossing into Sweden (385Kr), and the stunning Store Baelt bridge linking Zealand with Funen (240Kr). **Brobizz** is an electronic toll collection system that works with both bridges, plus –car ferries.

Denmark is a leading nation in electric vehicle use and has promised a ban on all petrol and diesel vehicles by 2030. The 2,050 EV charging points now exceeds the country's number of petrol stations. These charging points are some of the fastest, most high-powered in the world; cars can be fully recharged in less than 20 minutes. Despite these green credentials, Denmark doesn't have urban congestion charges (a measure voted down in Copenhagen), nor low emission zones or any system of closing streets in relation to pollution levels.

Brobizz
w brobizz.com

Rules of the Road

Foreign drivers must be at least 18 years of age. Children under 7 years, or smaller than 1.35 m (4.3 ft), must be in child seats and seat belts must be worn at all times. Drivers are required to carry a warning triangle. The use of mobile phones, even with headsets, is forbidden. Dipped headlights must be used at all times, even during daylight. British cars must be fitted with deflectors to adjust headlight angles so they do not blind oncoming motorists. When turning right, drivers must give away to cyclists on the inside.

The blood alcohol limit is the European standard of 0.05 per cent, which is stricter than in the UK and USA. Changing lanes without signalling can result in a fine of 1000Kr, payable on the spot. Payments for other traffic and parking offences, including speeding, may also be demanded in cash on the spot. Motorcyclists and passengers must both wear helmets.

Car drivers should be aware of cyclists, of whom there are many and who often have the right of way. This being said, they are not immune to road regulations. They cannot turn right at red lights and are forbidden on roadways where cycle paths exist.

Hitchhiking

Hitchhiking is forbidden on motorways and is generally not common practice in Denmark.

Cycling

Denmark is a country of cyclists, with infrastructures supporting this green mode of transport. It's easy to join the locals, especially in Denmark's cities. Copenhagen is the world's best cycling city, and is home to more bikes than cars. Sophisticated and comfortable electric bikes, with built in GPS, can be used across the capital with the **Bycyklen** scheme. For more choice and longer tours, **Copenhagen Bicycles** has everything from cargo carriers to carbon fibre racing bikes. Other cities have free or subsidized **City Bike** schemes too, notably Aarhus and Odense. Bike trails like the Copenhagen Green Belt and long-distance forest routes are best tackled on full-suspension mountain bikes from the Danish specialists **Mountain Bike Tours**.

Bycyklen
w bycyklen.dk
Copenhagen Bicycles
w copenhagenbicycles.dk
Aarhus City Bike
w aarhuskommune.dk

Odense City Bike
w cibi.dk
Mountain Bike Tours
w mtb-tours.com

Boats and Ferries

Car ferries are often faster, and can be more enjoyable, than driving. Within Denmark, in addition to the international car transports going to Germany, Sweden and Norway, Denmark has some two dozen smaller craft. These can take as little as four minutes, and traverse areas where no land crossing exists, as at Veno-Kleppen in Jutland, accessed by **Venoe Faergefart**. The oldest, and most quaint ferry is the Mellerup-Voer crossing in Jutland, run by **Randersfjord Faerger**.

Denmark also has a range of pleasure-only cruises. Some are on lakes, like Skanderborg Lake with the **MS Dagmar**. Others involve international liners touring Scandinavia. Some day-cruises can even be done on old wooden sailing ships; visit **United Sailing Ships** for more information. Companies such as **Get My Boat** offer experienced sailors all manner of craft to rent, from rowboats to sailing yachts.

Venoe Faergefart
w venoefaergefart.dk
Randersfjord Faerger
w randersfjord-faerger.dk
MS Dagmar
w dagmar.mono.net
United Sailing Ships
w unitedsailingships.com
Get My Boat
w getmyboat.com

SAILING THE NORDICS

Smyril Line
The Faroe Islands are perhaps one of Denmark's best kept secrets. This boat service sails from Hirtshals, North Jutland, to Tórshavn, the capital of the Faroe Islands. Check online for timetables.
w smyrilline.com

Fjordline
Head north to the epic landscape of Norway with this catamaran service, which runs from Hirtshals to Kristiansand and Bergen, via Stavanger, mid-May to mid-September.
w smyrilline.com

Scandlines
Hop on at Helingsør and, 20 minutes later, hop off at Sweden's Helsingborg.
w scandlines.dk

PRACTICAL
INFORMATION

A little local know-how goes a long way in Denmark. Here you will find all the essential advice and information you will need during your stay.

EMERGENCY NUMBERS

AMBULANCE	POLICE
112	**114**

FIRE SERVICE	ON-CALL PHYSICIAN
112	**1813**

TIME ZONE
CET/CEST Central European Summer Time runs from the last Sunday in March to the last Sunday in October.

TAP WATER
Unless posted otherwise, tap water in Denmark is safe to drink.

TIPPING

Waiter	Round up bill
Hotel Porter	10Kr per bag
Housekeeping	Not Expected
Concierge	Not Expected
Taxi Driver	Round up bill

Personal Security

Denmark poses no undue risks to travellers, though normal safety precautions should be observed to deter pickpockets and opportunist thieves. Certain districts, such as Christiania in Copenhagen, are best avoided at night. Travel insurance is advised.

Health

Denmark's healthcare service is excellent, but note that not all hospital emergency rooms are open 24 hours a day. It is strongly advised that travellers have personal medical insurance or an EHIC card (p271). Pharmacists are readily available and can give advice and over-the-counter medication. Pharmacies are generally open 24 hours a day; look for the *apotek* sign.

In an urgent situation that does not quite require an ambulance, call 1813 before going to an emergency room. This alerts an on-call physician or an appropriate hospital to your arrival. The 1813 service can also issue medical prescriptions, to be picked up at a nearby pharmacy.

Smoking, Alcohol and Drugs

Danes smoke considerably more than Britons, Americans and their Scandinavian counterparts. Chewing tobacco is also common and Denmark is famous for its manufacture of luxury pipes and pipe tobacco. Rather suprisingly, smoking is illegal at train stations and in indoor public spaces, with the exception of very small bars and pubs that do not s erve food.

Denmark's blood alcohol limit for drivers, at 0.05 per cent, is considerably stricter than those in the UK and USA, though standard for the EU. There is no lower limit for novice drivers. Beer and wine can be bought in shops from 16 years of age and above, but in bars only from 18 years.

Marijuana is illegal in Denmark though present in places such as Christiana in Copenhagen, where police raids are routine.

ID

Passports may be requested when checking into a hotel and some form of photo ID may be requested at any time by police. It is advisable to carry a photocopy of your passport. Drivers must carry valid driving licences at all times.

Local Customs

Danes are genuinely friendly and frankly outspoken. It's sensible to brush up on the rules of the road –whether a cyclist, driver or pedestrian – before your arrival. For more specifc advice, turn to Rules of the Road (p275). Make eye contact when raising a glass for a toast, and remember that this is a progressive country, where women's and LGBT+ rights are ubiquitous.

LGBT+ Safety

Like their Scandinavian neighbours, Denmark has long been at the forefront of the LGBT+ movement and was the first country in the world to legalize same-sex relationships. As a result, LGBT+ travellers should not face any issues when visiting Denmark. A number of parades and events are held each year in Copenhagen and Aarhus.
LGBT+
🆆 lgbt.dek

Visiting Churches and Cathedrals

Denmark does not have any dress codes for visiting its churches, but be sure to show respect.

Mobile Phones and WIFI

Phone signals are strong throughout Denmark, even on its 406 islands. Danish SIM cards can only be bought by Danish residents with a Danish Security Number, but pay-as-you-go cards are available for tourists. European travellers can use up to 15GB of their data allowance without being charged an additional fee. Libraries, hospitals and many businesses offer free Wi-Fi, as do all trains. Free hotspots can be found quickly on **Wi-Fi Space**.
Wi-Fi Space
🆆 wifispc.com/Denmark

Post

Denmark's PostNord has been closing regional offices, though the bright red postal boxes remain common. Postal services are often found in small shops and newsagents.

Taxes and Refunds

Travellers returning to countries outside the EU are eligible for VAT refunds, though only a limited number of shops in the main cities operate the scheme. Shoppers must spend a minimum of 300Kr per day in the same shop and get a VAT refund certificate at time of purchase. Goods must be presented to customs at the departure point. Refunds are operated by **Premier Tax Free**.
Premier Tax Free
🆆 premiertaxfree.com

Discount Cards

The **Copenhagen Card** offers unlimited travel on bus, train and metro, free museum admission and deals at many attractions and shops. The **City Pass** covers transport only. In Aarhus, the **Aarhus Card** provides free admission to 25 museums and sights, unlimited travel and free car parking.
Copenhagen Card
🆆 copenhagencard.com
City Pass
🆆 citypass.dk
Aarhus Card
🆆 go.bookaarhus.com

WEBSITES AND APPS

Bike & Stay DK
This cycling app provides routes and bike-friendly places to stay.
ART CPH
For Apple devices, this guide to art in Copenhagen includes invitations to free gallery shows.
Mobilbilletter
Locates your cheapest transport options.
Visit Denmark
Visitdenmark.com is a comprehensive website for your Danish adventure.

INDEX

Page numbers in **bold** refer to main entries.

2-Amino-5-Bromobenzotri fluoride (Hirst) 131

A

Aakirkeby **250**, 255
Aalborg 227, 231, **232-3**
  map 233
Aalborghus Slot **233**
Aarhus 11, 205, **208-11**
  hotels 209
  map 209
  restaurants 211
Aarhus O **210-11**
Abildgaard, Nicolai 33
Absalon, Bishop 170, 172, 177, 188
  Roskilde Domkirke 156
  statues of 102, 109
Absolute monarchy 55
Accommodation
  booking 271
  see also Hotels
Ærø 195, **203**
Ærøskøbing **203**
Agersø **182**
Air travel 272, 273
Alcohol 276-7
Alfred the Great 53
Allinge **248**
Amager (Copenhagen) **138**
Amalienborg Slot (Copenhagen) **74-5**, 88-9
Amusement parks 41
  Bakken 12, **162**
  BonBon-Land (Holme-Ostrup) **183**
  Fårup Sommerland **237**
  Joboland **253**
  LEGOLAND® 12, 41, 205, **214-15**
  Sommerland Sjælland 175
  Tivoli (Copenhagen) 12, 41, **94-5**
Ancher, Anna and Michael 32, 76, 234, 235, 237
Ancient monuments
  Bornholm burial mounds 243
  Bronze Age burial mounds (Limfjorden) 230
  Fyrkat 35, 227, **239**
  Grønjægers Høj 191
  Hindsholm burial chamber 201
  Jelling burial mounds 219
  Kong Asgers Høj **190-91**

Ancient monuments (cont.)
  Lindholm Høje 34, **238**
  mummies/bog bodies 52, 216, 217, 260
  Neolithic burial chamber (Grønnesse Skov) 163
  Neolithic burial mounds (Knudshoved Odde) 184
  Viking burial grounds 34
  see also Vikings
Ancient Road 45
Andersen, Hans Christian 12, **42-3**, 56, 102, 133
  Nyhavn houses (Copenhagen) 43, **104**
  Odense houses **198-9**
  statues 87, 103
  The Little Mermaid **82**
Apps 277
Architecture **36-7**
ARKEN Museum (Copenhagen) 33, **130-31**
ARoS Kunstmuseum (Aarhus) 32, **210**
Arresø **165**
Art **32-3**
Art galleries *see* Museums and galleries
Assens **200**
Assistens Kirkegård (Copenhagen) 133
ATMs 271
Axeltorv (Helsingør) 149

B

Bakeries 69
Bakken 12, **162**
Bang & Olufsen 37
Bars and cafés
  cocktail bars 67
  Copenhagen 87, 108, 109, 123, 132, 139
  craft beer bars and brew pubs 38
  Funen 198
  Greenland and the Faroe Islands 262
  pubs with a view 39
Beaches **46-7**
  Amager Strandpark (Copenhagen) 41, 138
  Bildsø Strand **183**
  family-friendly 41
  Skagen 10, 234-5
  Southern Zealand 189
Beer 38-9
Bendz, Wilhelm Ferdinand 85
Bicycle hire 275

Björk, Oscar 235
Black Diamond (Copenhagen) 36, 113, 116, 117
Blixen, Karen 49, **163**
BLOX (Copenhagen) **113**
Boats and ferries 275
Boat trips
  coastal boat cruises (Greenland) 263
  Postbåden 186
  Wadden Sea 213
Bohr, Niels 102
BonBon-Land (Holme-Ostrup) **183**
Bornholm 13, 20, **242-55**
  beaches 47
  cycling 44, 254-5
  hotels 249
  map 244-5
  restaurants 251
Bornholm School 32
Bornholms Kunstmuseum (Gudhjem) 32, **252**
Børsen (Copenhagen) **112**, 117
Botanisk Have (Copenhagen) **86**
Brahe, Tycho 136
Brandts (Odense) **199**
Brøndum's Hotel (Krøyer) 235
Burial grounds *see* Ancient monuments
Bus travel 274

C

Cafés *see* Bars and cafés
Calendar of events **50-51**
Canute the Great 54
Canute IV 54
Carbon neutral 44, 71, 116
Carlsberg Brewery (Copenhagen) 37, 132
Car rental 274
Castles and fortifications
  Aalborghus Slot **233**
  Dragsholm Slot **174**, 175
  Egeskov Slot 195, **200**
  Fyrkat 35, 41, 227, **239**
  Gåsetårnet & Danmarks Borgcenter (Vordingborg) 184-5
  Gavnø Slot **184**
  Gisselfeld Kloster 182
  Hammershus Slot **253**
  Kastellet (Copenhagen) **82-3**
  Korsø Fæstning 171
  Nyborg Slot 200
  Rosenholm Slot 241
  Selsø Slot **172-3**
  Sønderborg Castle 224

Castles and fortifications (cont.)
  Spøttrup Borg **231**
  Trelleborg **173**
  Valdemars Slot (Tåsinge)
    202
  Vallø Slot **192**
  Voergård Slot **239**
  see also Palaces
Cathedrals *see* Churches and
  cathedrals
Ceramics 36
Changing of the Guard
  (Copenhagen) 74, 88
Charlotte Amalie, Princess 139
Charlotte Amalie, Queen 104
Charlottenborg Slot
  (Copenhagen) **104–5**, 115
Charlottenlund Slot
  (Copenhagen) **139**
Children **40–41**, 275
Christian IX 75
Christian I 157
Christiania (Copenhagen) 119,
  124
Christian II 170, 187
Christianity 54
Christian IV 55, 150, 160
  Christianshavn (Copenhagen)
    119, **122**
  Copenhagen 71, 91
  Rosenborg Slot (Copenhagen)
    78–9
  Roskilde Domkirke 156, 157
Christiansborg Slot
  (Copenhagen) **98–9**, 116–17
Christiansen, Ole Kirk 214
Christianshavn (Copenhagen)
  47, 119, **122**
Christian V 106, 111, 160
Christian VII 74, 75
Christian VIII 75
Churches and cathedrals
  Alexander Nevsky Kirke
    (Copenhagen) 88
  Den Tilsandede Kirke **237**
  Domkirke (Aarhus) **211**
  Domkirke (Viborg) 240
  Elmelunde Kirke **190**
  etiquette 277
  Fanefjord Kirke **188**
  Jelling Kirke 219
  Marmorkirken (Copenhagen)
    84, 88
  Nykirke (Nyker) 250
  Nylars Kirke 250
  Østerlars Rundkirke
    (Bornholm) **246–7**
  Ribe Domkirke **212**
  Roskilde Domkirke **156–7**

Churches and cathedrals (cont.)
  Sankt Albans Kirke
    (Copenhagen) **83**
  Sankt Ansgars Kirke
    (Copenhagen) 89
  Sankt Bendts Kirke
    (Ringsted) 182
  Sankt Knuds Kirke (Odense)
    199
  Sankt Olai Kirke (Helsingør)
    149
  Sankt Petri Kirke
    (Copenhagen) **109**
  Tveje Merløse Kirke **168**
  Vor Frelsers Kirke
    (Copenhagen) **122–3**
  Vor Frue Kirke (Aalborg) **233**
  Vor Frue Kirke (Aarhus) **209**
  Vor Frue Kirke (Copenhagen)
    110
  see also Monasteries and
    convents
Cinema **48–9**
Cirkelbroen (Copenhagen) **125**
Cisternerne (Copenhagen) **137**
Closures 271
Clubs, Copenhagen 66
Coffee 69
Copenhagen 16, **58–139**
  bars and cafés 67, 87, 108,
    109, 123, 132, 139
  Beyond the Centre 63,
    126–39
  Central Copenhagen North
    62, **70–89**
  Central Copenhagen South
    62, **90–117**
  Christianshavn and Holmen
    63, **118–25**
  cycling 11, 44, 64–5
  food 68–9
  H.C. Andersen in 43
  history 54, 56
  hotels 85, 105, 125
  itineraries 22–3, 64–5
  map 60–61
  map: Beyond the Centre 127
  map: Central Copenhagen
    North 72–3
  map: Central Copenhagen
    South 92–3
  map: Christianshavn and
    Holmen 120–21
  nightlife 66–7
  public transport 274
  restaurants 69, 83, 110, 123,
    136, 139
  shopping 133
  urban beaches 47

Copenhagen (cont.)
  urban design 37
  walks 88–9, 114–17
Credit cards 271
Currency 270
Customs information 270
Cycling **44–5**
  A Cycling Tour of Bornholm
    254–5
  bicycle hire 275
  for children 40
  Copenhagen 11, 42, **64–5**
  Silkeborg Lake District **217**

D

Danelaw 53
Danevirke 53
Danish Architecture Centre
  (Copenhagen) **113**
Danish Riviera 46
Davids Samling (Copenhagen)
  86–7
Deconstructivism movement
  130
Degas, Edgar 96
  Little Dancer of Fourteen 97
Den Blå Planet (Copenhagen)
  138
Den Fynske Landsby (Odense)
  199
Den Gamle Bay (Aarhus) **211**
Den Tilsandede Kirke **237**
Derain, André, *Woman in a
  Chemise* 76
Design 13, **36–7**
Designmuseum Danmark
  (Copenhagen) 37, **80–81**, 89
Det Gamle Rådhus (Ribe) **212**
Det Kongelige Bibliotek
  (Copenhagen) **113**, 117
Det Kongelige Teater
  (Copenhagen) 43, **106**,
  115
Disabled travellers 271
Disko Bay 260, 261
Dogsledding 263
Dokk1 (Aarhus) **210**
Domkirke (Aarhus) **211**
Domkirke (Viborg) 240
Dragør (Copenhagen) **139**
Dragør Museum (Copenhagen)
  139
Dragset, Ingar *see* Elmgreen &
  Dragset
Dragsholm Slot **174**, 175
Drinks *see* Food and drink
Driving 274–5
Drugs 277

E

Ebeltoft **216**
Eckersberg, Christoffer Wilhelm 33, 56, 76, 85
Edward VII 83
Egeskov Slot 195, **200**
electricity supply 270
Eliasson, Olafur 32, 125, 131, 210
Elling Woman 52
Elmelunde Kirke **190**
Elmelunde Master 188, 190
Elmgreen & Dragset 33
    Han 148
Emergency numbers 276
Enlightenment 55
Entertainment
    Det Kongelige Teater (Copenhagen) 43, **106**, 115
    Katuaq Cultural Centre (Nuuk) 261
    Kulturværftet (Helsingør) **148**
    Musikhuset (Aarhus) **208**
    Ny Carlsberg Glyptotek (Copenhagen) 96
    Operaen (Copenhagen) **123**
    Skuespilhuset (Copenhagen) **107**
    Tivoli (Copenhagen) 94-5
    VEGA (Copenhagen) 66
    see also Nightlife
Erik of Pomerania 54, 149, 150, 185
Erik the Red 257
Esbjerg **223**
Eskilstrup **189**
Esrum Sø **165**
Etiquette 277
European Union 57
Eventyrhaven (Odense) **199**
Experimentarium (Copenhagen) **136**
Eysturoy **267**

F

Faaborg **201**
Fakse **192-3**
Falster 177, 188-9
Fanefjord Kirke **188**
Fano, Queen 188, 191
Fanø 205, **222**
Farming 31
Faroe Islands **266-7**
    history 56
    itinerary 28-9
    restaurants 267
    see also Greenland and the Faroe Islands
Fårup Sommerland **237**
Fejø **186-7**
Femø **186-7**

Ferries 275
Festivals and events
    A Year in Denmark **50-51**
    Viking 34
Film locations 49
Fjerritslev 231
Flakhaven (Odense) **199**
Folketinget (Copenhagen) **111**, 117
Food and drink
    Bornholm 13, 248
    Carlsberg Brewery (Copenhagen) 37, 132
    Copenhagen for Foodies **68-9**
    Danish wine **169**
    Denmark for Foodies **30-31**
    Denmark on Tap **38-9**
    Gården Madkulturhuset (Bornholm) **248**
    Høstet Sea Buckthorn Farm (Bornholm) **250**
    Nyborg Destillery 200
    Smørrebrød 10, **31**, 68
    Southern Zealand 190
    Visit Carlsberg (Copenhagen) 132
    see also Bars and cafés; Restaurants
Foraging 31
Fossils 180, 181, 193, 231
Fredensborg Slot 143, **165**
Frederick IX 57
Frederick II 150, 160
Frederick III 55, 75, 82, 160, 166
Frederick IV 78, 128, 165
Frederick V 71, 75, 84, 88
Frederick VI 55
Frederick VII 167, 193
Frederick VIII 75, 139
Frederiksberg Have (Copenhagen) **128-9**
Frederiksborg Slot (Zealand) 143, **160-61**
Frederikshavn **237**
Fredrikssund 143, **166**
Fregatten Jylland (Ebeltoft) 216
Frilandsmuseet (Lyngby) **162-3**
Fuglsang Kunstmuseum **190**
Funen 19, **194-203**
    bars and cafés 198
    cycling 45
    itinerary 26-7
    map 196-7
    restaurants 201
Fur 231
Fyrkat 35, 41, 227, **239**

G

Gade, Niels W. 56
Gammel Estrup **241**
Gården Madkulturhuset (Bornholm) **248**

Gavnø Slot **184**
Gefionspringvandet (Copenhagen) **85**
Geologisk Museum (Copenhagen) **86**
Giacometti, Alberto 11, 146
Gilleleje **164**
Givskud Zoo **218**
Gniben **175**
Godfred, King of Jutland 53, 54
Golden Age 32, 33, **56**
Gorm the Old 35, 53, 54, 219
Grabodre Kirkegard (Roskilde) **154-5**
Gråbrødretorv (Copenhagen) **108**
Grauballe Man 216
Greenland and the Faroe Islands 21, **256-67**
    activities 263
    bars and cafés 262
    history 55, 56
    itinerary 28-9
    map 258-9
    restaurants 262, 267
Grenen 227, 234
Gribskov 165
Grøn Jæger 188, 191
Grønnesse Skov **163**
Gudenå River 217
Gudhjem 247, **252**, 255

H

Haderslev **224-5**
Håkon of Norway 54
Hamlet 150, 241
Hammershøi, Vilhelm 33
Hammershus Slot **253**
Han (Elmgreen & Dragset) 148
Hanklit Cliffs (Mors) 230
Hansen, Constantin 76
Harald I (Bluetooth) 53, 54, 156, 173, 219
Harvest (Ring) 76
Hasle **249**
Havnebadet Islands Brygge (Copenhagen) 47, **137**
H.C. Andersens Barndomshjem (Odense) 42, **198**
H.C. Andersens Hus (Odense) 42, **198-9**
Health 276
Helligandsklostret (Aalborg) **233**
Helligdomsklipperne (Sanctuary Cliffs) (Bornholm) 247, **252**
Helsingør **148-51**
    map 149
Helsingør Bymuseum **148**
Henningsen, Poul 37, 80
Herning **218-19**
Hestetorvet (Roskilde) **155**

Hindsholm **201**
Hirschsprungske Samling
(Copenhagen) **85**
Hirst, Damien
2-Amino-5-
Bromobenzotrifluoride 131
Love's Paradox 131
Hirtshals **236**
Historic buildings
Agersø Mølle 182
Børsen (Copenhagen) **112**,
117
Den Gamle Gaard (Faaborg)
201
Det Gamle Apotek
(Langeland) 202-3
Det Gamle Hus (Gilleleje) 164
Det Gamle Rådhus (Ribe) **212**
Det Kongelige Bibliotek
(Copenhagen) **113**, 117
Dukkehuset (Ærøskøbing)
203
Folketinget (Copenhagen)
111, 117
Gammel Estrup **241**
H.C. Andersens
Barndomshjem (Odense)
42, **198**
H.C. Andersens Hus (Odense)
42, **198-9**
Jens Bangs Stenhus (Aalborg)
232
Knud Rasmussens Hus
(Hundested) 166, 167
Lungholm Gods (Tågerup)
187
Magasin du Nord
(Copenhagen) 114
Nørre Jernløse Mølle **170**
Polakkasernen (Tågerup) 187
Rådhus (Aarhus) **208**
Rådhus (Copenhagen) **102-3**
Rådhuset (Aalborg) **233**
Rundetaarn (Copenhagen)
105
Rungstedlund **163**
Skagen Grå Fyr **235**
Universitet (Copenhagen)
110
Vandtårnet (Esbjerg) 223
see also Castles and
fortifications; Churches
and cathedrals; Museums
and galleries; Palaces
Historiske Museum (Aalborg)
232
History **52-7**
Hitchhiking 275
Hjerl Hede Frilandsmuseum
238
Højbro Plads (Copenhagen) **109**
Højerup 180-81
Holbæk **169**

Holmen (Copenhagen) 119
Holstebro **238**
Hornbæk **164-5**
Horns Rev Lightship (Esbjerg)
223
Horsens **216-17**
Høstet Sea Buckthorn Farm
(Bornholm) **250**
Hotels
Bornholm 249
Copenhagen 85, 105, 125
Northern Jutland 236, 239
Northwestern Zealand 155,
167, 171, 175
Southern and Central Jutland
209, 215, 223
Southern Zealand and the
Islands 181, 185
Hundested **166-7**
Hygge 13, 37

I
Ice Age 52
ID 277
Illullisat Kangerlua **260**
Inderhavnsbroen (Copenhagen)
125
In the Month of June (Ring) 33
Insurance 270-71
Internet access 277
Inuits 101, 166, 257, 260, 261
Isakson, Karl 32
Itineraries **22-9**
1 Day by Bike in Copenhagen
64-5
2 Days in Copenhagen 22-3
3 Days in the Faroe Islands
28-9
4 Days in Zealand 24-5
7 Days in Jutland and Funen
26-7
A Cycling Tour of Bornholm
254-5
see also Walks

J
Jacobsen, Arne 36, 37, 80, 81
Jacobsen, Carl 82, 96
Jacobsen, Jacob Christian 39
Jægersborg Dyrehave **162**
Jægersborggade (Copenhagen)
133, 138
Jægerspris Slot **167**
Jalk, Grete 81
Jelling **219**
Viking Market 34
Jens Bangs Stenhus (Aalborg)
232
Joboland **253**
Jorn, Asger 11, 108, 131
Museum Jorn (Silkeborg) 217

Juel, Jens 33
Juel, Admiral Niels 177, 202
Jutes 205
Jutland
beaches 47
cycling 45
history 53-4
itinerary 26-7
see also Northern Jutland;
Southern and Central
Jutland

K
Kalmar Union 54, 55
Kalsoy **267**
Kalundborg **172**
Kangerlussuaq (Søndre
Strømfjord) **261**
Karmeliterklosteret Sankt
Mariae Kirke (Helsingør) **148**
Kastellet (Copenhagen) **82-3**
Kattegat 175, 230
Kayaking 263
Kerteminde **201**
Kiel, Treaty of 257
Kierkegaard, Søren 56, 80, 113,
133
Klint, Kaare 80, 81
Knudshoved Odde **184**
Knuthenborg Safari Park **192**
Købke, Christian 33, 85
View from Dosseringen 76
Koelbjerg Man 52
Køge 177, **193**
Køge Bay, Battle of 177, 202
Kolding **224**
Kong Asgers Høj **190-91**
Kongens Have (Copenhagen) **87**
Kongenshus Mindepark **238-9**
Kongens Nytorv (Copenhagen)
106, 114-15
Korsør **171**
Krigsmuseet (Copenhagen)
112-13, 116
Krogh, Christian 235
Kronborg Slot (Helsingør) 143,
150-51
Krøyer, Peder Severin 32, 76, 235
Brøndum's Hotel 235
Summer Evening near Skagen
32
Krøyers Plads (Copenhagen) 47,
124
Kulturværftet (Helsingør) **148**
Kunsten Museum of Modern Art
(Aalborg) **233**
Kunstforeningen GL STRAND
(Copenhagen) **108**
Kunsthal Charlottenborg
(Copenhagen) **104-5**, 115
Kusama, Yayoi 146
Kvindemuseet (Aarhus) **209**

L

Lalandia (Rødby) 41, **186**
Langeland 195, **202-3**
Language 271
  essential phrases 270
  phrasebook 286
Ledreborg Slot **168-9**
LEGOLAND® 12, 41, 205,
  214-15, 275
Lejre 143, **169**
LGBT+ 67, 277
Lille Bælt 195, 200, 224, 225
Limfjorden **230-31**
Lindholm Høje 34, **238**
Liselund Slot **190**
Little Dancer of Fourteen
  (Degas) 97
Little Mermaid, The
  (Copenhagen) **82**
Local customs 277
Locher, Carl 235
Løkken-Blokhus 227
Lolland 177, 185-7, 190-92
Louisiana Museum (Humlebæk)
  11, 32, 33, **146-7**
Love's Paradox (Hirst) 131
Lovns Bredning 231
Lutheranism 54, 55

M

Maps
  Aalborg 233
  Aarhus 209
  Bornholm 244-5
  Copenhagen 60-61
  Copenhagen: Beyond the
    Centre 127
  Copenhagen: Central
    Copenhagen North 72-3
  Copenhagen: Central
    Copenhagen South 92-3
  Copenhagen: Christianshavn
    and Holmen 120-21
  Denmark 14-15
  Faroe Islands 259
  Funen 196-7
  Greenland 258
  Helsingør 149
  Northern Jutland 228-9
  Northwestern Zealand 144-5
  Odense 199
  Rail Journey Planner 273
  Ribe 213
  Roskilde 155
  Southern and Central Jutland
    206-7
  Southern Zealand and the
    Islands 178-9
Margrete I **54**, 149, 155, 157
Margrethe II **57**, 74, 88, 98, 110,
  111

Mariager **241**
Maribo **185**
Marielyst 41, **189**
Marmorkirken (Copenhagen)
  84, 88
Marstal **203**
Marstrand, Nicolai Wilhelm 85
Matisse, Henri, *Portrait of
  Madame Matisse* 76
Medical Museion (Copenhagen)
  84, 88
Metro 274
Middeldercentret (Lolland)
  191
Mobile phones 277
Moesgård **216**
  Viking Moot 34
Møllestien (Aarhus) **208**
Møn 177, 188, 190-92
Monasteries and convents
  Esrum Kloster 165
  Helligandsklostret (Aalborg)
    233
  Karmeliterklosteret Sankt
    Mariae Kirke (Helsingør)
    148
  Øm Kloster 217
  Roskilde Kloster **155**
Money 271
Møns Klint **191**
Mønsted **240**
Moore, Henry 146
Mors Island 230
Mossø 217
Museums and galleries
  Ærø Museum (Ærøskøbing)
    203
  Andelslandsbyen Nyvang
    (Holbæk) 169
  Archaeology (Haderslev) 225
  ARKEN Museum
    (Copenhagen) 33, **130-31**
  ARoS Kunstmuseum (Aarhus)
    32, **210**
  Bornholms Forsvarsmuseum
    (Rønne) 251
  Bornholms Kunstmuseum
    (Gudhjem) 32, **252**
  Bornholms Museum (Rønne)
    251
  Brandts (Odense) **199**
  Danish Architecture Centre
    (Copenhagen) **113**
  Davids Samling (Copenhagen)
    86-7
  Den Fynske Landsby
    (Odense) **199**
  Den Gamle Bay (Aarhus) **211**
  Denmark's Sugar Museum
    (Nakskov) 186
  Designmuseum Danmark
    (Copenhagen) 37, **80-81**,
    89

Museums and galleries (cont.)
  Dragor Museum
    (Copenhagen) **139**
  Dúvugarðar Museum
    (Streymoy) 266
  Empiregården (Stege) 192
  Esbjerg Art Museum 223
  Experimentarium
    (Copenhagen) **136**
  Faaborg Museum 201
  Falsters Minder (Nykøbing F)
    188
  Fiddlers Museum 240
  Fiskeri-og Søfartsmuseet
    (Esbjerg) 223
  Flaske-Peters Samling
    (Ærøskøbing) 203
  Forsorgsmuseet (Svendborg)
    202
  Fredericia Museum
    (Haderslev) 225
  Frilandsmuseet (Herning)
    218, 219
  Frilandsmuseet (Lyngby)
    162-3
  Frilandsmuseet (Maribo) 185
  Fuglsang Kunstmuseum **190**
  Gåsetårnet & Danmarks
    Borgcenter (Vordingborg)
    184-5
  Geocenter Møns Klint 191
  Geologisk Museum
    (Copenhagen) **86**
  Geomuseum Faxe 193
  Glasmuseet (Ebeltoft) 216
  Gudhjem Museum 252
  Guinness World Records
    Museum (Copenhagen) 114
  Hammershus Visitor Centre
    253
  H.C. Andersens
    Barndomshjem (Odense)
    42, **198**
  H.C. Andersens Hus (Odense)
    42, **198-9**
  HEART Herning Museum of
    Contemporary Art 218, 219
  Helsingør Bymuseum **148**
  Hirschsprungske Samling
    (Copenhagen) **85**
  Historiecenter Dybbøl Banke
    (Sønderborg) 224
  Historiske Museum (Aalborg)
    232
  Hjerl Hede Frilandsmuseum
    238
  Holbæk Museum 169
  Holstebro Kunstmuseum 238
  Horsens Museum 216-17
  J.F. Willumsens Museum
    (Frederikssund) 166
  Johannes Larsen Museum
    (Kerteminde) 201

Museums and galleries (cont.)
Kalundborg Museum 172
Køge Museum 193
Koldkrigsmuseum
  (Langeland) 203
Kongelig Afstøbningssamling
  (Copenhagen) 89
Kongernes Jelling 219
Korsø By-og
  Overfartsmuseet 171
Krigsmuseet (Copenhagen)
  112-13, 116
Kunsten Museum of Modern
  Art (Aalborg) **233**
Kunstforeningen GL STRAND
  (Copenhagen) **108**
Kunsthal Charlottenborg
  (Copenhagen) **104-5**, 115
Kunstmuseet i Tønder 224
Kunstmuseet Trapholt
  (Kolding) 224
Kvindemuseet (Aarhus) **209**
Kystmuseet Bangsbo 237
Lejre Museum 169
Lolland-Falster Stiftsmuseet
  (Maribo) 185
Louisiana Museum
  (Humlebæk) 11, 32, 33,
  146-7
Mariager Museum 241
Mariager Saltcenter 241
Medical Museion
  (Copenhagen) **84**, 88
Middelaldercentret (Lolland)
  191
Moesgård **216**
Museet på Koldinghus
  (Kolding) 224
Museet Sofart (Helsingør) **149**
Museum of Contemporary
  Art (Roskilde) **154**
Museum Jorn (Silkeborg) 217
Museum Silkeborg 217
Museumsø (Roskilde) **158-9**
Museum Vestsjælland (Sorø)
  170, 171
Næstved Museum 183
Nationalmuseet
  (Copenhagen) 35,
  100-101, 116
National Museum (Nuuk) 261
NaturBornholm (Aakirkeby)
  250
Nikolaj Kunsthal
  (Copenhagen) **107**, 114
Ny Carlsberg Glyptotek
  (Copenhagen) **96-7**
Oluf Høst Museet (Gudhjem)
  252
private galleries 33
Ragnarock Museum for Pop,
  Rock & Youth Culture
  (Roskilde) **155**

Museums and galleries (cont.)
Ribe Kunstmuseum **212-13**
Ribes Vikinger **213**
Ribe Vikingecenter 35, 41, **213**
Ringkøbing-Skjern Museum
  219
Ripley's Believe It Or Not!
  (Copenhagen) **111**
Roskilde Museum **154**
Sæby Museum 237
Sagnlandet Lejre 143, 169
SAK Kunstbygningen
  (Svendborg) 202
Skagens Museum 32, 234
Søfartsmuseum (Marstal) 203
Søvn Landsins (Tórshavn)
  266
Statens Museum for Kunst
  (SMK) (Copenhagen) 33,
  76-7
Strandingsmuseet St George
  (Holstebro) 238
Thorvaldsens Museum
  (Copenhagen) 33, **112**, 116,
  117
Tidens Samling (Odense) **199**
Traktormuseum (Eskilstrup)
  189
Trelleborg **173**
Vadehavscentret (Ribe) 40,
  213
Vejle Museum 222
Viborg Museum 240
Vikingemuseet (Aarhus) **208**
Vikingeskibsmuseet
  (Roskilde) 41, 143, **158-9**
Visit Carlsberg (Copenhagen)
  132
Willemoesgården (Assens)
  200
Music
live 66
  see also Entertainment
Musikhuset (Aarhus) **208**
Myggedalen 260
Mykines **267**

N

Næstved **183**
Nakskov **186**
Nationalmuseet (Copenhagen)
  35, **100-101**, 116
National parks
Mols Bjerger National Park
  216
Thy National Park 47
Wadden Sea National Park 40
New Nordic cuisine 13, **30**, 69
Nibe 231
Nielsen, Kai 202
  Water Mother 96, 97
Nightlife, Copenhagen **66-7**

Nikolaj Kunsthal (Copenhagen)
  107, 114
noma (Copenhagen) 30, 69, 123,
  136
Nordic Noir 10, **48-9**, 137
Nordskoven **167**
Nørrebro (Copenhagen) **133**,
  138
Nørre Jernløse Mølle **170**
Northern Jutland 20, **226-41**
  hotels 236, 239
  itinerary 26-7
  map 228-9
Northern Lights 257, **261**
Northwestern Zealand 17,
  142-75
  beaches 46
  hotels 155, 167, 171, 175
  itinerary 24-5
  map 144-5
  restaurants 164, 175
Nuuk (Godthåb) **260-61**
Nyborg **200**
Ny Carlsberg Glyptotek
  (Copenhagen) **96-7**
Nyhavn (Copenhagen) **104**, 115
Nyker **249**
Nykøbing F **188**
Nylars **249**
Nyord **193**
Nysted **187**
Nytorv (Copenhagen) **111**

O

Odense 195, **198-9**
  H.C. Andersen in 42
  map 199
Odsherred **175**
Old Lille Bælt Bridge 224
Olsker **249**
Oluf III 170
Opening hours 271
Operaen (Copenhagen) **123**
Ørestad (Copenhagen) **138**
Øresund Bridge 127, **137**
Østerbro (Copenhagen) **133**
Østerlars Rundkirke (Bornholm)
  246-7
Outdoor activities, Greenland
  263

P

Palaces
Amalienborg Slot
  (Copenhagen) **74-5**, 88-9
Charlottenborg Slot
  (Copenhagen) **104-5**, 115
Charlottenlund Slot
  (Copenhagen) **139**
Christiansborg Slot
  (Copenhagen) **98-9**, 116-17

Palaces (cont.)
Fredensborg Slot 143, **165**
Frederiksberg Slot
(Copenhagen) 128-9
Frederiksborg Slot (Zealand)
143, **160-61**
Jægerspris Slot **167**
Kronborg Slot (Helsingør)
143, **150-51**
Ledreborg Slot **168-9**
Liselund Slot **190**
Rosenborg Slot (Copenhagen)
78-9
Roskilde Palace **154**
see also Castles and
fortifications
Parks and gardens
Amaliehaven (Copenhagen)
89
Assistens Kirkegård
(Copenhagen) 133
Botanisk Have (Copenhagen)
86
Eventyrhaven (Odense) **199**
Frederiksberg Have
(Copenhagen) **128-9**
Gavnø Slot **184**
Gisselfeld Kloster 182
Jægersborg Dyrehave **162**
Jesperhus Park 231
Kongens Have (Copenhagen)
87
Kongenshus Mindepark
238-9
Liselund Slot **190**
Rebild Bakker **240**
Tivoli (Copenhagen) 41,
94-5
Winter Garden (Ny Carlsberg
Glyptotek, Copenhagen)
96-7
see also Amusement parks
passports 270
Personal security 276
Phrase Book 286
Portrait of Madame Matisse
(Matisse) 76
Postal services 277
Prices
average daily spend 270
public transport 272
Public holidays 271
Public transport 272, **274**

Q

Qaanaaq (Thule) **262**

R

Råbjerg Mile **236**
Rådhus (Aarhus) **208**
Rådhus (Copenhagen) **102-3**

Rådhuset (Aalborg) **233**
Rådhuspladsen (Copenhagen)
103
Ragnarock Museum for Pop,
Rock & Youth Culture
(Roskilde) **155**
Rail travel 272-3
Randers **241**
Rasmussen, Knud **166**, 260
Rasmussen, Lars Løkke 57
Reasons to Love Denmark
10-13
Rebild Bakker **240**
Redzepi, René 30, 69, 123
Reformation 54
Refshaleøen Island
(Copenhagen)M **136**
Restaurants 30
beach restaurants with a
view 47
Bornholm 251
Copenhagen 69, 83, 110, 123,
136, 139
Funen 201
Greenland and the Faroe
Islands 262, 267
Northwestern Zealand 164,
175
Southern and Central Jutland
211, 213, 218, 225
Southern Zealand and the
Islands 185
see also Food and drink
Ribe 35, **212-13**
map 213
restaurants 213
Ribe Domkirke **212**
Ribe Kunstmuseum **212-13**
Ribes Vikinger **213**
Ribe Vikingecenter 35, 41,
213
Ringkøbing Fjord **219**
Ring, Laurits Andersen 33
Harvest 76
In the Month of June 33
Ringsted 177, **182**
Ripley's Believe It Or Not!
(Copenhagen) **111**
Road travel 272, **274-5**
Rømø 47, 205, **222**
Rønne **251**, 254
Rosenborg Slot (Copenhagen)
78-9
Roskilde 143, **154-9**
hotels 155
map 155
Roskilde Domkirke **156-7**
Roskilde Kloster **155**
Roskilde Museum **154**
Roskilde Palace **154**
Roskilde, Treaty of 55
Røsnæs **172**
Rules of the road 272, **275**

Rundetaarn (Copenhagen) **105**
Rungstedlund **163**
Russells Glacier 261

S

Sæby **237**
Safety
personal security 276
travel safety advice 270
Sakskøbing **185**
Sand dunes 236
Sankt Albans Kirke
(Copenhagen) **83**
Sankt Knuds Kirke (Odense)
199
Sankt Olai Kirke (Helsingør) **149**
Sankt Petri Kirke (Copenhagen)
109
Saxo Grammaticus 150
Schleswig Wars 56, 205
Scooter hire 275
Sculpture 33
Selsø Slot **172-3**
Shakespeare, William 150, 241
Shopping, Copenhagen 133
Silkeborg **217**
Silkeborg Lake District **217**
Skagen 227, **234-5**
beaches 10, 46, 234
Skagen Grå Fyr **235**
Skagen School 32, 76, 190, 234,
235
Skagerrak 227
Skibby **168**
Skiing 263
Skovgaard, P.C. 190
Skuespilhuset (Copenhagen)
107
Smoking 276
Smørrebrød 10, **31**, 68
Sønderborg **224**
Søndervig 47
Sorø **170-71**
Southern and Central Jutland 19,
204-25
hotels 209, 215, 223
itinerary 26-7
map 206-7
restaurants 211, 213, 218,
225
Southern Fjords (Greenland)
263
Southern Zealand and the
Islands 18, **176-93**
beaches 189
hotels 181, 185
itinerary 24-5
map 178-9
restaurants 185
Special needs, travellers with
271
Spøttrup Borg **231**

Sprogø Island 172
Stændertorvet (Roskilde) **154**
Statens Museum for Kunst
    (SMK) (Copenhagen)
    33, **76-7**
Stege **192**
Stengada (Helsingør) **149**
Stevns Klint **180-81**
Store Bælt 172, 173, 195
Store Bælt Bridge **173**
Street food 31
Streymoy **266**
Strøget (Copenhagen) **107**
Summer Evening near Skagen
    (Krøyer) 32
Suså River **183**
Svaneke **248**
Svendborg **202**
Svinninge **175**
Svinninge Modeljernbane 175

T

Tågerup **187**
Tap water 276
Tårnborg **170**
Tasermiut Fjord 263
Tasiilaq (Ammassalik) **262**
Tåsinge 195, **202**
Taxes 277
Taxis 274
Telephone services 277
Television series 48-9
Theatres *see* Entertainment
Thirty Years War 55
Thorvaldsen, Bertel 99, 102
    Thorvaldsens Museum
        (Copenhagen) 33, **112**,
        116, 117
Tidens Samling (Odense) **199**
Time zone 276
Tipping 276
Tivoli (Copenhagen) 12, 41, **94-5**
Tollund Man 53, 217
Tønder **224**
Tórshavn **266**
Torssuqatoq Fjord 263
Trains *see* Rail travel
Trams 274
Travel
    getting around **272-5**
    safety advice 270
Trelleborg 143, **173**
Tveje Merløse Kirke **168**
Tycho Brahe Planetarium
    (Copenhagen) **136-7**

U

Universitet (Copenhagen) **110**
Utzon Center (Aalborg) **232-3**
Utzon, Jørn 36, 232
Uummannaq **260**

V

Vaccinations 271
Vadehavscentret (Ribe) 40, **213**
Vágar **267**
Valdemar dynasty 177, 184
Valdemar I the Great 184, 224
Valdemar IV 170, 184
Vallø Slot **192**
VAT refunds 277
Vejle **222**
Vesterbro (Copenhagen) 33,
    132, 138
Vestmanna 266
Viborg **240**
View from Dosseringen
    (Købke) 76
Vikings 12, **34-5**, **53-4**
    Fyrkat 35, 41, 227, **239**
    Greenland 257
    Kongernes Jelling 219
    Lindholm Høje **238**
    Ribes Vikinger **213**
    Ribe Vikingcenter
        35, 41, **213**
    Trelleborg **173**
    Vikingemuseet (Aarhus) **208**
    Vikingeskibsmuseet
        (Roskilde) 41, 143, **158-9**
Visas 270
Voergård Slot **239**
Vordingborg 177, **184-5**
Vor Frelsers Kirke (Copenhagen)
    122-3
Vor Frue Kirke (Aalborg) **233**
Vor Frue Kirke (Aarhus) **209**
Vor Frue Kirke (Copenhagen) **110**

W

Wadden Sea 40, 47, 205, 213
Walks
    A Short Walk Around
        Amalienborg Slot
        (Copenhagen) 88-9
    A Short Walk Around
        Christiansborg Slot
        (Copenhagen) 116-17
    A Short Walk Around Kongens
        Nytorv (Copenhagen)
        114-15
    Fjordstien (Zealand) 168
Water Mother (Nielsen) 96, 97
Websites 277
Wegner, Hans 37, 81
Weie, Edvard 32
Wi-Fi 277
Wildlife
    for children 40
    Den Blå Planet (Copenhagen)
        138
    Fiskeriets Hus (Ringkøbing)
        219

Wildlife (cont.)
    Fjord & Bælt (Kerteminde)
        201
    Givskud Zoo **218**
    Greenland wildlife safaris 263
    Guldborgsund Zoo
        (Nykøbing F) 188
    Knuthenborg Safari Park **192**
    Krokodille Zoo (Eskilstrup)
        189
    Nordsøen Oceanarium
        (Hirtshals) 236
    Randers Regnskov 241
    Vadehavscentret (Ribe)
        40, **213**
    Zoologisk Have (Copenhagen)
        129
Wine **169**, 190
Woman in a Chemise (Derain) 76
World War I 56
World War II 56, 243

Z

Zahrtmann, Kristian 190
Zealand *see* Northwestern
    Zealand; Southern Zealand
    and the Islands
Zoologisk Have (Copenhagen)
    129
Zoos *see* Wildlife

PHRASE BOOK

IN AN EMERGENCY

Can you call an ambulance?	Kan du tilkalde en ambulance?	kann do till-kalleh ehn ahm-boo-lang-seh?
Can you call the police?	Kan du tilkalde politiet?	kann do till-kalleh po-ly-tee'd?
Can you call the fire brigade?	Kan du tilkalde brand-væsenet?	kann do till-kalleh brahn-vaiys-ned?
Is there a telephone here?	Er der en telefon i nærheden?	e-ah dah ehn tele-fohn ee neya-hethen?
Where is the nearest hospital?	Hvor er det nærmeste hospital?	voa e-ah deh neh-meste hoh-spee-tahl

USEFUL PHRASES

Sorry	Undskyld	ons-gull
Goodnight	Godnat	goh-nad
Goodbye	Farvel	fah-vell
Good evening	Godaften	goh-ahf-tehn
Good morning	Godmorgen	goh-moh'n
Good morning (after about 9am)	Goddag	goh-dah
Yes	Ja	yah
No	Nej	nye
Please	Værsgo/ Velbekomme	vehs-goh/ vell-beh-commeh
Thank you	Tak	tahgg
How are you?	Hvordan har du det?/ Hvordan går det?	voh-dann hah do deh?/voh-dan go deh?
Pleased to have met you	Det var rart at møde dig	deh vah rahd add meutheh die
See you!	Vi ses!	vee sehsl
I understand	Jeg forstår	yay fuh-stoah
I don't understand	Jeg forstår ikke	yay fuh-stoah egge
Does anyone speak English?	Er der nogen, der kan tale engelsk?	e-ah dah noh-enn dah kann tah-leh eng-ellsgg?
on the left	til venstre	till vehn-streh
on the right	til højre	till hoy-reh
open	åben	oh-ben
closed	lukket	luh-geth
warm	varm	vahm
cold	kold	koll
big	stor	stoah
little	lille	lee-leh

MAKING A TELEPHONE CALL

I would like to call...	Jeg vil gerne ringe til...	yay vill geh-neh ring-eh till...
I will telephone again	Jeg ringer en gang til	yay ring-ah ehn gahng till

IN A HOTEL

Do you have double rooms?	Findes her dobbelt-værelser?	feh-ness he-ah dob-belld vah-hel-sah?
with bathroom	Med bade-værelse	meth bah-the-vah-hel-sah
with washbasin	Med hånd-vask	meth hohn-vasgg
key	nøgle	noy-leh
I have a reservation	Jeg har en reservation	yay hah ehn res-sah-vah-shohn

SIGHTSEEING

cathedral	domkirke	dom-kia-keh
church	kirke	kia-keh
museum	museum	muh-seh-uhm
railway station	banegård	bah-neh-goh
airport	lufthavn	luhft-havn
train	tog	toh
ferry terminal	færgehavn	fah-veh-havn
a public toilet	et offentligt toilet	ehd off-end-ligd toa-led

SHOPPING

I wish to buy...	Jeg vil gerne købe...	yay vill geh-neh kyh-beh...
Do you have...?	Findes der...?	feh-ness de-ah...?
How much does it cost?	Hvad koster det?	vath koh-stah deh
expensive	dyr	dyh-ah
cheap	billig	billy
size	størrelse	stoh-ell-seh
general store	købmand	keuhb-mann
greengrocer	grønthandler	grund-handla
supermarket	supermarked	suh-pah-mah-keth
market	marked	mah-keth

EATING OUT

Do you have a table for... people?	Har I et bord til... personer?	hah ee ed boah till... peh-soh-nah?
I wish to order...	Jeg vil gerne bestille...	yay vill geh-neh beh-stilleh...
I'm a vegetarian	Jeg er vegetar	yay eh-ah veh-gehta
children's menu	børnemenu	byeh-neh-meh-nye
starter	forret	foh-red
main course	hovedret	hoh-veth-red
dessert	dessert	deh-seh'd
wine list	vinkort	veen-cod
May I have the bill?	Må jeg bede om regningen?	moh yay beh-theh uhm rahy-ning-ehn

MENU DECODER

brød	bread	bruth
danskvand	mineral water	dansg vann
fisk	fish	fesgg
fløde	cream	flu-theh
grøntsager	vegetables	grunn-saha
is	ice cream	ees
kaffe	coffee	kah-feh
kartofler	potatoes	kah-toff-lah
kød	meat	kuth
kylling	chicken	killing
laks	salmon	lahggs
lam	lamb	lahm
leverpostej	liver paté	leh-vah-poh-stie
mælk	milk	mailgg
oksekød	beef	ogg-seh-kuth
ost	cheese	ossd
pølse	sausage	pill-seh
rejer	shrimps	rah-yah
røget fisk	smoked fish	roy-heth fesgg
saftevand	squash	sah-fteh-vann
salat	salad	sah-lad
salt	salt	sald
sild	herring	sil
skaldyr	shellfish	sgall-dya
skinke	ham	sgeng-geh
smør	butter	smuah
sodavand	fizzy drink	sodah-vann
svinekød	pork	svee-neh-kuth
te	tea	teh
torsk	cod	tohsgg
vand	water	vann
wienerbrød	Danish pastry	vee-nah-bryd
æg	egg	egg
øl	beer	uhl

NUMBERS

0	nul	noll
1	en	ehn
2	to	toh
3	tre	tray
4	fire	fee-ah
5	fem	femm
6	seks	seggs
7	syv	siu
8	otte	oh-deh
9	ni	nee
10	ti	tee
20	tyve	tyh-veh
30	tredive	traith-veh
40	fyrre	fyr-reh
50	halvtreds	hahl-traiths
60	tres	traiths
70	halvfjerds	hahl-fyads
80	firs	fee-ahs
90	halvfems	hahl-femms
100	hundrede	hoon-dreh-the
200	tohundrede	toh-hoon-dreh-the
1,000	tusind	tooh-sin-deh
2,000	totusinde	toh-tooh-sin-deh